Third Edition

SPORTS SPEED

George Blough Dintiman, EdD
Professor Emeriti, Virginia Commonwealth University
Cofounder of National Association for Speed and Explosion

Robert D. Ward, PED
Director Sports Science, AdvoCare
Former Strength and Conditioning Coach, Dallas Cowboys

Human Kinetics

Library of Congress Cataloging-in-Publication Data

Dintiman, George B.
   Sports speed / George Blough Dintiman, Robert D. Ward. -- 3rd ed.
        p. cm.
Includes bibliographical references and index.
   ISBN 0-7360-4649-6 (soft cover)
   1. Physical education and training. 2.   Sprinting. 3.   Speed.   I.
Ward,
Robert D., 1933- II. Title.
   GV711.5.D56 2003
   613.7'07--dc21

                                                            2003008731

ISBN: 0-7360-4649-6

The Web addresses cited in this text were current as of June 5, 2003, unless otherwise noted.

Acquisitions Editor: Ed McNeely; **Developmental Editor:** Cynthia McEntire; **Assistant Editor:** John Wentworth; **Copyeditor:** Patricia MacDonald; **Proofreader:** Kathy Bennett; **Indexer:** Gerry Lynn Messner; **Permission Manager:** Toni Harte; **Graphic Designer:** Andrew Tietz; **Graphic Artist:** Tara Welsch; **Art and Photo Manager:** Dan Wendt; **Cover Designer:** Jack W. Davis; **Photographer (cover):** Tom Roberts; **Photographer (interior):** Tom Roberts unless otherwise noted; **Illustrator:** Mic Greenberg; **Printer:** Phoenix Color

We thank St. Mark's School of Texas in Dallas for assistance in providing the location for the photo shoot for this book.

Human Kinetics books are available at special discounts for bulk purchase. Special editions or book excerpts can also be created to specification. For details, contact the Special Sales Manager at Human Kinetics.

Printed in the United States of America   10   9   8   7   6   5   4   3   2

Human Kinetics
Web site: www.HumanKinetics.com

United States: Human Kinetics
P.O. Box 5076
Champaign, IL 61825-5076
800-747-4457
e-mail: humank@hkusa.com

Canada: Human Kinetics
475 Devonshire Road, Unit 100
Windsor, ON N8Y 2L5
800-465-7301 (in Canada only)
e-mail: orders@hkcanada.com

Europe: Human Kinetics
107 Bradford Road
Stanningley
Leeds LS28 6AT, United Kingdom
+44 (0)113 255 5665
e-mail: hk@hkeurope.com

Australia: Human Kinetics
57A Price Avenue
Lower Mitcham, South Australia 5062
08 8277 1555
e-mail: liaw@hkaustralia.com

New Zealand: Human Kinetics
Division of Sports Distributors NZ Ltd.
P.O. Box 300 226 Albany
North Shore City, Auckland
0064 9 448 1207
e-mail: blairc@hknewz.com

This book is dedicated to the memory of the incomparable Tom Landry (September 11, 1924–February 12, 2000), football coach of the Dallas Cowboys from 1960 to 1989; Bob Hayes (December 20, 1942–September 18, 2002), Olympic 100-meter gold medalist and NFL wide receiver; and John Unitas (May 7, 1933–September 11, 2002), NFL Hall of Fame quarterback and one of the greatest legends of the 20th century. All three men turned the NFL upside down with their talent. Coach Landry brought his industrial engineering skills and integrity to NFL football to achieve greatness. Bob brought his bullet-like sports speed to the game and introduced fear into unfortunate defensive backs assigned to cover him. John brought his magic golden arm and competitive spirit to popularize the NFL and the game of pro football. Their innovations will live on in the way football is played today and in the future.

CONTENTS

PREFACE

Although we have entered a new sports millennium, the single greatest concern of athletes and coaches in soccer, football, basketball, baseball, rugby, lacrosse, field hockey, and most other team sports has not changed. In fact, new awareness that the right kind of training can produce dramatic changes has increased emphasis on the improvement of playing speed, or the speed of all movement in sports, including starting, stopping, cutting, accelerating, changing direction, delivering or avoiding a blow, sprinting, and split-second decision making during sports competition. *Sports Speed*, *Third Edition*, takes a new approach, providing a complete program for the improvement of each phase of movement in team sports. Each section has been thoroughly updated and new chapters have been added.

Sports Speed doesn't focus on helping athletes accelerate faster and sprint faster in a vacuum or a straight line. Seldom will athletes have the luxury of running this way during competition. This new book provides a complete program to improve playing speed for specific sports. It is designed to train athletes for the movements and skills that must be performed at high speed in their sports. It covers all aspects of training to help athletes perform every skill and movement required during competition faster and quicker.

Chapter 1 examines the art and science of playing speed in team sports and describes the overall plan for the use of our holistic speed improvement program in team sports. Chapter 2 examines all aspects of assessing speed to identify each athlete's strengths and weaknesses in order to accurately determine the major focus points for a specific sport. The assessment program includes separate tests for various sports such as those administered at the NFL, NBA, MLB, and pro soccer combines. Existing tests have been updated and refined, and new tests have been added to measure starting, stopping, cutting, and other sport-specific conditioning factors. Chapter 2 provides a comprehensive battery of tests for coaches and athletes in baseball, basketball, football, soccer, and other team sports for a thorough evaluation of weaknesses and strengths to assist in player selection and improvement.

Beginning in chapter 3, we cover all aspects of training to improve playing speed, including foundation training (chapter 3), strength and power training (chapter 4), ballistics and plyometrics (chapter 5), sport loading (chapter 6), and speed endurance (chapter 7). Chapter 8 deals with recovery technologies that will accelerate recovery from workouts. These technologies include the nutritional aspects of recovery between workouts and competition to help athletes return to the next practice session and game with their energy systems in high gear.

A complete sport-specific sprint-assisted training program is presented in chapter 9. Chapters 10, 11, and 12 cover the key aspects of starting and stopping, cutting and accelerating, and sprinting form and technique. Many new drills and training techniques are presented.

Finally, chapter 13 includes a record-keeping system that keeps careful tabs on exactly what was done at each workout to identify the areas where additional work is needed and to compare test scores at the end of both the four-week and eight-week training periods. Chapter 13 also presents periodized sport-specific speed programs to help athletes in various sports focus on a complete approach, workout by workout, leading up to the start of the competitive season. The entire speed improvement program is based on the concept of periodization, which is easily adapted to any team sport.

ACKNOWLEDGMENTS

We would like to thank John G. Turek, head cross-country and track and field coach at St. Mark's School of Texas for organizing and conducting the photo sessions and Wisteria Nicole Gillham, Garland Hampton, and Innis Buggs who volunteered their time and energy to be photo subjects for this book.

George wishes to thank his wife Carol Ann Dintiman and his daughter Lynne R. Dintiman for their assistance; colleague and friend Dr. Sergei Beliaev, sport scientist and CEO of supersportssystem.com for sharing his futuristic thinking and new concepts of training elite athletes; Fred Caro, former Edinboro University of Pennsylvania football and wrestling coach; Outer Banks of North Carolina "think tank" colleagues Henry Blaha, Don Brown, Charles Butler, Dick Kerr, William Howell, Frank Karkuff, Ed Miller, and Clay Richardson; and Bev Tucker MD for his excellent free and willing medical advice.

Bob wishes to thank Dan Inosanto, martial artist and friend, who laid the foundation for the application of martial arts to other sports; Dr. Reg McDaniel of Mannatech, Inc., for scientific support; Larry McBryde of Southwest Ergonomics for biomechanical consultation; Steve Davison for moving science to the athletic conditioning program by providing Inertial Impulse Systems to train for explosive movement off the field; Randy White for his unparalleled commitment to being a master in his art; Tex Schramm, who supported a coaching environment at the Dallas Cowboys and encouraged creative thinking; Dr. Ralph Mann for his insight and tenacity in taking sport into the 21st century; Dr. John Cooper, educator and friend, for launching me on a lifelong journey toward sport analysis with practical observations and science as companions; Dr. Jim Counsilman, sport scientist and swim coach from Indiana University, for his creative application of the sciences to sport; Bert Hill, friend, collegiate and professional conditioning coach, and present director of endorsements for AdvoCare for his knowledge and support; Charley Baker, friend and track coach, who helped me apply the sport speed concepts to masters competition; Dr. Barry Sims for nutrition materials; Todd Nadeah of SmartVest for sport loading programs; Dr. Sam Symmauk for his guidance on chiropractics; Gary Butler for the section on massage; and the many other heroes, friends, athletes, and coaches who contributed to my understanding of how to play faster in any sport. Finally, to my wife Joyce, I give thanks beyond measure.

In addition, we thank the people at Human Kinetics who committed themselves to the careful review, editing, and production of this book, in particular Ed McNeely and Cynthia McEntire. They provided us with valuable insight and guidance in all phases of the creation of this book, from the first written word to the last details of organization, design, illustration, and production.

Chapter 1

PLAYING SPEED

*T*hrough the years, coaches and athletes recognized the importance of speed and quickness but were convinced that they were genetic qualities no one could improve. As a result, speed training did not exist for team sports but was relegated to track coaches and those interested in sprinting events. Even among sprint coaches, emphasis was placed on the improvement of form and conditioning (wind sprints and other interval sprint training programs) to produce an athlete with upper- and lower-body movement in tune with the kinesiological principles of sprinting and then condition that athlete through repeated sprints longer and shorter than the distance of the sprinting event. At the university and pro levels, team coaches recruited fast, quick athletes rather than trying to improve speed and quickness in athletes with superior playing skills.

As long as the United States continued to win the 100-, 200-, and 400-meter dash in the Olympics, American training techniques went unquestioned, and the use of the old methods continued. When Valeri Borzov won the 100-meter dash in the 1972 Olympics, dethroning American sprint supremacy, the United States realized that there was more to improving speed than genetics and conditioning. As early as 1963, however, we began to challenge and test both the genetic theory and the two-prong approach to speed improvement involving form and muscular endurance training. We recognized that sprinting speed was increased not only by improving form (the start and mechanics of sprinting), holding maximum speed longer, and reducing the slowing effect at the end of a sprint (interval sprint training) but also by improving acceleration and taking faster and longer steps. None of the training programs in use during the 1960s had much impact on the latter two target areas, yet these were the most important.

Although weight training and weightlifting seeped into organized sports programs in the United States from various spots around the country, Bob Hoffman, the world's foremost weightlifting coach, probably had the greatest influence on our respective work in speed improvement and in today's conditioning programs. As early as the 1960s, we and others were independently testing our own conditioning and speed improvement theories. Our work during this time began to focus on analyzing the effectiveness of training the neuromuscular system. If the muscles involved in sprinting were forced to move faster than ever before through methods such as sprint-assisted training, speed-strength training, and high-speed stopping, starting, cutting, and accelerating, could we permanently increase the number of steps an athlete takes per second and improve stride length? During his speed camps in the 1960s, Dr. George Dintiman towed athletes behind a motor scooter and automobile to force faster and longer steps. Dr. Dintiman began publishing his work on improving speed (Dintiman 1964, 1970, 1980, 1984) and, with Bob Ward, published the first edition of *Sports Speed* in 1988 and the second edition in 1997.

In the mid-1970s, Bob Ward joined the Dallas Cowboys to become the first NFL strength and conditioning coach with full coaching status. Dr. Ward revolutionized the way football players were evaluated and selected and the way they concentrated on strength training, speed training, and general conditioning. Many of his special training techniques are still used by NFL teams.

The rest is history. Genetics is now considered only one factor in determining maximum speed potential. It is also widely accepted that athletes do not reach their potential unless they use a complete approach to improving playing speed. Athletes and coaches in practically all sports now follow our holistic speed improvement program. Speed coaches have been hired at all levels of competition, even professional levels, and the sports world is aware that, with the proper training, athletes can dramatically improve both speed and quickness. Together, in this book, we have developed a comprehensive program designed to improve playing speed in any sport.

A Holistic Approach to Speed Improvement

Every athlete can improve starting, stopping, and cutting speed, acceleration, and overall playing speed. Although it is true that genetics is important, keep in mind that heredity only deals the cards; environment and training play the

© Human Kinetics

Athletes in all sports can improve playing speed.

hand. Regardless of genetic makeup, any athlete can get faster with proper training. On the other hand, even genetically gifted athletes will not reach their potential unless they follow the complete playing speed improvement program described in this book. This holistic program includes all aspects of conditioning and sport-specific speed training; it progresses from a solid foundation of strength, power, and aerobic fitness to ballistics, plyometrics, speed strength, speed endurance, and sprint-assisted training. Every aspect of speed improvement is emphasized in a 12-month macrocycle and an 8-week preseason microcycle designed to help athletes reach near-peak performance at the start of the competitive season.

Regardless of the sport, there are only five ways to improve playing speed and anticipatory awareness of the athlete over short distances:

1. Improve starting ability from a stationary three-point, four-point, or standing position or moving posture (walking, jogging, or striding) and acceleration to maximum speed.
2. Increase stride length.
3. Increase the number of steps taken per second (stride rate).
4. Improve speed endurance.
5. Improve sprinting form and technique.

These areas are not equally important to athletes in all sports. Basketball, soccer, rugby, lacrosse, and field hockey players, and defensive backs and linebackers in football, for example, are generally moving at one-quarter to one-half speed when they go into a full-speed sprint, rather than from a stationary position such as a baseball player or football player in another position. For these athletes, starting technique is not nearly as important as acceleration, stride rate, stride length, and speed endurance. For baseball and football players, starting techniques from the batting box, field positions, and turf are important. Although improving speed endurance will not make an athlete faster, it will keep the athlete from slowing down because of fatigue after repeated short sprints

© Human Kinetics

A baseball player has to have great starting speed to be able to accelerate quickly from the batter's box.

or at the end of a long sprint of 80 yards or more. This quality is important to most team sport athletes.

Study table 1.1 carefully. The key speed improvement areas for each sport, listed in order of importance, will help you understand the test scores in chapter 2 and focus on the programs for your sport. If, for example, test scores indicate the need to improve starting technique for a defensive back on a football team, ignore that finding and concentrate on areas that are critical to this position.

Table 1.2 identifies the specific training programs that will bring about the changes necessary to improve speed for your sport in the five key areas identi-

Table 1.1 **Speed Improvement Attack Areas for Team Sports**

Sport	Attack areas by priority	Comments
Baseball	1. Starting, accelerating, stopping, and cutting 2. Stride rate 3. Stride length 4. Speed endurance 5. Sprinting form	A baseball player will not approach maximum speed unless he hits a triple or an inside-the-park home run. Starting ability and acceleration should receive major emphasis. Speed endurance comes into play on a triple, on an inside-the-park home run, or when baserunning from first to home.
Basketball	1. Starting, accelerating, stopping, and cutting 2. Stride rate 3. Speed endurance 4. Stride length 5. Sprinting form	Most explosive action occurs after some movement (jog, bounce, slide) has occurred. Maximum speed is not reached. High-speed starting, accelerating, stopping, and cutting should receive the major emphasis. A high level of speed endurance is needed to maintain speed and quickness as a player makes repeated short sprints throughout the game.
Football	1. Sufficient force 2. Starting, accelerating, stopping, and cutting 3. Stride rate 4. Speed endurance 5. Stride length 6. Sprinting form	Starting and accelerating from a three-point, four-point, or standing position for 5 to 25 yd. is critical to every position. High-speed stopping and cutting is performed by every player throughout the game. A player sprints faster in the open field by increasing stride rate and length. Speed endurance training prevents players from slowing down because of fatigue at the end of a long run or after repeated short sprints.
Soccer	1. Starting, accelerating, stopping, and cutting 2. Stride rate 3. Stride length 4. Speed endurance 5. Sprinting form	Soccer is a game of starting, accelerating for 15 to 25 yd., and high-speed stopping as a player approaches the ball or an opponent. Speed endurance prevents players from slowing down after repeated short sprints.

Table 1.2 — Speed Improvement Through Training Programs

Area of improvement	Training program
Sufficient force Improved starting, accelerating, stopping, and cutting	Sport-specific starting form training Muscle imbalance training Start, stop, and cut training Speed-strength training Sport loading Sprint-assisted acceleration training
Increased stride length	Speed-strength training Muscle imbalance training Plyometrics Sport loading Sprint-assisted training Form training Flexibility training
Increased number of steps taken per second (stride rate)	Sprint-assisted training Quick feet training Muscle imbalance training Speed-strength training
Improved sprinting technique	Form training Speed-strength training
Improved speed endurance	Pickup sprints, hollow sprints, and interval sprint training Sport loading Maximum effort training Ballistics

Note: Assuming the athlete already possesses an acceptable level of strength, power, and body fat.

fied in table 1.1. Your task is to master the training concepts associated with each program. Keep in mind that speed improvement does require a holistic approach. In other words, each training program is important and produces results when used with other training programs to train all key areas associated with the improvement of playing speed.

Move on to chapter 2 for a complete assessment of strengths and weaknesses and to identify the factors that keep athletes from sprinting faster in their sports.

ASSESSING SPEED

C hapter 2 is divided into two sections. First we introduce a comprehensive testing battery designed to identify strengths and weaknesses and form the basis for a personal speed improvement program. Then we look at team sport combine tests used by professional teams in baseball, basketball, football, and soccer to aid in draft selection and player signings. Both test areas concentrate on the unique aspects associated with playing speed, or the speed at which skills are performed during competition in team sports.

Comprehensive Testing Battery

The first step toward getting faster is to work with a friend or coach to test the seven general areas of the comprehensive test battery: sprinting speed (starting speed, acceleration, mph speed, and speed endurance, all in one 120-yard run); starting, stopping, and cutting; strength; stride length; flexibility; explosive power and quickness; and body composition.

Evaluating these seven areas provides all the information needed to identify key strengths and weaknesses associated with speed improvement. Later when developing a workout schedule, return to this chapter and complete the advanced testing program for a more detailed analysis.

Test scores mean nothing unless the athlete gives maximum effort on every trial. This provides meaningful scores that can be used to prepare an effective speed improvement program based on individual needs. The more accurate the test scores, the easier it is to identify the key factors that are limiting speed. Loafing or loading (providing only partial effort in order to show more improvement on a later test) only hurts. The end result could be a program that emphasizes areas where the athlete has already reached optimum performance. Focusing on these areas while neglecting weaknesses may not improve sprinting or playing speed.

The following sections provide a thorough explanation of the purpose, procedure, and interpretation of results for each of the seven test areas. Make a copy of the test score sheet (table 2.1) and record your scores.

Table 2.1

Name: _____ Age: _____ Height: _____ Weight: _____

Sport: _____ Position: _____ Testing date: _____

Test	Score	Standard	Weakness (yes or no)
Sprinting speed and speed endurance Stationary 40-, 80-, and 120-yard dash		Everyone can improve these times. Scores are used to find weak areas.	Yes
20 yards (first timer)	_____		
40 yards (first timer)	_____		
Flying 40 yards (second timer)	_____		
60 yards (third timer)	_____		
80 to 120 yards (second timer)	_____		
120 yards (third timer)	_____		
Speed endurance Flying 40-yard time minus 80- to 120-yard time	_____	No more than .2 second difference between times.	_____
NASE repeated sprints (20, 30, or 40 yards)	_____ _____ _____ _____ _____ _____ _____ _____ _____	No more than .3 second difference among the 10 trials.	_____
Starting, stopping, and cutting Start, stop, and cut test	_____	Under 14.0 seconds for junior high school; under 13.0 for high school; under 12.0 for college; under 11.0 for professionals.	_____

(continued)

7

Table 2.1 (continued)

Test	Score	Standard	Weakness (yes or no)
Strength			
Leg strength to body weight ratio		Multiply body weight	
Double-leg press	_____	by 2.5. Leg press score should be higher.	_____
Hamstrings and quadriceps		If right and left leg	
Leg extension (quads)		scores differ by	
Right	_____	more than 10 lb., a	_____
Left	_____	weakness exists in the low scoring leg.	_____
Double-leg curl (hamstrings)	_____	Score should be	_____
Double-leg extension (quads)		at least 80% of leg extension score.	
Single-leg kickback		If right and left leg	
Right	_____	scores differ by	_____
Left	_____	more than 10 lb., a weakness exists in the low scoring leg.	_____
Stride length			
Stride length test		For males, score	
Right	_____	should be 1.14 times	_____
Left	_____	height, plus or minus 4 inches. For females, score should be 1.15 times height or 2.16 times leg length (see also table 2.3).	_____
		Right and left leg push-off stride length score should not differ by more than 5%.	_____
Flexibility			
Sit-and-reach test	_____	College-age males should score at least 15.50; college-age females should score at least 16.25.	_____
Practical ROM tests	_____	Successfully complete each test.	_____

Test	Score	Standard	Weakness (yes or no)
Explosive power and quickness			
Standing triple jump	_____	Males: at least 20 feet (junior HS), at least 25 (senior HS), at least 28 (college and up). Females: at least 15 (junior HS), at least 20 (senior HS), at least 23 (college and up).	_____
Quick hands	_____	Males: at least 47 (junior HS), at least 60 (senior HS), at least 80 (college and up). Females: at least 33 (junior HS), at least 42 (senior HS), at least 57 (college and up).	_____
Quick feet	_____	Males: at least 3.8 (junior HS), at least 3.3 (senior HS), at least 2.8 (college and up). Females: at least 4.2 (junior HS), at least 3.8 (senior HS), at least 3.4 (college and up).	_____
Right and left leg hops Right Left	_____ _____	2.5 and under is excellent; 2.6 to 3.0 is good; higher than 3.0 means strength power training is needed. A difference greater than .2 between right and left legs shows a power imbalance.	_____ _____

(continued)

Test	Score	Standard	Weakness (yes or no)
Body composition			
Skinfold tests		See table 2.4 for percent body fat. Males who exceed 15% and females who exceed 20% should consult a physician for advice before beginning any weight loss program.	
Biceps	_____		_____
Triceps	_____		_____
Subscapula	_____		_____
Suprailiac	_____		_____
Total	_____		_____
Percent body fat	_____		_____
Form and technique		Form errors from video of 40-yard dash and coach's observations (side, front, rear views)	
Starting form		1. 2. 3	
Sprinting form		1. 2. 3.	
Aerobic fitness			
1.5-mile run	_____	Males: less than 225 lb., 10:01 to 12:00 is good, 8:30 to 10:00 is excellent; 226 to 300 lb., score should be 12:01 to 14:00; 301 lb. or more, score should be 14:01 to 15:30. Females: less than 150 lb., score should be 12:30 to 14:00; 151 to 200 lb., score should be 14:01 to 15:30.	_____
Stride rate and acceleration			
Stride rate	_____	Use stride length and flying 40 scores to find stride rate using table 2.5. Everyone can improve stride rate.	YES
Acceleration	_____	No more than .7 difference between stationary 40-yard time and flying 40-yard time.	_____

Test	Score	Standard	Weakness (yes or no)
Advanced testing			
NASE Future 40	_____	Score provides an estimate of potential for improvement. Add .3 second to approximate how fast the 40-yard dash should eventually be completed.	_____
Single-leg extension Right Left	_____ _____	Find 1RM for each arm and leg. Scores for right and left should not differ by more than 10%.	_____ _____
Single-leg curl Right Left	_____ _____		_____ _____
Single-leg kickback Right Left	_____ _____		_____ _____
One-arm barbell curl Right Left	_____ _____		_____ _____
One-arm military press Right Left	_____ _____		_____ _____

If your score in a test area didn't meet the minimum standards, check the training programs that you need to follow to eliminate the weakness.

Test	Training programs
Sprinting speed and speed endurance	Speed endurance training Speed-strength training
Starting, stopping, and cutting	High-speed quickness training
Strength	Speed-strength training Plyometrics
Stride length	Sprint-assisted training Plyometrics Speed-strength training
Flexibility	Concentrated stretching program

(continued)

Table 2.1   (continued)

Test	Training programs
Explosive power and quickness	Speed-strength training Plyometrics
Body composition	Consult a health professional
Form and technique	Form training
Stride rate	Sprint-assisted training Plyometrics Speed-strength training
Start and acceleration	Sport loading Sprint-assisted training Form training Plyometrics Ballistics Speed-strength training
Muscle balance	Speed-strength training Plyometrics

Sprinting Speed and Speed Endurance

Two tests are used to analyze sprinting speed and speed endurance: the stationary 40-, 80-, and 120-yard dash and the National Association of Speed and Explosion (NASE) repeated sprints. Both tests look at sprinting speed, but the NASE repeated sprints are more sport-specific. We will start with the stationary 40-, 80-, and 120-yard dash.

STATIONARY 40-, 80-, AND 120-YARD DASH

The stationary 40-, 80-, and 120-yard dash provides information on numerous phases of sprinting speed and quickness including the start, acceleration, maximum speed (miles per hour and feet per second), and speed endurance (sustained speed).

Mark a 120-yard route with flags and finish tapes at 20, 40, 60, 80, and 120 yards (figure 2.1). Timers are stationed at 40, 80, and 120 yards. Each timer has a stopwatch that permits two separate times (split). If available, an electronic timing system can be used.

Assume a three-point football stance or a four-point track stance. Sprint full speed for the entire 120 yards, running through each tape without slowing or changing form. Continue sprinting for 10 yards beyond the last tape.

The first timer (40 yards) and third timer (120 yards) start their watches on your first muscular movement forward. The first timer stops his watch when the flag draped over the 20-yard mark moves (split time) and again when the flag at the 40-yard mark moves. The third timer stops his watch when the flag at the 60-yard mark moves (split time) and again when you cross the finish line (120 yards).

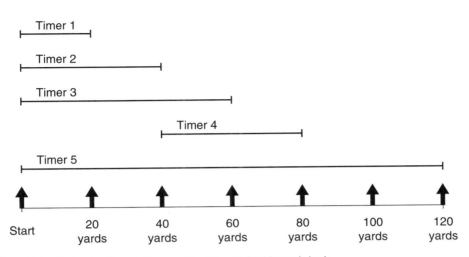

Figure 2.1 Setup for the stationary 40-, 80-, and 120-yard dash.

The second timer (80 yards) starts his watch when the flag at 40 yards moves and stops it for a split time when the flag at 80 yards moves. This is the flying 40-yard dash. He stops it again when you cross the finish line (120 yards).

The first timer records the 20-yard and 40-yard times on the test score sheet (table 2.1). The third timer records the time from the start to the 60-yard mark (split) and the start to the 120-yard mark on the test score sheet. The second timer records the time from the 40-yard mark to the 80-yard mark and the time from the 80-yard mark to the 120-yard mark.

Keep in mind that everyone can improve in the 40-yard dash, so no matter what your time was, it will get better with training. The importance of this test also varies for athletes in different sports.

With only one 120-yard sprint, you already know a lot about yourself. You can now evaluate your 40-yard dash time and speed endurance. Additional information from the 120-yard sprint will be used later to determine acceleration time and steps per second (stride rate).

SPEED ENDURANCE

The speed endurance score compares your flying 40-yard time (40- to 80-yard dash time) to your 80- to 120-yard dash time. If both scores are the same, or almost the same, it means you are in excellent anaerobic condition to repeatedly sprint a short distance during a baseball, basketball, football, soccer, rugby, lacrosse, or field hockey game without slowing down. If your flying 40 time and your time from 80 yards to 120 yards (also a flying 40) differ by more than .2 second, write *yes* in the Weakness column for speed endurance on the test score sheet.

NASE REPEATED SPRINTS

The NASE repeated sprint test of 20, 30, or 40 yards is a more sport-specific test to evaluate speed endurance for team sports that require repetitions of short sprints.

Table 2.2   Guidelines for Sprint Distances and Rest Intervals for Different Sports

Sport	Average sprint distance (yd.)	Typical interval between sprints (sec.)
Baseball, softball	30	30 to 60
Basketball	20	10 to 15
Football	10 to 40	25 to 30 (huddle time)
Soccer, lacrosse, rugby, field hockey	10 to 40	5 to 15
Tennis	5 to 10	3 to 5 (same point) 20 to 30 (between points) 60 (between games)

Use the guidelines in table 2.2 to determine the length of the sprint and the rest interval between each of the 10 repetitions for your sport.

Complete 10 repetitions of the average distance sprinted in your sport. After each repetition, rest the typical number of seconds that occur between sprints during competition. Record each score in the order they are completed. Ideally, the best and worst times should not differ by more than .3 second. If a greater difference exists, write *yes* in the Weakness column.

Starting, Stopping, and Cutting

The start, stop, and cut test measures your ability to start and accelerate quickly, to execute high-speed stops and backward and forward sprints, and to make a 90-degree cut.

START, STOP, AND CUT TEST

Mark off a 10-yard square in the gymnasium or on the athletic field (see figure 2.2). Assume a two-point (standing) or three-point starting stance in the bottom left of the square (point A). Sprint forward for 10 yards before coming to a complete stop inside a two-by-two-foot box in the upper left corner of the 10-yard square (B). Execute the stop by planting your right foot then left foot, then sprint backward toward the starting area. Plant your left foot inside box C. Execute a side shuffle for 10 yards to the right. At box D, plant your right foot to allow a powerful push-off and sprint to box E. Plant your left foot in box E to stop, push off, and execute a final forward sprint to the finish line (F).

The timer starts the watch with your first muscular movement and stops it when you cross the finish line. The best time of two trials is recorded.

Your time provides an indication of explosive stopping and starting action, power, acceleration, agility, and quickness for team sports. Accelerating from a stationary position and executing two high-speed stops and starts, a backward

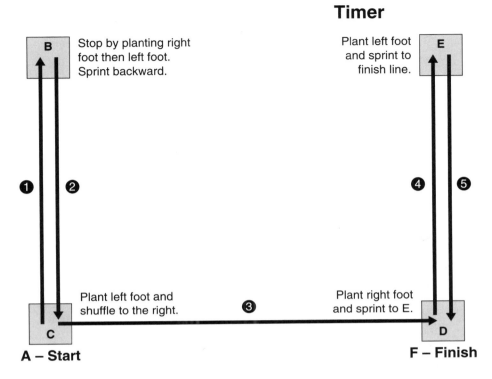

Figure 2.2 Setup for the start, stop, and cut test.

sprint, and two high-speed cuts and sprints simulate conditions that commonly occur during competition.

Strength

LEG STRENGTH TO BODY WEIGHT RATIO

The objective of the leg press to body weight ratio test is to find the maximum amount of weight you can press for one repetition. Record this amount on the test score sheet (table 2.1).

Adjust the seat on a Universal®, Nautilus®, or similar leg press station or free weight squat stand until your knees are bent at right angles. The objective is to identify the amount of weight you can lift for one repetition (1RM), and record that lift in pounds. On your first attempt, use an amount of weight equal to two times your body weight. If that amount is too little, rest three to four minutes and add weight before trying again. If that amount is too much, rest three to four minutes and remove weight before trying again. Add or remove 10 pounds at a time until you locate the amount, within 5 to 10 pounds, that you can leg press one time. Divide your body weight into the total pounds lifted to find your leg strength to body weight ratio.

Your leg strength to body weight ratio indicates how easily you can get and keep your body moving at high speeds. This ratio is extremely important for speed improvement over short distances. A good ratio is 2.5 to 1, or a leg press score two and one-half times body weight. For example, for someone who weighs 150 pounds, a leg press score of at least 375 pounds (150 × 2.5 = 375) is a good score. At college and professional levels of competition, ratios of 3 to 1 and 4 to 1 (three and four times body weight) are desirable. If your score is less than two and one-half times your body weight, write *yes* in the Weakness column.

HAMSTRING AND QUADRICEPS STRENGTH

A speed-strength imbalance between two opposing muscle groups such as the quadriceps (agonists) and the hamstrings (antagonists) may be a limiting factor in the development of speed. Conditioning and training for team sports traditionally cause greater strength increases in the quadriceps than in the hamstrings. Hamstring strength is the weak link in sprinting and often needs to be increased. Unfortunately, the majority of athletic movements and exercises—such as the leg press, leg extensions, high knee lifts, jogging, sprinting, and numerous calisthenics—strengthen the quadriceps while few exercises (leg curls) strengthen the hamstrings. This imbalance is an important factor in limited sprinting speed in athletes.

For both the leg extension test and the leg curl test, you want to find your 1RM. Complete the leg extension test by sitting with your back straight while grasping both sides of a Universal or Nautilus bench. Hook both feet under the leg press pad and extend your legs. To complete the leg curl test, lie on your abdomen and hook both heels under the leg curl pad. Grasp the sides of the seat or the handles with both hands, and flex your legs to your buttocks.

Your task is to find your 1RM in the same manner described in the leg press to body weight ratio test. Begin with an amount of weight you know you can complete for three to five repetitions as a warm-up. Add 5 to 10 pounds at three- to four-minute intervals until you find the weight you can extend only once. Record the score on the test score sheet (table 2.1).

Divide leg extension score, in pounds, into leg curl score to find your ratio. For example if leg extension score is 100 pounds and leg curl score is 50 pounds, the ratio is 50 divided by 100, or 50 percent. A score of less than 75 percent is low and indicates the need to focus on strengthening the hamstrings.

Ideally, leg extension scores (quadriceps) and leg curl scores (hamstrings) would be the same. In almost every athlete, however, the quadriceps are much stronger than the hamstrings. The average leg curl score of 1,625 middle school and high school football players tested was less than 50 percent of the leg extension score. Such an imbalance is associated with injuries such as hamstring muscle pulls and reduced performance in sprinting short distances.

Experts also feel that the speed strength of the hamstring muscle group is the weakest link in most athletes and should be improved to 80 to 100 percent of the speed strength of the quadriceps group. A minimum of 75 to 80 percent is recommended for the prevention of injury.

SINGLE-LEG KICKBACK

The purpose of the single-leg kickback test is to examine and compare the force you exert against an area similar to a starting block and the ground during the accelerating phase of sprinting. It also allows you to compare the force exerted by each leg.

Stand to the side of a leg press station, facing away from the leg pad. Place one foot on the pad and bend your knee to a right angle before exerting as much force as possible to reach a full leg extension. Repeat the procedure until you find your 1RM, then switch legs.

If right and left leg scores differ by more than 1 pound, write *yes* in the Weakness column (table 2.1). Emphasize this exercise in your weight training routine until sufficient improvement is noted.

Stride Length

Finding your ideal stride length is an important part of achieving maximum speed potential. Understriding or overstriding may adversely affect your overall speed in short distances. Speed can be improved by increasing stride length and maintaining the same stride rate (steps per second).

STRIDE LENGTH TEST

Place two markers 25 yards apart on a smooth dirt surface approximately 50 yards from the starting line. (The soft dirt surface will allow the runner's footprint to be seen. Runners reach maximum speed before arriving at and sprinting through the 25-yard area.) On the first trial, two helpers identify your footprints and measure and record your stride length to the nearest inch from the tip of the left toe to the tip of the right toe. On the second trial, the measurement is taken from the tip of the right toe to the tip of the left toe. This provides two unique aspects of stride length and permits a comparison of the push-off power from the left foot on one trial and from the right foot on the other trial, which helps determine imbalances.

Find your ideal stride length from table 2.3 for your age group. Locate your height in inches on the vertical column. Your ideal stride length appears to the right under your age group. If your measured stride length on either trial is less than this range, you need to engage in a program to increase stride length.

Compare the stride length of the two trials: one with a left foot push-off and one with a right foot push-off. If one is more than 2 to 3 inches longer than the other, you are generating more push-off power on that foot. This difference should also show up on your leg kickback test. If your stride length is greater than this range and you are sprinting without overstriding, do not change your stride. If your score indicates that you are overstriding, the form drills in chapter 12 will help you achieve the most efficient stride length. Sprint-assisted training, form training, plyometrics, and speed-strength training will increase stride length.

Table 2.3   **Estimate of Ideal Stride Length by Age and Gender**

Height (in.)	Stride length (in.)		
	Males (9 to 16)	Males (17+)	All females
50	53 to 61	59 to 67	54 to 62
51	54 to 62	61 to 69	55 to 63
52	55 to 63	62 to 70	56 to 64
53	56 to 64	63 to 71	57 to 65
54	58 to 66	64 to 72	58 to 66
55	59 to 67	66 to 74	59 to 67
56	60 to 68	67 to 75	60 to 68
57	61 to 69	68 to 76	62 to 70
58	62 to 70	69 to 77	63 to 71
59	63 to 71	71 to 79	64 to 72
60	64 to 72	72 to 80	65 to 73
61	66 to 74	73 to 81	66 to 74
62	67 to 75	74 to 82	67 to 75
63	68 to 76	76 to 84	68 to 76
64	69 to 77	77 to 85	70 to 78
65	70 to 78	78 to 86	71 to 79
66	71 to 79	79 to 87	72 to 80
67	72 to 80	81 to 89	73 to 81
68	74 to 82	82 to 90	74 to 82
69	75 to 83	83 to 91	75 to 83
70	76 to 84	85 to 93	76 to 84
71	77 to 85	86 to 94	78 to 86
72	78 to 86	87 to 95	79 to 87
73	79 to 87	88 to 96	80 to 88
74	80 to 88	89 to 97	81 to 89
75	82 to 90	91 to 99	82 to 90
76	83 to 91	92 to 100	83 to 91
77	84 to 92	93 to 101	85 to 93
78	85 to 93	95 to 103	86 to 94
79	86 to 94	96 to 104	87 to 95
80	87 to 95	97 to 105	
81	88 to 96	98 to 106	
82	90 to 98	100 to 108	
83	91 to 99	101 to 109	
84	92 to 100	102 to 110	

Flexibility

To achieve maximum speed potential, you must possess an adequate range of motion in the shoulders, hips, and ankles. Flexibility in these areas is affected by joint structure. Ball-and-socket joints (hip and shoulder) have the highest range of motion (ROM); the wrist is one of the least flexible joints with an ROM of 80 degrees, less than the 130 degrees of the knee joint. Additional factors that affect ROM include excess muscle bulk (decreases ROM); age (decreases flexibility); gender (females are more flexible than males); connective tissue such as tendons, ligaments, fascial sheaths, and joint capsules; injuries (restrict movement); and existing scar tissue (decreases ROM).

Flexibility testing is essential for the preparation of an individualized speed improvement program based on weaknesses. Flexibility tests also reveal excessive range of motion or joint laxity that may predispose athletes to injury. Once an optimum level of flexibility is developed, athletes should focus on other training areas while maintaining this flexibility.

Because flexibility is joint-specific, a single test does not provide an accurate assessment of ROM. It is also impractical to measure the ROM of every joint. In addition, the flexibility of some joints is not critical to sprinting speed. The following tests, which can be completed easily with little equipment, provide important information on ankle flexion and extension, shoulder flexibility, and hamstring flexibility.

SIT-AND-REACH TEST

The sit-and-reach test measures the flexibility of the lower back and the hamstring muscle group, the group of muscles located on the back of the upper leg. An optimal level of flexibility in both areas is important for the improvement of playing speed.

After warming up to elevate body temperature as indicated by perspiration, remove your shoes and sit on the floor with your hips, back, and head against a wall, legs fully extended, feet in contact with a sit-and-reach box. Place one hand on top of the other so the middle fingers are together. Slowly lean forward as far as possible. Without bouncing, slide your hands along the measuring scale on top of the box. Your hands should reach at least slightly beyond your toes.

Complete four trials and record your best score to the nearest one-quarter inch. If a sit-and-reach box is not available, you can build one by attaching a yardstick to the top of a 12-by-12-inch square box. The yardstick extends exactly 9 inches from the front of the box where the feet are.

The sit-and-reach test provides an indication of hamstring flexibility. If your score falls below the 50th percentile for your age, flexibility training is needed five or six times a week. Males 17 years or older should score at least 13.50; females 17 years or older should score at least 13.75.

PRACTICAL ROM TESTS

You can quickly assess the range of motion in the ankle, elbow and wrist, groin, hip, neck, and shoulder in less than five minutes by self-administering these practical tests. After performing the tests, record your scores on the test score sheet.

To test the ankle, lie on your back with both legs extended and the backs of your heels flat on the floor. Point your toes down away from your shins, attempting to reach a minimum of 45 degrees (halfway to the floor). Now point your toes toward your shins to a minimum of right angles. Compare the flexion and extension of the right and left ankles.

To test the elbow and wrist, hold your arms straight with palms up and little fingers higher than your thumbs.

To test the groin, stand on one leg and raise the other to the side as high as possible. You should be able to achieve a 90-degree angle between your legs.

To test the hips, stand and hold a yardstick or broom handle with hands shoulder-width apart. Without changing your grasp, bend down and step over the stick with both feet, one foot at a time, and then back again.

To test your neck, you should be able to use your chin to sandwich your flattened hand against your chest.

To test your shoulders, stand and attempt to clasp your hands behind your back. Reach over one shoulder with one hand and reach up from behind the other shoulder with the other hand. Repeat, reversing arm positions.

If you failed any of the practical tests, include stretching exercises in your warm-up that are designed to improve the ROM in these areas.

Explosive Power and Quickness

STANDING TRIPLE JUMP

The standing triple jump provides a noninvasive technique (without resorting to muscle biopsy) to estimate fast-twitch muscle fiber percentage in key areas. High scores are associated with starting acceleration in sprinting and explosive power, quickness, and speed over short distances.

From a standing long jump position, jump forward as far as possible using a two-foot takeoff, landing on only one foot before immediately jumping to the opposite foot, taking one final jump, and landing on both feet. Practice the standing triple jump test at low speeds until you master the technique. The movement is identical to the triple jump in track and field, except for the use of a two-foot takeoff (as in a standing broad jump). You must jump off both feet to initiate the test for successful completion. Record the best of five trials on your test score sheet.

The standing triple jump provides an indication of genetic potential to become a fast sprinter. Don't be discouraged if you have a low score; low scores can be improved. Some athletes may score high in this test and still not record excellent times in sprinting tests such as the 40-yard dash. These people may be very explosive and quick to change direction and accelerate to full speed without possessing the maximum speed of faster athletes.

QUICK HANDS

The quick hands test provides information on the presence or absence of fast-twitch muscle fibers in the muscles involved in moving the arms and hands rapidly. This test indicates your potential ability to use your upper extremities. Although heredity plays a major role in the ability to move quickly, proper training can improve speed and accuracy of upper extremity performance.

Find a padded surface that can be hit such as a boxing bag, football dummy, or martial arts or boxing focus gloves. Stand with palms flat against the equipment, arms extended. Step an inch or so closer so the length of your reach will emphasize speed and not hitting force. Have someone time you for 20 seconds as you strike the object with the palm of your hand as many times as you can. Focus on executing a firm and quick hit. The timer should count the number of strikes as well as tell you when to start and stop. Do the test twice and record the best trial on the score sheet.

The quick hands test provides an indication of genetic potential to become a fast player. This test shows how quickly you are able to strike your opponent. If your score is below the standard, you can improve by performing the test daily in practice.

QUICK FEET

The quick feet test provides information on the presence or absence of fast-twitch muscle fibers in the muscles involved in sprinting and indicates potential to execute fast steps (stride rate) and quick movements. Although hereditary factors such as limb length, muscle attachments, and proportion of fast-twitch fibers place a limit on maximum potential, everyone can improve speed and quickness.

Place 20 two-foot-long sticks or a 20-rung stride rope on a grass or artificial turf field. (A football field with each yard marked can also be used.) Space sticks exactly 18 inches apart for a total distance of 10 yards. Pump arms vigorously in a sprint-arm motion and use little knee lift while running the 10 yards without touching the sticks. The timer starts the stopwatch when your foot first touches the ground between the first and second stick and stops the watch when contact is made with the ground beyond the last stick. Record the best of two trials.

Like the standing triple jump and quick hands test, the quick feet test provides an indication of genetic potential to become a fast sprinter. Keep in mind that low scores can be improved.

RIGHT AND LEFT LEG HOPS

Right and left leg hops provide an excellent assessment of speed strength and explosive power in each leg. High scores are associated with a higher stride length during sprinting.

After a 15-yard flying start, begin a one-legged hop at the start tape and continue hopping 20 yards to the finish tape. Flags are used on start and finish tapes, as in the flying 120-yard dash (see page 12). The test involves an all-out effort, first on the dominant leg and then on the nondominant leg.

Right and left leg hops allow you to compare the explosive power of your dominant and nondominant leg so that you can focus on the less explosive limb, if necessary, to correct the imbalance. If your score fails to meet the standards, write *yes* in the Weakness column.

Body Composition

The purpose of body composition tests is to determine whether your body fat percentage falls within an acceptable range. Excess fat and pounds restrict speed and movement.

For optimum sprinting speed in sports competition, body fat should not exceed 10 percent for men and 15 percent for women. Useless fat weight, an added burden to be moved at high speed, slows down an athlete.

Unless underwater weighing equipment is available, the most accurate and practical method of determining body fat percentage is through the skinfold technique. Because a major portion of fat storage lies just under the skin, measurements in millimeters can be used to predict total body fat.

SKINFOLD TESTS

Body fat can be measured by determining the thickness of four skinfolds. Firmly grasp a fold of skin and subcutaneous fat (just under the skin) with your thumb and forefinger, pulling it away and up from the underlying muscle. Attach the jaws of the calipers one centimeter below your thumb and forefinger. All measurements should be taken on the right side of the body while the athlete is standing. Practice taking measurements with a partner, measuring the four areas described until you consistently get a similar score on each attempt.

✦ Triceps. With the arm resting comfortably at the side, take a vertical fold parallel to the long axis of the arm midway between the tip of the shoulder and the tip of the elbow.

✦ Biceps. With the arm resting comfortably at the side, take a vertical fold halfway between the elbow and the top of the shoulder on the front of the upper arm.

✦ Subscapula. Take a diagonal fold across the back, just below the shoulder blade.

✦ Suprailiac. Take a diagonal fold following the natural line of the iliac crest, just above the hip bone.

Record the following information to complete your evaluation:

1. Total the four skinfold measures in millimeters. Record this total on the test score sheet.

2. Find the percent of body fat based on this total from table 2.4. Record the percentage on the test score sheet.

3. Determine the amount of weight, if any, that should be lost to improve sprinting speed.

Although the ideal percentage of body fat may be somewhat lower for optimum sprinting speed, reasonable values fall between 10 and 15 percent for males and

Table 2.4   **Fat As a Percentage of Body Weight Based on the Sum of Four Skinfolds, Age, and Gender**

Age	17 to 29	16 to 29	30 to 39		40 to 49		50+	
			Body fat (%)					
Skinfold total (mm)	Male	Female	Male	Female	Male	Female	Male	Female
15	4.8	10.5						
20	8.1	14.1	12.2	17.0	12.2	19.8	12.6	21.4
25	10.5	16.8	14.2	19.4	15.0	22.2	15.6	24.0
30	12.9	19.5	16.2	21.8	17.7	24.5	18.6	26.6
35	14.7	21.5	17.7	23.7	19.6	26.4	20.8	28.5
40	16.4	23.4	19.2	25.5	21.4	28.2	22.9	30.3
45	17.7	25.0	20.4	26.9	23.0	29.6	24.7	31.9
50	19.0	26.5	21.5	28.2	24.6	31.0	26.5	33.4
55	20.1	27.8	22.5	29.4	25.9	32.1	27.9	34.6
60	21.2	29.1	23.5	30.6	27.1	33.2	29.2	35.7
65	22.2	30.2	24.3	31.6	28.2	34.1	30.4	36.7
70	23.1	31.2	25.1	32.5	29.3	35.0	31.6	37.7
75	24.0	32.2	25.9	33.4	30.3	35.9	32.7	38.7
80	24.8	33.1	26.6	34.3	31.2	36.7	33.8	39.6
85	25.5	34.0	27.2	35.1	32.1	37.5	34.8	40.4
90	26.2	34.8	27.8	35.8	33.0	38.3	35.8	41.2
95	26.9	35.6	28.4	36.5	33.7	39.0	36.6	41.9
100	27.6	36.4	29.0	37.2	34.4	39.7	37.4	42.6
105	28.2	37.1	29.6	37.9	35.1	40.4	38.2	43.3
110	28.8	37.8	30.1	38.6	35.8	41.0	39.0	43.9
115	29.4	38.4	30.6	39.1	36.4	41.5	39.7	44.5
120	30.0	39.0	31.1	39.6	37.0	42.0	40.4	45.1
125	30.5	39.6	31.5	40.1	37.6	42.5	41.1	45.7
130	31.0	40.2	31.9	40.6	38.2	43.0	41.8	46.2
135	31.5	40.8	32.3	41.1	38.7	43.5	42.4	46.7

(continued)

Table 2.4   **(continued)**

| Skinfold total (mm) | Body fat (%) | | | | | | | |
| | 17 to 29 | 16 to 29 | 30 to 39 | | 40 to 49 | | 50+ | |
	Male	Female	Male	Female	Male	Female	Male	Female
140	32.0	41.3	32.7	41.6	39.2	44.0	43.0	47.2
145	32.5	41.8	33.1	42.1	39.7	44.5	43.6	47.7
150	32.9	42.3	33.5	42.6	40.2	45.0	44.1	48.2
155	33.3	42.8	33.9	43.1	40.7	45.4	44.6	48.7
160	33.7	43.3	34.3	43.6	41.2	45.8	45.1	49.2
165	34.1	43.7	34.6	44.0	41.6	46.2	45.6	49.6
170	34.5	44.1	34.8	44.4	42.0	46.6	46.1	50.0
175	34.9			44.8		47.0		50.4
180	35.3			45.2		47.4		50.8
185	35.6			45.6		47.8		51.2
190	35.9			45.9		48.2		51.6
195				46.2		48.5		52.0
200				46.5		48.8		52.4
205						49.1		52.7
210						49.4		53.0

Note: In two-thirds of the measurements, the error was within ±3.5 percent of the body weight as fat for the women and ± 5 percent for the men

Reprinted, by permission, from J.V.G.A. Dumin and J. Womersley, 1974, "Body Fat Assessed from Total Body Density and Its Estimation from Skinfold Thickness." *British Journal of Nutrition* (Cambridge: Cambridge University Press), 32.

15 and 20 percent for females. Growing athletes falling within these ranges do not need to diet.

For example, Ted is a 17-year-old athlete who weighs 185 pounds. His four skinfold measurements are 3, 4, 9, and 9 millimeters. Ted's total is 25 millimeters (3 + 4 + 9 + 9). In this example, move down the first vertical column to 25 and over to the 17 to 29 age group for males in column two. Ted has about 10.5 percent fat; he is already at his ideal percent of body fat.

Ideal body fat for athletes depends on age, sport, and position. For optimum sprinting speed, athletes should strive for 10 to 15 percent (males) and 15 to 20 percent (females) or lower. Although some body fat is essential for life (3 to 4 percent for men and 10 to 12 percent for women), athletic performance (including speed and quickness) and health can be adversely affected by excess body fat.

Dieting to lose body fat can be very dangerous and is not recommended for growing athletes or anyone without careful supervision. The maximum rate of weight loss for athletes is 1 percent of body weight per week (1 to 2 pounds for those weighing 200 pounds or less). This rate requires a 500 to 1,000 calorie deficit each day. Faster rates of weight loss, losing more than 5 percent of total weight, or weight loss programs exceeding four weeks may result in loss of lean muscle mass, dehydration, and overtraining and may cause changes in vitamin and mineral status that could hinder performance. A sound weight loss program requires careful supervision and a combination of caloric restriction, slow weight loss, and regular exercise, including strength training to avoid loss of lean muscle mass and to add muscle weight while losing fat weight. Consult your coach and physician (and parents if you are under 18) before beginning any weight loss program.

Form and Technique

The checklist in chapter 10 and the descriptions of ideal form in chapter 12 can be used to evaluate form in the start, during acceleration or the drive phase, and while sprinting at maximum speed. Slow motion video analysis of your 40-yard dash and a coach's observation of technique will also provide valuable insight into counterproductive factors in your style that do not contribute to efficient forward movement.

Aerobic Fitness

A high level of aerobic fitness is important to every team sport athlete, including football players and other athletes who predominantly make short high-speed sprints during competition. All sports have an aerobic component, and attaining a high level of cardiovascular fitness will aid performance and also expedite the removal of lactic acid accumulated during repetitive anaerobic activity. The 1.5-mile run will measure cardiovascular fitness.

© Mark Friedman/SportsChrome

Short high-speed sprints are common in football.

1.5-MILE RUN

Begin with a general warm-up that produces perspiration, followed by five to eight minutes of stretching. Next, complete six laps around a quarter-mile track. In many sports, standards vary according to position, with large athletes of 225 to 400 pounds permitted more time to complete the test.

Your time provides an indication of aerobic fitness and your ability to perform continuous exercise in sports such as soccer, rugby, lacrosse, and field hockey. In addition, excellent scores suggest faster recovery between sprints in these same sports and football.

Stride Rate and Acceleration

You now have enough information to find out two more important things about yourself: how many steps you take per second and how well you accelerate from a stationary position to full speed.

FIGURING STRIDE RATE

Figuring out your stride rate allows you to compare the number of steps you take per second with faster sprinters, even Olympic-caliber sprinters such as Tim Montgomery and others who take between 4.5 and 5 steps per second. It also determines whether stride rate is an area of weakness for you that requires special attention in your training program.

To determine how many steps you take per second while sprinting, use the stride rate matrix in table 2.5. Find your stride length in inches on the vertical column. Now move to the right until you locate your flying 40-yard dash time on the horizontal column. Circle the point where these two scores intersect. This is your stride rate. Record the score on your test score sheet.

You can also calculate stride rate with some simple math using your flying 40-yard dash time and stride length: 1,440 inches (40 yards) divided by stride length (in inches) divided by flying 40-yard dash time equals stride rate (steps per second).

The stride rate of champion male sprinters approaches 5 steps per second; champion female sprinters average 4.48 steps per second. Because everyone can benefit from improved stride rate, sprint-assisted training, speed-strength training, and plyometrics are checked on the test score sheet, regardless of your score. This training program will improve stride rate.

ASSESSING ACCELERATION

Acceleration scores help you interpret your 40-yard dash time as well as predict how much you should improve.

Subtract your flying 40-yard time from your stationary 40-yard time and record the score to the right of Start and Acceleration on your test score sheet.

One way to find out how fast you should be sprinting a 40-yard dash is to add .7 second to your flying 40-yard time. For example, if your stationary 40-yard time is 4.9 and your flying 40 is 4.0, you should be sprinting the stationary 40-yard dash in 4.7, not 4.9. The .2-second difference is probably due to faulty starting techniques.

The difference between your stationary 40-yard dash and your flying 40-yard dash is the time delay required to accelerate. If there is more than a .7-second difference between these two scores, check ballistics, plyometrics, sport loading, speed-strength training, sprint-assisted training, and form training on your test score sheet. These training programs will improve your acceleration time.

Advanced Testing Program

The advanced testing program is designed for athletes competing at the high school, college, and professional levels. The program requires more specialized equipment and coaches who are familiar with these procedures.

Speed Potential

The NASE has developed a test to predict speed potential. This test helps estimate just how much you can improve.

NASE FUTURE 40

Have a coach or friend test you in the 40-yard dash from a stationary start using surgical tubing to tow you as fast as possible. Connect the belt securely around your waist, with the other belt attached to a partner. With your partner standing 10 yards in front of the finish line, back up and stretch the tubing exactly 30 yards until you reach the starting line; assume a three-point or track stance. The timer at the finish line starts the watch on your first muscular movement and stops it when you cross the finish line. After you sprint 5 yards, your partner sprints as fast as possible away from you to give you additional pull throughout the test. Record your score on the test score sheet. Decreasing your time .3 to .4 of a second provides an estimate of what you will be capable of after several months of training.

Muscle Balance

The prime movers in sprinting (knee extensors, hip extensors, and ankle plantar flexors) tend to become well developed as a result of normal sprint training. Muscle balance testing to compare the strength of opposing muscle groups is important to prevent injury and guarantee maximum speed of muscle contraction and relaxation. Muscle imbalances can slow you down. These tests can easily be completed by you and a partner, coach, or trainer.

Table 2.5   Stride Rate Matrix

Stride length (in.)	Flying 40-yard dash time (sec.)																				
	3.6	3.7	3.8	3.9	4.0	4.1	4.2	4.3	4.4	4.5	4.6	4.7	4.8	4.9	5.0	5.1	5.2	5.3	5.4	5.5	5.6
50	8.0	7.7	7.5	7.3	7.2	7.0	6.8	6.7	6.5	6.4	6.2	6.1	6.0	5.9	5.7	5.6	5.5	5.4	5.3	5.2	5.1
51	7.8	7.6	7.4	7.2	7.0	6.8	6.7	6.5	6.4	6.2	6.1	6.0	5.8	5.7	5.6	5.5	5.4	5.3	5.2	5.1	5.0
52	7.6	7.4	7.2	7.1	6.9	6.7	6.5	6.4	6.3	6.1	6.0	5.8	5.7	5.6	5.5	5.4	5.3	5.2	5.1	5.0	4.9
53	7.5	7.3	7.1	6.9	6.7	6.6	6.4	6.3	6.1	6.0	5.9	5.7	5.6	5.5	5.4	5.3	5.2	5.1	5.0	4.9	4.8
54	7.4	7.2	7.0	6.8	6.6	6.5	6.3	6.2	6.0	5.9	5.8	5.6	5.5	5.4	5.3	5.2	5.1	5.0	4.9	4.8	4.7
55	7.2	7.0	6.9	6.7	6.6	6.4	6.2	6.0	5.9	5.8	5.7	5.6	5.4	5.3	5.2	5.1	5.0	4.9	4.8	4.7	4.6
56	7.1	6.9	6.7	6.6	6.4	6.3	6.1	6.0	5.8	5.7	5.5	5.4	5.3	5.2	5.1	5.0	4.9	4.8	4.7	4.6	4.5
57	7.0	6.8	6.6	6.5	6.3	6.1	6.0	5.9	5.7	5.6	5.5	5.4	5.3	5.2	5.1	5.0	4.9	4.8	4.7	4.6	4.5
58	6.9	6.7	6.5	6.4	6.2	6.0	5.9	5.8	5.6	5.5	5.4	5.3	5.2	5.1	5.0	4.9	4.8	4.7	4.6	4.5	4.4
59	6.8	6.6	6.4	6.3	6.1	6.0	5.8	5.7	5.6	5.4	5.3	5.2	5.1	5.0	4.9	4.8	4.7	4.6	4.5	4.4	4.3
60	6.7	6.5	6.3	6.2	6.0	5.9	5.7	5.6	5.4	5.3	5.1	5.0	4.9	4.8	4.7	4.6	4.5	4.4	4.3	4.2	4.1
61	6.6	6.4	6.2	6.1	5.9	5.7	5.6	5.5	5.4	5.3	5.1	5.0	4.9	4.8	4.7	4.6	4.5	4.4	4.3	4.2	4.1
62	6.4	6.3	6.2	6.0	5.9	5.7	5.6	5.4	5.3	5.2	5.0	4.9	4.8	4.8	4.6	4.5	4.4	4.3	4.3	4.2	4.1
63	6.3	6.1	6.0	5.8	5.7	5.6	5.5	5.3	5.2	5.1	5.0	4.9	4.8	4.7	4.6	4.5	4.4	4.3	4.2	4.1	4.0
64	6.2	6.1	5.9	5.8	5.6	5.5	5.4	5.2	5.1	5.0	4.9	4.8	4.7	4.7	4.5	4.4	4.3	4.2	4.1	4.0	4.0
65	6.2	6.0	5.8	5.7	5.6	5.4	5.3	5.2	5.0	4.9	4.8	4.7	4.6	4.6	4.4	4.3	4.2	4.1	4.0	4.0	3.9
66	6.1	5.9	5.7	5.6	5.5	5.3	5.2	5.1	5.0	4.9	4.7	4.6	4.5	4.5	4.4	4.3	4.2	4.1	4.0	3.9	3.8
67	6.0	5.8	5.7	5.6	5.4	5.3	5.1	5.0	4.9	4.8	4.7	4.6	4.5	4.4	4.3	4.2	4.1	4.0	3.9	3.9	3.8
68	5.9	5.7	5.6	5.4	5.3	5.2	5.0	4.9	4.7	4.6	4.5	4.4	4.3	4.3	4.2	4.1	4.0	3.9	3.8	3.7	3.7
69	5.8	5.6	5.5	5.3	5.2	5.1	5.0	4.9	4.8	4.6	4.5	4.4	4.3	4.3	4.2	4.1	4.0	3.9	3.9	3.8	3.7
70	5.7	5.6	5.4	5.3	5.1	5.0	4.9	4.8	4.7	4.6	4.5	4.4	4.3	4.2	4.1	4.0	4.0	3.9	3.8	3.7	3.7
71	5.6	5.5	5.3	5.2	5.1	5.0	4.8	4.7	4.6	4.5	4.4	4.3	4.2	4.1	4.1	4.0	3.9	3.8	3.8	3.7	3.6
72	5.6	5.4	5.3	5.1	5.0	4.9	4.8	4.7	4.6	4.4	4.3	4.3	4.2	4.1	4.0	3.9	3.8	3.8	3.7	3.6	3.5
73	5.5	5.3	5.2	5.1	4.9	4.8	4.7	4.6	4.5	4.4	4.3	4.2	4.1	4.0	4.0	3.9	3.8	3.7	3.6	3.6	3.5
74	5.4	5.3	5.1	5.0	4.9	4.8	4.6	4.5	4.4	4.3	4.2	4.1	4.0	4.0	3.9	3.8	3.7	3.6	3.5	3.5	3.4
75	5.3	5.2	5.1	4.9	4.8	4.7	4.6	4.5	4.4	4.3	4.2	4.1	4.0	3.9	3.8	3.8	3.7	3.6	3.5	3.4	3.4

76	5.3	5.1	5.0	4.9	4.7	4.6	4.5	4.4	4.3	4.2	4.1	4.0	3.9	3.8	3.8	3.7	3.6	3.6	3.5	3.4	3.3
77	5.2	5.0	4.9	4.8	4.7	4.6	4.5	4.4	4.3	4.2	4.1	4.0	3.9	3.8	3.7	3.7	3.6	3.5	3.4	3.4	3.3
78	5.1	5.0	4.9	4.7	4.6	4.5	4.4	4.3	4.2	4.1	4.0	3.9	3.8	3.8	3.7	3.6	3.5	3.5	3.4	3.4	3.3
79	5.1	4.9	4.8	4.7	4.6	4.5	4.3	4.2	4.2	4.1	3.9	3.9	3.8	3.7	3.6	3.6	3.5	3.4	3.4	3.3	3.2
80	5.0	4.9	4.8	4.6	4.6	4.4	4.3	4.2	4.1	4.0	3.9	3.8	3.8	3.7	3.6	3.5	3.5	3.4	3.3	3.3	3.2
81	4.9	4.8	4.7	4.6	4.5	4.4	4.3	4.1	4.1	4.0	3.9	3.8	3.7	3.6	3.6	3.5	3.4	3.3	3.3	3.2	3.2
82	4.9	4.8	4.6	4.6	4.5	4.4	4.2	4.1	4.0	3.9	3.8	3.8	3.7	3.6	3.6	3.5	3.4	3.3	3.3	3.2	3.2
83	4.8	4.7	4.6	4.5	4.4	4.3	4.2	4.1	4.0	3.9	3.8	3.7	3.6	3.6	3.5	3.4	3.4	3.3	3.2	3.1	3.1
84	4.7	4.6	4.5	4.4	4.4	4.2	4.2	4.0	4.0	3.9	3.8	3.7	3.6	3.5	3.5	3.4	3.3	3.3	3.2	3.1	3.0
85	4.7	4.6	4.5	4.4	4.3	4.2	4.1	4.0	3.9	3.8	3.7	3.7	3.6	3.5	3.4	3.3	3.3	3.2	3.1	3.1	3.0
86	4.7	4.5	4.4	4.3	4.3	4.1	4.1	3.9	3.9	3.8	3.7	3.6	3.5	3.5	3.4	3.3	3.2	3.2	3.1	3.0	3.0
87	4.6	4.5	4.4	4.3	4.2	4.1	4.0	3.9	3.8	3.8	3.7	3.6	3.5	3.4	3.3	3.3	3.2	3.1	3.1	3.0	2.9
88	4.6	4.4	4.3	4.2	4.2	4.0	4.0	3.8	3.8	3.7	3.6	3.5	3.5	3.4	3.3	3.2	3.2	3.1	3.0	3.0	2.9
89	4.5	4.4	4.2	4.2	4.1	4.0	3.9	3.8	3.7	3.7	3.6	3.5	3.4	3.3	3.3	3.2	3.1	3.1	3.0	2.9	2.8
90	4.4	4.3	4.2	4.1	4.1	3.9	3.9	3.7	3.7	3.6	3.5	3.4	3.4	3.3	3.2	3.2	3.1	3.0	3.0	2.9	2.8
91	4.4	4.3	4.1	4.1	4.0	3.9	3.8	3.7	3.6	3.6	3.5	3.4	3.3	3.3	3.2	3.1	3.1	3.0	3.0	2.8	2.8
92	4.4	4.3	4.1	4.0	4.0	3.8	3.8	3.6	3.6	3.5	3.4	3.4	3.3	3.2	3.2	3.1	3.0	3.0	2.9	2.9	2.8
93	4.3	4.2	4.1	4.0	3.9	3.8	3.7	3.6	3.5	3.5	3.4	3.3	3.3	3.2	3.1	3.0	3.0	3.0	2.9	2.8	2.8
94	4.3	4.1	4.0	3.9	3.9	3.7	3.7	3.6	3.5	3.4	3.3	3.3	3.2	3.1	3.1	3.0	3.0	2.9	2.9	2.8	2.7
95	4.2	4.1	4.0	3.9	3.8	3.7	3.6	3.5	3.4	3.4	3.3	3.2	3.2	3.1	3.1	3.0	2.9	2.9	2.8	2.8	2.7
96	4.2	4.1	4.0	3.9	3.8	3.7	3.6	3.5	3.4	3.4	3.3	3.2	3.2	3.1	3.0	3.0	2.9	2.8	2.8	2.7	2.6
97	4.1	4.0	3.9	3.8	3.7	3.6	3.5	3.4	3.3	3.3	3.2	3.2	3.1	3.1	3.0	2.9	2.9	2.8	2.8	2.7	2.7
98	4.1	4.0	3.9	3.8	3.7	3.6	3.5	3.4	3.3	3.3	3.2	3.1	3.1	3.0	3.0	2.9	2.8	2.8	2.7	2.7	2.6
99	4.0	3.9	3.8	3.7	3.6	3.6	3.4	3.3	3.3	3.2	3.1	3.1	3.0	3.0	2.9	2.9	2.8	2.8	2.7	2.6	2.6
100	4.0	3.9	3.8	3.7	3.6	3.5	3.4	3.3	3.3	3.2	3.1	3.1	3.0	3.0	2.9	2.9	2.8	2.7	2.7	2.6	2.6
101	4.0	3.9	3.8	3.7	3.6	3.5	3.4	3.3	3.2	3.2	3.1	3.0	3.0	3.0	2.9	2.8	2.8	2.7	2.7	2.6	2.6
102	3.9	3.8	3.7	3.6	3.5	3.4	3.3	3.2	3.2	3.1	3.1	3.0	2.9	2.9	2.8	2.8	2.7	2.7	2.6	2.6	2.5
103	3.9	3.8	3.7	3.6	3.5	3.4	3.3	3.2	3.1	3.1	3.0	3.0	2.9	2.9	2.8	2.7	2.7	2.6	2.6	2.5	2.5
104	3.9	3.7	3.6	3.6	3.4	3.4	3.2	3.1	3.1	3.0	3.0	2.9	2.9	2.8	2.8	2.7	2.6	2.6	2.6	2.5	2.4
105	3.8	3.7	3.6	3.5	3.4	3.3	3.3	3.2	3.1	3.0	2.9	2.9	2.8	2.8	2.7	2.7	2.6	2.6	2.5	2.5	2.4
106	3.8	3.6	3.6	3.5	3.4	3.3	3.2	3.1	3.0	3.0	2.9	2.9	2.8	2.7	2.7	2.6	2.6	2.5	2.5	2.4	2.4
107	3.7	3.6	3.5	3.4	3.3	3.2	3.1	3.0	2.9	2.8	2.8	2.8	2.7	2.7	2.6	2.6	2.5	2.5	2.4	2.5	2.4
108	3.7	3.6	3.5	3.4	3.3	3.2	3.1	3.0	3.0	2.9	2.8	2.8	2.7	2.6	2.6	2.5	2.5	2.5	2.4	2.4	2.3

Prepared by Lynne R. Mohn.

Testing for 1RM (maximum amount of weight with which you can execute just one repetition) allows quick, easy comparison of the strength of your left and right limbs using the single-leg extension, single-leg curl, single-leg kickback, one-arm curl (biceps), one-arm military press (triceps), and one-leg press (quadriceps). For each test, select a weight that you can lift comfortably. Add weight in subsequent trials until you find the weight that you can lift correctly just one time (1RM). Three trials with a three-minute recovery period between each trial are needed to find the true 1RM. Compare the scores of your right and left leg and right and left arm in each test. If there is a difference of more than 10 pounds in the leg tests or 5 pounds in the arm tests, write *yes* in the Weakness column.

✦ Single-leg extension (quadriceps): Find and compare your 1RM for each leg.

✦ Single-leg curl (hamstrings): Find and compare your 1RM for each leg.

✦ Single-leg kickback: Find and compare your 1RM for each leg. If scores differ by more than 5 to 10 pounds, your stride length will be affected, producing a shorter stride. If this occurs, examine your stride length scores to see if there is also a significant difference between these scores when you push off with a different foot. If so, it is important to focus on a speed-strength training program that will eliminate this deficiency in the weak leg.

✦ One-arm barbell curl (biceps): Using the underhand grip in a standing position, raise the barbell from thighs to chest and return it, keeping the body erect and motionless throughout the movement. Record your 1RM.

✦ One-arm military press (triceps): Using the overhand grip in a standing position, raise the dumbbell or barbell from the shoulder to an overhead position until the elbow is locked. Record your 1RM.

Table 2.6 lists some reported values for joint agonist-antagonist ratios at slow isokinetic speeds. Your coach or trainer can test you in any of these areas where an imbalance is suspected. Your task is to find the 1RM for both movements and compare your ratio to those on the chart. Because of differences in muscle mass, you can expect some disparity (no more than 10 percent) between muscle groups such as the quadriceps and hamstrings and the plantar flexors and dorsiflexors.

In general, the further the joint agonist-antagonist muscle balance ratio is from 1:1, the more you need to be concerned. A hamstring/quadriceps ratio of 1:2 or a plantar flexion/dorsiflexion ratio of 4:1 is an indication of a speed-strength weakness that could be limiting sprint speed. Specific weight training exercises and the proper prescription of sets, repetitions, weight, and recovery intervals can improve the ratio.

Table 2.6   Agonist-Antagonist Ratios for Slow Concentric Isokinetic Movements

Joint	Muscles	Desirable torque ratio at slow speed
Ankle	Plantar flexion/dorsiflexion (gastrocnemius, soleus, tibialis anterior)	3:1
Ankle	Inversion/eversion (tibialis anterior, peroneals)	1:1
Knee	Extension/flexion (quadriceps/ hamstrings)	3:2
Hip	Extension/flexion (spinal erectors, gluteus maximus, hamstrings/iliopsoas, rectus abdominis, tensor fasciae latae)	1:1
Shoulder	Flexion/extension (anterior deltoids/ trapezius, posterior deltoids)	2:3
Shoulder	Internal rotation/external rotation (subscapularis/supraspinatus, infraspinatus, teres minor)	3:2
Elbow	Flexion/extension (biceps/triceps)	1:1
Lumbar spine	Flexion/extension (psoas, abdominal muscles/spinal erectors)	

Note: Values are a summary of numerous studies of slow-speed concentric isokinetic movements.

Reprinted, by permission, from D. Wathen, 1994, Muscle Balance. In *Essentials of Strength Training and Conditioning*, edited by T. Baechle (Champaign, IL: Human Kinetics), 425.

Other Tests

Strength curve testing. Dr. Stan Plagenhoef has developed testing procedures to measure changes in leverage and muscle mass as a limb is moved through a range of motion. Anatomical strength curves reflect the body's ability to produce muscle contractile force at given points in the range of motion. These strength curves are used to determine how far above or below the strength potential a person falls. Data collected on Olympic sprinters such as Carl Lewis, Leroy Burrell, Chris Jones, and Lamont Smith allow valuable comparisons to athletes in other sports who are striving to improve sprinting speed. Strength curves can also be used to compare the right and left side of the body (dominant to nondominant side).

On-field analysis (playing speed). For sprinting analysis, this sophisticated system uses an Olympic champion sprinter as a basis for creating a digital athletic model of performance. Performances are recorded in the computer with values assigned to points of movement. The performance of an athlete is recorded in the computer and compared with the database of the digital model of the Olympic champion. The result is graphically displayed through differences in performance characteristics such as leg lift, arm swing, stride length, and leg extension.

Digitized analysis is also used for on-field performance to provide a complete analysis during competitive play. Coaches interested in the On-Field Analysis System should contact Dr. Bob Ward at www.sportsscience.com.

Muscle Fiber Types

All athletes possess three types of muscle fiber:

+ Slow-twitch red (type I) muscle fiber develops force slowly, has a long twitch time and a low power output, is fatigue-resistant (high endurance), and has high aerobic capacity for energy supply, but it has limited potential for rapid force development and anaerobic power.

+ Fast-twitch red (type IIa) is an intermediate fiber type that can contribute to both anaerobic and aerobic activity. It develops force moderately quickly and has moderate twitch time, power output, fatigability, aerobic power, force development, and anaerobic power.

+ Fast-twitch white (type IIb) fiber develops force rapidly and has a short twitch time, a high power output, fatigability (low endurance), low aerobic power, and high anaerobic power.

Although slow-twitch fibers cannot be changed into fast-twitch fibers, most of the intermediate fibers (type IIa) can be converted to the faster type IIb fibers through training. This conversion aids explosive movements such as sprinting.

Speed of arm and leg movements is specific to the limb, as are the type and direction of movements with the limb. Training programs to improve speed therefore must involve the muscles and specific movements of sprinting.

Comparing the speed strength of left limb to right limb, agonist to antagonist, upper body to lower body, and strength to total body weight provides valuable information to the athlete who wants to improve speed by focusing on her weaknesses or limiting factors.

You now have enough information to design a speed improvement program just for you. For each score on the comprehensive test, write *yes* in the Weakness column on the test score sheet if you failed to meet the standard specified. If you write *yes* for a test, also check the programs listed in table 2.1 for that test area. These are the specific training programs you need to follow to eliminate the weakness areas. Each program is described in detail in chapters 7 and 9 through 12.

Team Sport Combine Tests

Predraft testing programs in team sports, such as the NFL Combine for pro football prospects, have become extremely important; scores can have a dramatic effect on the draft round, signing bonus, salary, and other specifics in a contract. A poor combine 40-yard dash time, for example, can and has cost potential high-round picks millions of dollars. So much emphasis is placed on the 40-yard dash and some other tests that prospects are forced to practice and train for specific tests for months before the scheduled combine. As a result, combine training centers have sprung up throughout the United States for this purpose. Specific player position skills tests are also becoming more and more important, and scores in these areas can be improved with training and practice.

Your best opportunity to score high on the 40-yard dash and other speed and quickness tests in the combine for your sport is to complete the comprehensive test battery described in this chapter and follow our sport-specific speed improvement program for 6 to 10 weeks to eliminate weaknesses and improve speed.

Practice and training for the specific tests used in the combine for your sport will also greatly increase your chances of achieving a higher rating for the draft. This section describes each test and scoring procedure in pro combine or tryout centers in baseball, basketball, football, and soccer. Study this section carefully, and master the techniques for each test in your sport before attending a combine or tryout.

NFL Combine Tests

The NFL Combine includes physical tests and specific one-on-one drills that are filmed but not included as part of the grading system. A video manual is available to help players prepare for the NFL Combine. The following physical tests are included:

+ 40-yard dash—Each player runs twice; test is filmed; best time is scored by pro scouts.

+ 225-pound bench press—All players, except kickers, complete as many repetitions as possible.

+ 20-yard short shuttle—All players, except kickers, are timed twice, once while shuttle running to the left and once to the right. Both times are scored and the drill is filmed.

+ Vertical jump—Test is conducted using the Vertec® measuring device. Each player jumps twice; highest jump is scored.

+ Height and weight—Height is measured to one-eighth of an inch, weight to the nearest pound.

✦ Full body video portrait—Provides a visual image of body type and build. Players are filmed from the front and back wearing shorts only.

Phase II of the combine includes specific one-on-one drills that are filmed but are not part of the grading system.

✦ Quarterbacks are filmed in isolation performing three-, five-, and seven-step drops and throws to wide receivers in one-on-one coverage against defensive backs.

✦ Running backs and tight ends compete against linebackers in man coverage during a one-on-one passing drill.

✦ Wide receivers compete against defensive backs in man coverage during a one-on-one passing drill.

✦ Linemen are timed in the 10-yard and 20-yard dash before completing several cone drills to evaluate foot speed and quickness. They compete in one-on-one competition during run block/react and pass rush/block drills. Helmets are worn during blocking drills.

✦ Punters complete the baseline strength test and kicking tests (hang time, distance, and get-off time for six punts over two rounds) and random selection scenario test (ability to perform six different types of punts during two rounds—direction right, direction left, deep center, deep nose over, straight pooch, and float pooch). Top punters in these tests may be asked to perform additional punts.

✦ Kickers perform kickoffs (hang time, location, and distance for three consecutive kicks) and field goals (eight field goals over four rounds at randomly selected distances from 30 to 55 yards). The most successful kickers may be asked to perform additional field goals and kickoffs.

✦ Long snappers perform seven snaps from 7 and 15 yards and are graded for time and accuracy.

Players are graded on a 5- to 10-point scale:

✦ 9.00 to 10.00 points—Player significantly exceeds minimum pro standard (pro player).

✦ 8.00 to 8.99—Player meets or exceeds minimum pro standard (pro prospect).

✦ 7.00 to 7.99—Player scores slightly below minimum pro standard (potential pro prospect).

✦ 6.00 to 6.99—Player scores below minimum pro standard (college-level player).

✦ 5.00 to 5.99—Player scores significantly below minimum pro standard (below college-level player).

Height and weight measurements and the results of the four physical tests determine a player's score in each of the four test grades—size (height and weight), speed (40-yard dash), quickness (both shuttle run times), and strength (bench press and vertical jump test). The four athletic test grades are averaged to arrive at a player's final test grade (FTG). Players with an FTG equal to or greater than 8.00 are pro-rated.

Table 2.7 shows the minimum standards by position. The minimum pro standard in each category equals a grade of 8.00. Higher than the minimum pro standard receives a score between 8.01 and 10.00; scores below the minimum fall between 5.00 and 7.99.

Punters are graded based on averages for touch-to-toe, hang time, and distance during open-field punting. The pro standard minimum for touch-to-toe is 1.40 seconds and is considered 20 percent of the punter's final test grade (FTG). The pro standard minimum for hang time is 4.25 seconds (40 percent of FTG); the minimum for distance is 42 yards (40 percent of FTG).

Kickers are graded based on field goals made and average kickoff hang time and distance. The kickoff grade is based on distance (50 percent) and hang time (50 percent). The field goal grade is based on a starting value of 5.00, with each successful kick increasing the grade by the point values listed in table 2.8. The FTG is based 70 percent on field goal grade and 30 percent on kickoff grade.

Table 2.7   **NFL Combine Minimum Standards by Position**

Position	Height	Weight	40-yd. dash	Shuttle run	Bench press	Vertical jump
Quarterback	6'1"	200	4.90	4.50	10	28
Running back	5'10"	185	4.65	4.35	12	30
Fullback	5'11"	220	4.75	4.35	14	28
Wide receiver	5'11"	180	4.65	4.29	8	30
Tight end	6'2"	230	4.85	4.55	18	28
Cornerback	5'10"	180	4.60	4.29	10	30
Safety	5'11"	190	4.70	4.29	10	30
Outside linebacker	6'1"	220	4.80	4.50	18	28
Inside linebacker	6'1"	230	4.85	4.50	18	28
Defensive end	6'2"	270	5.00	4.60	20	26
Defensive tackle	6'3"	275	5.20	4.75	24	24
Nose tackle	6'2"	275	5.20	4.79	24	24
Offensive guard	6'2"	275	5.15	4.79	24	24
Offensive tackle	6'3"	275	5.25	4.79	24	24
Center	6'1"	275	5.20	4.79	24	24

Table 2.8   **Point Values for Grading Kickers**

Category	Pro minimum	Distance (yd.)	Point value
Kickoff hang time	3.85 sec.	30	.25
Kickoff distance	62 yd.	35	.35
Field goals		40	.45
		45 (left hash)	.75
		45 (right hash)	.75
		50 (left hash)	.80
		50 (right hash)	.80
		55	.85

Long snappers are graded based on average time and accuracy for seven snaps at each distance. Accuracy is scored based on the following scale:

+ 1 Excellent—Holder makes no adjustment.
+ 2 Good—Holder makes minor adjustment.
+ 3 Poor—Holder makes major adjustment.
+ 4 Uncatchable—Snap is wild or short.

The minimum pro standards (8.00 grade) for a 7-yard snap are .28 seconds (time) and 1.29 (accuracy). The minimum standards for a 15-yard snap are .75 seconds (time) and 1.57 (accuracy).

Pro Soccer Combine Tests

A standardized pro soccer combine test battery is not available. Individual teams and coaches use their own tests to evaluate current and potential players.

Soccer players repeatedly sprint from a walk or slow jog for 5 to 25 yards during competition. Top players may cover over 2,000 yards in one game. A solid aerobic foundation is considered very important in aiding recovery from lactic acid buildup after repeated sprints.

To test aerobic endurance, players perform a 12-minute run or a beep test. To test anaerobic capacity, tall cones are set up 30 yards apart. Players use a standing start then sprint back and forth (total of 60 yards) five times, touching the tops of the cones each time. A time of 57 to 58 seconds is considered excellent, 59 to 60 seconds is considered good, and 61 to 63 seconds is considered weak. Players also perform a 40-meter sprint. Two cones are placed 40 meters apart. The best time is recorded. Testers use a radar gun to determine how fast a player can run.

Muscular endurance is tested using a 30-second bent-knee sit-up test and a push-up test. For the sit-up test, the spotter places a palm on top of the player's knees. The player touches the spotter's hand for each repetition. For the push-up test, the spotter places a hand just above the floor underneath the player's chest. The player's chest touches the spotter's hand with each repetition. The sit-and-reach test described earlier in this chapter is also used. To test leg power, players perform three consecutive bounds using a two-foot takeoff. The 1RM bench and leg press are used to test strength.

Major League Baseball (MLB) Combine Tests

MLB uses the following speed tests and standards: 60-yard dash (under 7.0 seconds); crack of bat to first base, to second base, to third base; first to second base, second to third base, and second to home plate (under 7.0 seconds). Some teams use a shuttle run.

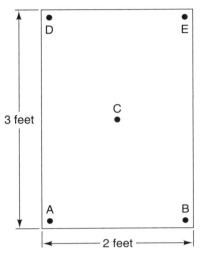

Figure 2.3 Setup for the quick feet test.

The quick feet test used by the Houston Astros was developed by Dr. Gene Coleman, strength and conditioning coach for the Astros. A two-by-three-foot rectangle is taped on the floor with a three-inch dot in each corner and one in the middle of the rectangle (see figure 2.3). Players must perform five repetitions of each drill as fast as possible, without resting between sets or between drills.

1. **Up and back.** Stand at one end of the rectangle with the left foot on dot A and the right foot on dot B. Jump off both feet and land on dot C with both feet at the same time. Immediately jump off both feet and land with one foot on dot D and one foot on dot E. Jump backward and come back in the same way. Finish by landing with the left foot on dot A and the right foot on dot B.

2. **Right foot.** With the left foot on dot A and right foot on dot B, jump to dot C, landing on the right foot. Then, in order, jump to dots D, E, C, A, and B, always landing on the right foot. End with the right foot on dot B.

3. **Left foot.** With the right foot on dot B, jump to dot C, landing on the left foot. Then, in order, jump to dots D, E, C, A, and B, always landing on the left foot. End with the left foot on dot B.

4. **Both feet.** With the left foot on dot B, jump to dot C, landing on both feet. Then, in order, jump to dots D, E, C, A, and B, always landing on both feet. End with both feet on dot B.

5. **Turn around.** With both feet on dot B, jump to dot C, landing on both feet. Jump forward and land with the left foot on dot D and right foot on dot E. Quickly jump up and turn 180 degrees, facing the other way, and land with the right foot on dot D and left foot on dot E. Jump and land on dot C with

both feet and then jump to dots A and B, landing with the right foot on dot A and the left foot on dot B. Spin 180 degrees and repeat the drill.

A good time is 60 seconds or less. After completing the drill, the player is allowed to rest for two to three minutes and repeat, completing three sets.

Skills tests include an arm strength test (tested using a radar gun) in which the player catches fly balls and throws 270 feet to home, a ground ball test in which pitchers throw from the mound and players field the ground balls (velocity is checked with the radar gun), a catcher test in which catchers throw to second base (the timer begins the stopwatch when the catcher receives the ball and stops the watch when the ball reaches second base), batting practice (8 to 10 swings per hitter), and a live game.

Finally, players complete a mental skills assessment questionnaire that includes measures of traits and abilities that sport psychologists have found to be associated with high-level performance in baseball and other sports.

NBA Combine Tests

The following test was developed and is administered by the National Basketball Conditioning Coaches Association (NBCCA).

For the no-step vertical jump, a Vertec device is used. Players complete two trials with no foot movement permitted (no shuffle step, side step, drop step, or gather step allowed), only a straight down and straight up movement. If an athlete reaches a new height on the second attempt, a third attempt is granted.

For the maximum vertical jump test, a maximum approach distance is measured from the free throw line, extended in a 15-foot arch to the baseline. Athletes may take as many steps toward the Vertec device as they feel necessary to attain their maximum vertical jump as long as they start within the 15-foot arch. A one- or two-foot takeoff may be used, and the best of two trials is recorded.

For the pro lane agility drill, cones are placed at each of the four corners of the pro foul lane (16 feet by 19 feet, baseline to foul line). The player begins in the lower left corner of the lane. The player sprints toward the top of the lane, going around the cone in a right defensive slide, then goes to the edge of the lane and around the cone, then backpedals to the foul line, around the cone, then defensive slides to the left. He touches the floor, feet even with the cone at the starting position. The player changes direction to his right, then defensive slides around the cone and sprints to the top of the lane. He defensive slides to the left around the cone and backpedals past the original starting position. The fastest time of two attempts is recorded. One false start (including knocking over a cone, cutting the corner of the drill, sprinting sideways instead of defensive sliding, not touching the line at the change of direction point at the start/finish line, or simply falling down) is permitted without penalty. Two coaches begin timing on the athlete's first movement. The coaches average their readings to get the official time for the trial.

For the three-quarter court sprint, the player starts in a two-point stance (standing start) then sprints from baseline to opposite foul line. Timing begins on the athlete's first movement. Four coaches time each of two sprints, with high and low scores eliminated and middle two times averaged and recorded as the official time. One false start is permitted.

The Acuflex® sit-and-reach box is used to administer the sit-and-reach flexibility test. The toes (without shoes) are zero. Anything past the toes is a positive reading; anything not reaching the toes is a negative reading. The middle fingers of both hands are lined up on top of each other. Knees are kept in a locked position as the athlete takes a deep breath, blows out, reaches beyond the toes, holds the position for one count, then repeats the movement. The best of two attempts is recorded.

The final test is the 185-pound maximum repetition (1RM) bench press. After a warm-up that consists of 10 push-ups followed by a 60-second rest and five repetitions of the bench press with 135 pounds followed by a 90-second rest, the athlete completes as many consecutive repetitions as possible of the bench press with 185 pounds. Two spotters are used. One provides a liftoff, counts the number of repetitions, and makes sure each repetition is locked at the top. The second spotter makes certain that the athlete's glutes stay in contact with the bench (no arching).

Chapter 3

FOUNDATION TRAINING

*T*he foundation training that appeared in the first edition of *Sports Speed* served as a fragmented all-systems preparation period. In this edition, a periodization model has been added to the training. A periodization model is an integrated system that considers all the elements of performance required for competition in team sports. The outcome of foundational training is superior training and better performance in your sport.

Fundamentally, foundation training is the root system that supports and sustains every play in any sport. No doubt a time will come during play that shows a player's weaknesses (limiting factors). A careful examination of these situations will establish whether a direct connection exists between weakness in sport performance and a deficiency that could be worked on.

This chapter establishes a list of core activities based on how many basic movement patterns a person can develop. A good way to understand foundation training is to take a close look at a space shuttle launch. Initially, the shuttle is stationary on the launch pad, even after ignition. However, subtle movements are taking place as the shuttle's nervous system (its computer) sends instructions to put all subsystems in motion in preparation for launch. In addition, the astronauts are preparing for the launch. Physical educators call these actions before takeoff, in relation to the shuttle, nonlocomotor movements. The shuttle hasn't moved from the launch pad even though the astronauts and shuttle's systems are in motion and preparation for launch.

Likewise, any actions you make on the field of play without moving your body off the field are nonlocomotor skills (flexing, extending, rotating, bending, shifting, swaying, and faking). These movements are as important to play as nonlocomotor movements are for a perfect launch. Locomotor skills, on the other hand, are basic total body actions requiring movement through space (blocking, catching, changing direction, hitting, falling, leaping, pulling, pushing, rolling, running, sliding, starting, stopping, tackling, and throwing).

These basic movement patterns can be likened to the alphabet (which can be organized into words, phrases, sentences, and paragraphs) or to musical notes (which can be combined into scales and chords). Once you learn the basic elements of movement, you can make limitless combinations to form new and creative solutions to the problems faced when competing in sports.

Foundation training provides a solid, conceptual, and practical foundation to help accelerate you to the final steps of speed improvement.

Foundation training identifies core activities including many of the movement patterns performed with the feet, hands, and so on. Playing basketball, boxing, dancing, playing handball, fencing, doing gymnastics, hurdling, jumping, kicking, practicing martial arts, running, throwing, walking, and wrestling require many of these basic patterns. These activities have been tagged as core exercises by some because they contain many of the elements of comprehensive human movement. Remember, these activities must be specifically applied to specific sport needs. It is good to include these activities in physical education programs in school, in after-school extracurricular activities, and as specifically recommended in the rest of this book.

General Preparation

The first part of foundation training is called general preparation. The objective is to increase the body's resources to optimum levels before beginning the trip to faster running and playing speeds. In many programs, it is unlikely that the body's resources have been developed to threshold or optimum levels. Therefore, athletes should follow a threshold-based program that takes into account all the body's resources to produce an integrated program. Awareness, reactions, reflexes, quickness and control of body segments in all directions, quickness of close-range movements in all directions, basic movement elements of the body, basic movement elements required for sports (movement patterns, hand-eye and foot-eye coordination), power, sustained power output, speed in all directions, maximum strength, muscular strength endurance, anaerobic conditioning, and aerobic conditioning are all vital in sport performance.

Foundational training includes other organizational elements necessary for the operation of the total program. Use one of the variety of programs suggested for each of the basic elements. Get involved in the training process by adding your own ideas to the methods. The major outcome of foundational training is to optimize the performance quality of the essential resources required for your sport. You can be confident that you will accomplish this outcome if you successfully carry out the suggestions included in this chapter in combination with the assessments in chapter 2.

Foundational Training Sport Check

Before venturing too far into program planning, take a close look at your test results from the assessments taken in chapter 2. Then complete the Sport Check Scorecard in this chapter. Your assessment information list includes the basic testing program, the advanced testing program, and the sport check scorecard. These assessments are extremely important because you will build your playing speed training on this foundation.

The basic and advanced testing programs do not collect data about resources in actual game or sport conditions. To build an effective training program, you need to measure how effectively you use all of the necessary resources during game conditions. (Because sprinting is described in detail by the measurements of the testing programs, few additional measurements are required for a comprehensive assessment of pure sprinting.)

Computer software is a good tool to use to measure the specifics of an athlete's performance. The On-Field Analysis System (OFAS) is a computer graphic and software package. It was used to track NFL, Senior Bowl, and East-West College all-star game players as they played in order to develop a scientific grading system. The goal was to provide an objective method to precisely identify how players use their resources during games. Grades are based on objective sources. The OFAS yields the most objective and precise time motion analysis available. Contact OFAS at www.sportsscience.com for information. Other computer-based biomechanical systems have been designed to improve sport performance. Peak Performance Technologies in Englewood, Colorado, is leading the development and distribution of such systems. In addition, professional soccer teams in Europe are using scientific computer programs to evaluate players and the game.

The Coaching Association of Canada's National Coaching Certification Program: Level 3 Coaching Theory manual illustrates the use of a much simpler time motion analysis system to get important sport-specific training information for grading and training. The association's program includes observing games with a stopwatch, paper, and pencil to chart the action on the field. The program's objective is to determine the time, motion, and intensity involved in the sport. Using this method, coaches are able to calculate the average velocity, high- and low-intensity velocity, and schedules of repetitions. Players and coaches can use this method to evaluate the sport and individual performances. Coaches and players can make better estimates of the aerobic and anaerobic requirements of the sport by studying actual games. Sport-specific training programs and drills also can be created to duplicate the elements of the game. If you are interested in this time motion analysis method, contact the Coaching Association of Canada at 141 Laurier Avenue West, Suite 300, Ottawa, Ontario, Canada, K1P 5J3.

The sport check scorecard can be customized to fit your sport by using a combination of biomechanics and time motion measurement methods. These methods assess higher level game skills to get a better understanding of how athletes are integrating their basic resources into more complex sport-related functions. Scorecards identify, assess, and track performance.

Use the sport check scorecard as a conceptual guide. The scorecard divides the absolute performance curve into 10 labeled categories. The underlying structure of the curve is based on an absolute performance scale rather than one that has been adjusted for age. Both absolute and age-related values are important tools for program development. For more information about age-related performance scales, write the National Association for Sport and Physical Education, 1900 Association Drive, Reston, Virginia, 20191.

Sport Check Scorecard

The scorecard (table 3.1) is a 10-level scoring scale you can use to monitor achievement. Scoring starts at the beginner level and proceeds progressively to the master level, which only highly accomplished athletes achieve. Do not be confused by the names given to each level. An athlete who has spent a short time in a sport is generally classified as a beginner or novice, even though, by virtue of genetics, this athlete may have a better performance score than an athlete who has been involved in the sport for some time. The scoring scale includes the whole spectrum of performance. These questions will help you determine the assessment process and see how you compare with the best.

+ What sport or skill is being assessed?
+ Why are the measurements important?
+ Where am I in growth and development (chronological or performance age)?
+ When and how often will my measurements be taken?
+ How will the measurements be collected and used?

The 10-level sport check evaluates 11 basic elements: sport-specific tasks, proper breathing mechanics, combat breathing, training the brain, body control, sport hitting power, starting power, driving power, high-speed quickness, maximum playing speed, and sustained power output endurance base. Each of these elements is vital to success in playing more quickly and faster or sprinting at high speeds.

Table 3.1 **Sport Check Scorecard**

Level—Class	Percent level	Present score
10—Master	99+	
9—Elite	96 to 98	
8—Advanced	90 to 95	
7—Intermediate	79 to 89	
6—Above average	60 to 78	
5—Average	40 to 59	
4—Below average	21 to 39	
3—Apprentice	11 to 20	
2—Novice	3 to 10	
1—Beginner	0 to 2	

Sport-Specific Tasks

Sport-specific tasks should be determined and prioritized with the help of a professionally qualified person in your sport. Each of the tasks that make up your sport should be grouped and evaluated according to four questions:

1. How frequently is the task done?
2. How difficult is the task to complete?
3. How critical is the task to performance?
4. How much is required for the task?

A scientifically based program requires an in-depth study of the sport before a training prescription can be developed. Knowing the importance of each task involved in the sport enables you to allocate appropriate training time. Schellas Hyndman, men's varsity soccer coach at Southern Methodist University, provided four sample soccer sport check scorecards. We have modified them in tables 3.2 through 3.4 in an effort to prioritize basic techniques. Use these four focus areas to help you construct a scorecard for your sport: technique frequency, difficulty, and importance; technique scoring and resource recognition; physical dimensions, thresholds, and limiting factors; and physical dimensions performance report for program assessment.

Table 3.2 is an example of a soccer goalkeeper's scorecard. Tables 3.3 and 3.4 list the physical dimensions required for soccer. Scores can be based on any familiar system that you presently use: grades A through F, scores of 1 to 10, or scores of 0 to 100 (as shown in table 3.1). The system shown in table 3.1 is our recommendation. Whichever method you use, be consistent.

Careful study of the information in the scorecards will give the coach and player a sound basis for constructing an evaluation and training program based on the specific skills required for the sport and the limiting factors holding the player back. Remember, training must match the requirements of your sport if it is to be effective. In addition, limiting factors in performance must also be corrected. This assessment should be coupled with the basic and advanced testing programs found in chapter 2.

Proper Breathing Mechanics and Combat Breathing

Breathing is an essential human function that plays a major role in the production of energy at sleep, rest, or play. Not many of us have been trained to use the most efficient mechanics for meditating, relaxing, or executing the basic tasks of daily life. Most of us walk around each day with limited breathing skills. Athletes cannot afford inadequate skill in any aspect of breathing. Relaxing, starting in sprinting, body contact, hitting or punching, blocking, running, sprinting, and throwing all require specific breathing skills.

Proper breathing requires proper mechanics. First breathe through the nose to warm and filter air. During times of high oxygen demand, breathe through the

Table 3.2   **Soccer Goalkeeper Scorecard**

Defensive techniques	Score	Resource

1. Scooping
   Ground balls at the keeper
   Ground balls to either side		

2. Catching
   Catching below chest height
   Catching at chest height
   Overhead catching		

3. Falling/diving
   Simple falling
   Footwork leading to dive
   Diving for low shots
   Power diving—high shots
   Forward diving		

4. Boxing
   Two fisted to change direction
   One fisted to keep direction
   One fisted to change direction
   One elbow to keep direction
   One elbow to change direction
   Two elbows to keep direction
   Two elbows to change direction
   Boxing under pressure		

5. Deflecting
   With one hand around post
   With one hand over crossbar
   With one elbow to keep direction
   With one elbow
   With two elbows
   With two hands		

6. Breakaways
   Sliding at opponent
   Holding a long barrier
   Throwing the body to block a shot
   Stand-up technique		

7. Soccer playing skills
   Play outside of penalty area (general)
   Heading
   Playing to a teammate
   Interception of "thru passes"
   Dealing with back passes		

(continued)

Table 3.2   **(continued)**

Defensive techniques	Score	Resource

8. Range
   Judgment of flighted balls
   Ability to extend play		

Distribution and attacking techniques	Score	Resource

1. Throwing
   Bowling
   Sidearm sling
   Overhead "baseball" throw		

2. Kicking out of hand
   Volley
   Drop kick		

3. Goal kick and free kick
   Short range
   Long range		

Tactics	Score	Resource

1. Positioning/angle play
   In the goal—on the goal line
   Outside of goal area		

2. Reading the game
   In the goal—immediate danger
   Outside of goal area—secondary danger
   Outside of penalty area		

3. Breakaways One-on-one duels		

4. Penalty kicks
   Tactical concerns
   Reflex action		

Courtesy of Schellas Hyndman, Southern Methodist University. Modified by Bob Ward.

nose and mouth. Regulate the release of air through the mouth during contact and high-output skills, such as body contact, hitting in baseball, punching in boxing, or throwing in any sport.

Use the lower portions of the lungs to breathe when sleeping, meditating, relaxing, and during times of maximum oxygen transfer. To make sure you are breathing from the diaphragm, put your hand on your abdomen. If it moves inward and outward with each breath, you are breathing from your diaphragm. Watch the way babies breathe. Do their bellies go in and out?

Raise and roll your shoulders back to provide additional volume for combat breathing. Increase chest volume by maximizing breathing during periods of

	Raw score	Threshold	Limiting factor
Sleep HR zone (22 to 30%)			
Resting HR zone (30 to 35%)			
Aerobic zone (70 to 80% max)			
Anaerobic zone (80 to 90% max)			
Maximum zone (90 to 100% max)			
Coordination/flow (general)			
Open/target focus			
Timing and judgment			
Kinesthetic sense			
Rhythm			
Footwork			
Handwork			
Reactions/reflexes			
Quickness			
Agility			
Kicking power			
Kicking distance			
Hitting power			
Throwing distance			
Vertical jumping			
Horizontal jumping			
Speed			
Strength			
Muscle balance			
Sustained power output			
Range of motion			
Injury recovery			
Recovery from game workout			

Table 3.4   Physical Dimensions Performance Report

	Time	Rate	Duration	Rest	HR zone
Sleep HR zone (22 to 30%)					
Resting HR zone (30 to 35%)					
Aerobic zone (70 to 80% max)					
Anaerobic zone (80 to 90% max)					
Maximum zone (90 to 100% max)					
Coordination/flow (general)					
Open/target focus					
Timing and judgment					
Kinesthetic sense					
Rhythm					
Footwork					
Handwork					
Reactions/reflexes					
Quickness					
Agility					
Kicking power					
Kicking distance					
Hitting power					
Throwing distance					
Vertical jumping					
Horizontal jumping					
Speed					
Strength					
Muscle balance					
Sustained power output					
Range of motion					
Injury recovery					
Recovery from game workout					
Total					

high oxygen demand, for protection from the forces of contact, and for high force output. This added volume requires the use of all the intercostal muscles of the rib cage.

Training the Brain

In the past, training the brain to react quickly by using the latest technology had been overlooked. Amazing human feats have demonstrated that, through training, athletes can gain more control over their nervous systems than people ever dreamed possible. I'm sure we've all seen a yogi on a bed of nails. Recently I saw a yogi get inside a very small box that was then lowered into ice water for five minutes. When the box was pulled out of the water, the yogi emerged slowly, unraveling himself from the box alive and unharmed.

To accelerate speed to uncommon levels, tap into this kind of performance enhancing total body control. Keep up on the latest information. The computer age has brought all forms of sophisticated devices to the laboratory and the field. Software and equipment have come along to monitor body functions. Heart rate monitors are now available with computer interfaces and software to collect and evaluate information for each heart beat and its relation to the next beat. The sport science lab is really taking the field. Today's coaches are lucky to have immediate and powerful objective information for training their athletes. This information confirms what many scientists, coaches, and parents have felt for a long time: Use it or lose it, don't use it early and you'll never get the max, or start using it at any age and get some of it back. Some of the more important findings from these studies will help you sprint faster and play at higher speeds.

Technology has given us immediate and precise information about all forms of sport. One example is the disqualification of Linford Christie in the 100-meter finals at the 1996 Olympics for a second false start. His gun-to-leaving-the-blocks time was below human capability. This time difference was used to confirm that he had jumped the gun. However, the time difference was so close to human capability that without today's timing devices it would have been impossible to determine. During the preparation meets for the 2000 Olympics, Michael Johnson was highlighted on the TV and Internet as using science to evaluate how he was performing during competition. Real-time data were used for rapid evaluation and implementation. On-field evaluations can present immediate and objective information. This specific information about how players are moving on the field is necessary for player evaluation, selection, and training. Game action and sprinting take place at such high speeds that thinking before acting interferes with performance. Players must react to the situation and ask questions later.

Brain research and the practical playing experiences of elite athletes reveal a state of high artistic and sport performance. Many have described it as being in an effortless state called "the zone." Research reveals that the zone, also known as the flow state, is associated with lower heart and breathing rates coupled with brainwave frequencies of 8 to 13 hertz. Too much or not enough stress can adversely affect performance. You must be able to control stress levels for maximum performance. The best way to control stress is to get into the zone. The information and techniques provided in this chapter will help you achieve control over stress in your sport and in life. According to John Douillard (1995) in *Body, Mind, and Sport*, "The coexistence of opposites—rest and alertness, composure and vigorous exercise—is the formula for the zone."

One of the most common faults of many athletes is trying too hard. Invariably, the harder you try, the tighter you get, which is opposite of what you want. If the athlete is in the zone before performing, the proper muscle control or optimal coordination reaches superlative heights. Is there any question why the zone is the most critical performance principle for the beginner or elite athlete? You cannot compete if you are fighting yourself every step of the way. A common error in sport occurs when performers monitor the response they just made rather than being open to receive a signal for the next action. We call this open state *alertness*. You can manage the load of information by learning to play in a flow state.

Athletes can control visual awareness in such a way that they can see everything in the visual field. The running back who sees all defensive players in position and then runs to daylight is using a technique called *open focus*. This technique is similar to the ultimate camera that takes a clear picture, without a shutter, of anything, even when another picture is being taken at the same time. Can you imagine the luxury of processing all incoming information and sorting out what you need at any one moment? Obviously, performance would improve dramatically. One way to improve visual awareness is by doing turns or rolls while a coach throws a ball and you recover body control. Another way is to juggle or use a mini-trampoline as a rebounder of two or more objects. With practice, you will be able to juggle more balls, increase the area of visual recognition, and manage other sensory input with improving ability.

We have all experienced an adaptation to high-speed travel. Driving 70 miles per hour initially seems fast because of acceleration and the relative speed and position of other cars or objects in the field of vision. However, in a short period of time, this sensation is replaced by a sense that 70 miles per hour is not fast at all. This feeling is the exact playing sensation you want to have on the field. The programs for speed of movement and speed of thought provide drills and exercises that will help improve this flow state on and off the field. The best way to develop this slowing sensation is to incorporate the skills you learned in combat breathing and visual awareness. Your goal is to increase the area from which you are able to take in information. Once you have learned to expand your field of focus, perception of motion tends to slow down.

Training both sides of the body by developing near equal skill in both hands and feet appears to improve skill levels by producing higher levels of synchrony, or coordination, in the nervous system. It is not uncommon to find that sensory processing or skill dominance varies on left and right sides of the body. Differences can be found in every paired organ system: the brain, eyes, ears, hands, and feet. Further, research shows that hand preference affects the tissue (muscle, tendons, ligaments, capillaries, arteries, and veins) composition of the upper limbs in all age groups. Significant tissue changes have been shown to occur in bone density and the fat-free soft tissues of exercised limbs. In addition to these tissues changes, you can expect to gain the functional skills required for your sport or everyday tasks.

Research by Larry Brown of Mechano-Physics and Bob Ward has shown that sprinters and cyclists produce uneven amounts of power output with their legs. This is an example of dominant and recessive motor patterns that can limit speed of movement. The suggested corrective activities and training programs can help. The sport check assessments in this chapter, along with the assessments in chapter 2, will help correct deficiencies. As a simple challenge, select a few skills that you know are important in your sport, and learn to do them well on both sides of the body. For instance, you could use your trail leg as the lead leg over the hurdle, jump off of the other leg in the long jump or high jump, throw a football with your weaker arm, or dribble a basketball with your less accomplished hand.

Computer games help assess neuromuscular and brain function and train the neuromuscular system. Alternate hand and foot patterns and running patterns (e.g., left arm and right leg) have been programmed into the games. These specific patterns, rhythms, and distractions are used to systematically guide players to higher levels of handwork and footwork. A powerful advantage of using scientific games is their ability to record correct responses. There is good evidence that specific benefits (structural and functional changes in the nervous system) are gained by playing these games that may help you sprint faster or play faster. If you are interested in receiving more information about these kinds of computer games, visit www.sportsscience.com.

Body Control: The ABCs of Movement

The major objective of a body control program is to develop a large vocabulary of movement. The larger your vocabulary, the greater the chances of increasing your ability to move more quickly and faster in a variety of directions and solve many problems on the field. The ability to use all body parts, in all movement patterns, in a variety of game situations, when called on to do so, is the ultimate goal of a body control program.

We recommend a 75-minute video developed in the NFL by Bob Ward, Randy White, and Valentine Espiricueta called *Creating Big Plays.* The ancient secrets of many martial arts masters have been used to create the program. The benefits of the program have been demonstrated for the past 25 years by the outstanding play of many professional and collegiate athletes. The same principles that worked for them will work for you. If you are interested in this applied martial arts program, contact www.sportsscience.com.

Sport Hitting Power

Randy White, one of the most formidable defensive players to ever take the field in the NFL, needed instruction on how to improve his ability to hit properly with his hands. Randy came to the Dallas Cowboys as a highly recognized and decorated player. You would think that if you asked him to hit a bag with his left hand, right hand, or both together, you'd better step back, but this was not the case. The results of this simple test convinced Randy and his coaches that he should begin a training program to improve his hitting power.

The point is that any skill is relative to the method used to form its value. Until an objective measurement tool (like a thermometer or stopwatch) is developed to score sport hitting power, error will be present. A player can get by without having to fully develop master levels of skill if the competition doesn't demand it. Randy did improve his hitting power when he played for the Cowboys. A recent NFL Toughman boxing match in Las Vegas demonstrated that a well-learned skill such as hitting can be retained for some time with a little work. Randy knocked out his opponent in the first few seconds of the second round with a sizzling short left hook.

Starting Power

Starting power is the ability to get moving in the appropriate direction in the most efficient way. A sprinter reacting to the starting gun, a linebacker moving to fill the hole in reaction to a running play, or a Chicago Bull fast-breaking down the court for a two-point layup are all examples of actions that require

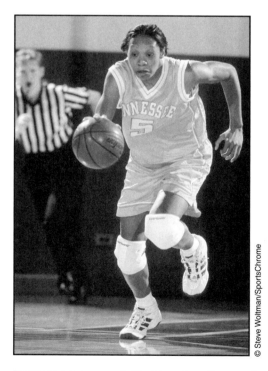

Beginning a successful fast break on the court requires good starting power.

© Steve Woltman/SportsChrome

a lot of starting power if the player is to be successful. If you move close to your opponent, you'd better be able to move quickly or you're in big trouble! Starting power plays a major role in the outcome of the contest.

Some of the best advice for improving this ability came from martial artist Bruce Lee. Lee suggested that athletes use his quickness principle of a small phasic bent-knee position to move quickly into an attack, evasion, or retreat. In sports that allow movement, this means that you keep your body in a slow movement pattern, which helps you overcome the inertia that makes it harder to get started from a still position. Some coaches call it dancing in your shoes. In sports where the athlete must remain still, such as the start in swimming and track or the offensive lineman position in football before the snap, the small phasic bent-knee position can take place in the mind—think movement.

Driving Power

Driving power applies to contact sports such as football, rugby, soccer, and basketball where initial contact is made and then the player has to follow through to clear an area by moving the opponent out of the way. Some sports considered noncontact may also involve incidental, permissible, or illicit contact. No matter how contact originates, physical properties must be managed to minimize or avoid potential injury.

Once contact is made, driving power is the ability of the player to maintain the contact and move the opponent in the appropriate direction. Repeated drills against a challenging opponent in many situations are the best way to develop driving power. This is why intersquad scrimmages are so effective and are the preferred method for high-level development.

High-Speed Quickness

High-speed quickness is the ability to adjust quickly to an opponent's movements. Ideally, coaches like to have athletes with outstanding speed and quickness. However, many athletes who do not have the fastest raw sprinting speed are able to make up for their lack of speed because they have a good grasp of the game. When these athletes are a reasonable distance from the action, their high-speed quickness comes into play and allows them to get the job done. Soccer and man-to-man basketball are two excellent crossover training sports to develop high-speed quickness for any sport. Select playing situations in your sport and apply the concept by covering your opponent as tightly as possible.

Maximum Playing Speed

Maximum playing speed is the ability to run at top speed in a sport. All of the tests in chapter 2 give you the necessary information to assess maximum playing speed potential and identify and fix weaknesses.

OFAS has analyzed more than 40 NFL and college all-star football games. This sophisticated software package, coupled with computer graphics techniques, found that all players, no matter what position, averaged playing speeds well below their maximum sprinting speeds during the game. Table 3.5 summarizes OFAS' findings. A careful study of table 3.5 reveals that speed is not a limiting factor for playing football. Speed is very important, however; work hard on playing quickness, and it will bring you the greatest dividends.

Sustained Power Output Endurance Base

Spartans say that any army may win while it still has its legs under it; the real test comes when all strength is fled and the men must produce victory on will alone.

Steven Pressfield, *Gates of Fire*

Table 3.5   **Speed Performance Comparisons**

Performer	Average 40		Best game		40 test	
	Feet per sec.	Time (sec.)	Feet per sec.	Time (sec.)	Feet per sec.	Percentage
Olympic sprinter	38	4.1	40	3.9	40.0	100
Wide receiver	24	5.7	30	4.7	31.8	75 to 94
Running back	21	6.5	29	4.8	31.1	68 to 93
Defensive back	20	6.7	28	5.0	30.6	65 to 92
Tight end	19	7.1	27	5.1	31.0	61 to 88
Linebacker	18	7.4	26	5.4	29.3	61 to 89
Quarterback	14	9.2	21	6.5	29.0	51 to 72
Defensive lineman	12+	9.7	21	6.5	28.3	46 to 71
Offensive lineman	12+	9.9	20	6.7	27.7	43 to 72

Watch for this hidden Spartan strength in the games you watch. See if the victory goes to those teams that have the ability to persevere. Therefore, sustained power output must have a very important place in a training program. Ideally, a training program should have provisions for developing acceptable levels of fitness before the season. The circulatory and respiratory systems should be brought to levels that can easily handle the specific demands of the sport.

Aerobic cycles and exercises have been proposed for training and evaluating aerobic fitness. However, most sports are not purely aerobic. In fact, most sports are anaerobic. In addition, some researchers have noted a negative influence of high aerobic exercise programs on explosiveness. Therefore, we recommend that most of the running in your training program match the speed demands of your sport with appropriate intervals between sprints.

The suggested time motion analysis methods and the sport check scorecard developed for your sport will give you the necessary information to develop an appropriate workout program. It is important to consider other problems, such as how weight control could influence how you use aerobic exercises in your program. If you are overweight, follow the nutritional program in chapter 8. Also, spend more training time doing interval and aerobic training to help burn more calories. Start early in the off-season so there will be plenty of time to get your weight under control; don't go on any crash diet programs.

Adequate aerobic conditioning is a necessary resource for sport. How much conditioning is adequate is the question. If your sport is continuous with bursts of speed and little recovery time, higher levels of aerobic performance are in order. Your sport evaluation will determine what level you need to attain. In general, strive to meet the standards given in the following sections, never falling below the category of good even when untrained and always striving for the category of excellent or superior when highly trained for your sport.

Anaerobic/Aerobic Foundation

To evaluate aerobic foundation and test it throughout the season, the 1.5-mile test is a good, easy-to-administer test for continuous moving sports such as soccer and basketball. However, we favor faster-paced tests, such as that shown in the lower part of table 3.6.

The following tests are run at a faster pace than the 1.5-mile test. They are excellent field tests for assessing anaerobic/aerobic fitness.

Speed Endurance: Long

The following tests are good for analyzing speed endurance for the majority of anaerobic sports or longer sprinting distances.

✦ 300-yard shuttle (or gassers, which are done from sideline to sideline on a football or soccer field). Run two 5-by-60-yard continuous shuttles. Rest one minute between sets. Keep track of the drop-off between the first and second shuttle.

✦ 100-meter repeat runs. Run 10-by-100 meters at 85 to 88 percent of your best 100-meter time. Take 60 seconds to walk back to the starting line between each run. Keep a graph of the times. Plot your best 100-meter and working 100-meter scores once a month.

✦ 200-meter repeat runs. Run two 4-by-200 meters at 90 percent maximum speed. Rest one minute between repetitions and two minutes between sets. Keep a graph of the times; plot them once a month.

Table 3.6   **Aerobic Test Scores**

1.5-mile test		
Men	Under 8:45 (470 points)*	Superior
Women	Under 9:45 (340 points)	Superior
Men	8:45 to 10:15 (290 points)	Excellent
Women	9:45 to 10:45 (250 points)	Excellent
Men	10:16 to 12:00 (130 points)	Good
Women	10:46 to 13:00 (60 points)	Good
2 × 880 yd., rest 5 min., repeat		
Men	Under 2:25 (470 points)	Superior
Women	Under 2:42 (340 points)	Superior
Men	2:25 to 2:49 (290 points)	Excellent
Women	2:42 to 3:04 (250 points)	Excellent
Men	2:50 to 3:15 (130 points)	Good
Women	3:05 to 3:30 (60 points)	Good

* Points based on computerized training programs, Garner and Purdy.

Note: The 200-meter and 100-meter runs are excellent distances for training and evaluation. The 100- and 200-meter runs discussed in the previous section are two of the many possibilities available.

This test or workout was designed for sports that have a work/rest cycle of play. However, it is an excellent workout for training speed endurance for most sports. Do 10 repetitions of each.

+ Speed positions: 15-second run with a 60-second walk back
+ Medium positions: 16-second run with a 60-second walk back
+ Slower positions: +17-second run with a 60-second walk back

Speed Endurance: Short

The 40-yard sprint is good for analyzing speed endurance for short sprinting distances. Run 10-by-40 yards at more than 90 percent maximum speed with 30 seconds of rest after each sprint. Use a heart rate monitor, if possible, for a more comprehensive assessment of heart rate response during and after each 40-yard sprint and the recovery after the set of 10 40-yard sprints.

Foundation training serves as a sneak preview of things to come and is an orientation course that prepares you for the rigors ahead. Certain goals should be established as a result of your sport check scorecard and the simple tests found in chapter 2. Each goal will serve as a guide for improving basic fitness before advancing to the next step. The next section will lead you through the necessary steps for developing a foundation training program. It also allows you the flexibility of writing more advanced programs in the future.

Organizing Foundation Training

Periodization is a way of organizing training so that peak condition occurs during the times of peak competition. The Russians led the way in scientific training plans. Essentially, they broke training into three phases: endurance (building an endurance base first), strength, and power. Thus the training year was broken down into three four-month cycles. The goal was to have the athlete peak one time per year in concert with important competitions.

Sports Speed has taken current periodization science to develop a 10-phase training year (macrocycle) that can be used as a model for all sports. The phases selected are common periods in the training year of most sports in the United States and can be easily identified. The example shown in table 3.7 was developed by Bob Ward for the Dallas Cowboys when he was their conditioning coach under Coach Landry. It is a yearly plan that can be easily applied to any level for baseball, basketball, football, and soccer.

Mesocycles cover weeks of training. Normally, a mesocycle will be four to eight weeks long. Table 3.8 is an example of how volume and intensity can be spread out over the weeks.

Mesocycles manage weeks; microcycles manage days. Table 3.9 shows four different ways that the days of the week can be managed for a workout schedule of three days per week.

Table 3.7   **Phase Definitions for NFL Football**

Phase	Weeks %	Name	Purpose
I	1 to 6 11.5%	Transition	Active rest. Adaptation theory tells us that the body has only so much energy in the short term and long term to handle the demands placed on it mentally, physically, and environmentally.
II	7 to 11 9.6%	Prep to vet camp Team check I	Regain fitness levels. Changes in performance involve a multiyear process: One year builds on another. It is much easier to retain a fitness level than it is to gain a fitness level.
III	12 to 15 7.6%	First quarter Team check II	Develop new levels of performance • Basic resources
IV	16 to 19 7.6%	Second quarter Team check III	• Sport-specific skills • Training skills can't begin too early • Quality would determine when to
V	20 to 23 7.6%	Third quarter Team check IV	begin and amount of training • Key principle: Seek to integrate
VI	24 to 27 7.6%	Fourth quarter Team check V	training factors into sport skills
VII	28 to 33 11.5%	Training camp Team check VI	Stressful integration of sport-specific skills • Putting it all together • High level of repeatability (sustaining % max)
VIII	34 to 41 15.3%	First half season Team check VII	Maintenance
IX	42 to 49 15.3%	Second half season Season team check VIII	Match difficulty of schedule with the workload. Some team matchups allow you to work through the game by doing higher levels of work.
X	50 to 52 5.7%	Playoffs	Superadaptation. Ideally, you'd like to be able to make great jumps in performance, but practically, it's unlikely that super increases in performance can be made at this time. Experience tells us that playing resources wane after a long and arduous season. Therefore, this makes recovery extremely important at this time.

Percentages are approximations.

Table 3.8   **Sample Four-Week, Six-Week, and Eight-Week Mesocycle**

	4 weeks	6 weeks	8 weeks
Week 1	High	High	High
Week 2	Medium	Medium	Medium
Week 3	High	High	High
Week 4	Easy competition testing	Medium	Medium
Week 5	Active rest	High	High
Week 6	Rest	Easy competition testing	Medium
Week 7		Active rest	High
Week 8		Active rest	Easy competition testing

Leo Costa of Optimum Training Systems cites Bulgarian research that presents a provocative insight into the effects of practice session length on testosterone levels in the blood. He states, "Bulgarian researchers found that there was a 79 to 83 percent drop in blood testosterone levels after 39 to 43 minutes of hard exercise." Does this mean that the athlete may still have the desire and motivation, but the body doesn't have the resources to support such intent? Chapter 8 will cover the implications for recovery.

Setting Objectives and Selecting Exercises

Complete the test score sheet (table 2.1, page 7). Develop a list of the areas you need to work on, listing them in order of importance to your main objective. Complete the conditioning program schedule in table 3.10. Place the sport-specific list on this sheet in the spaces provided. Each exercise is recorded in the day and time period of your choice. This record becomes the workout schedule of exercises that will remove any of your measured weaknesses. It is important to commit yourself to the program by writing your name in the space provided. To assure that all the necessary elements will be adequately perfected, they should be placed in a daily schedule.

The first thing to understand about putting together a foundation training program is that every good workout should have a primary purpose. A workout is similar to any work of art, be it a book, a dance, or a play. There is a beginning, a main purpose, and an ending. The beginning prepares the way for the main purpose, and the ending gets you back as close as possible to a normal level of body function. This theme is evident in every step of the sports speed program. You can determine the purpose of the workout by first making a list of all the critical tasks that need to be accomplished. Then arrange this list in order of each item's importance. Finally, allocate the time you have available to practice each item based on its importance.

Table 3.9   **Sample Microcycle: Work Out Three Days a Week**

	Cycle intensity			
	High	**Tapered**	**Cycloid**	**Intuitive**
Day 1	High	High	High	Intensity based on how the athlete feels at the time of the workout
Day 2				
Day 3	High	Medium high	Medium easy	
Day 4				
Day 5	High	Medium easy	High	
Day 6				
Day 7	Rest	Rest	Rest	

Table 3.10   **Conditioning Program Schedule**

Name _____ Height _____ Weight _____ % Fat _____

Date _____ Time _____

Time	Monday	Tuesday	Wednesday	Thursday	Friday	Saturday	Sunday
7:00							
8:00							
9:00							
10:00							
11:00							
12:00							
1:00							
2:00							
3:00							
4:00							
5:00							
6:00							
7:00							

To train energy systems to match those used in the sport of choice, it is important to select conditioning activities that utilize the same energy systems. Therefore, we collected the information shown in table 3.11 to help you select the types of exercise that match those used in your sport. Energy system, time, and distance ranges are given to assist in the selection process.

Table 3.11

	High rate of energy No or low body movement	Mix of high and medium rate High body movement	Medium rate High body movement	Low rate Medium body movement
Characteristics	Start Static Stationary body movement Limited movement Low rate < 1 fps to 1	Maximum speed Speed strength Primary training ground for most sports Medium rate to 30+ fps Burst intermittent rest	Sustained high capacity Speed endurance Submaximal	Sustained low capacity
Energy system	Anaerobic/Aerobic 80/20% initial 30 sec.	Anaerobic/Aerobic 80/20% initial 30 sec.	Anaerobic/Aerobic 45/55% 60 to 90 sec.	Anaerobic/Aerobic 30/70% 120 to 192 sec.
Impact	< 100 msec.			
Short time	100 to 300 msec.			
Level of intensity	High (98 to 100%)	High (90 to 98%)	Medium (75 to 90%)	Medium (60 to 75%)
		Assign percent of energy system used in your sport		
Distance	Limited	0 to 300 yd.	440 to 1,000 yd.	880+ yd.
Time	90 to 300 msec.	1 to 60 sec.	1 to 2 min.	2 to 30+ min.
Reference	Start	Start to 300 yd.	400 to 1,000 yd.	Mile plus
Recovery	Full	Full	Heart rate 120 bpm or based on goal	Heart rate 120 bpm
Perception (awareness)	Reaction Reflexes Total body Hands Elbows Feet	Abrupt (.3 to 2 sec.) Acceleration Brief (2 to 10 sec.): • 20-yd. sprint • 40-yd. sprint • Flying 40 yd. • 80-yd. sprint • Leg • Bench press (etc.)	Prolonged (60+ sec.) Sustained output 880-yd. run Mile run Anaerobic threshold $\dot{V}O_2max$	Prolonged (60+ sec.) Sustained output 880-yd. run Mile run 1.5-mile run $\dot{V}O_2max$

Power	Reaction Quickness Vertical jump Standing long jump Standing triple jump Puds Weight throws Snatch Clean Jerk	Long term (10 to 60 sec.) Agility 110 yd. 220 yd. 300 yd. 440 yd. Dips 20 sec. Chin-ups 20 sec. Sit-ups 60 sec. (etc.)		Interval training Speed play Distance Ultra circuit
Activities	Applied martial arts Neck wrestling Acceleration Sprinting Hopping Jumping Throwing	Applied martial arts Running Running (loaded) Gymnastics Free weights Concentric and eccentric Isokinetic	Running Applied martial arts Sports Circuit training Super circuit	
Equipment and facilities	Gymnastics Medicine balls Puds Various weights Hammer/shot/discus Olympic bar Selected machines	Gymnastics Martial arts Free weights Machines	Track	Track Field

Note: Multidimensional sport skills and drills can be used creatively to develop general and specific athletic ability and motor fitness needed for the sport. If team sport training can be improved in specific sport activities, then focus should be directed to those elements that need nonspecific off-field development.

General Warm-Up

An adequate structured warm-up period of 10 to 30 minutes is best. First exercise the large muscle groups with activities such as jogging or striding that cause perspiration and raise core temperature one to two degrees. Next perform stretching exercises: static (stretching to the maximum range of motion and holding that extreme position for 10 to 30 seconds), dynamic (stretching movements specific to the action of sprinting), or PNF (proprioceptive neuromuscular facilitation, which alternates contraction and relaxation of both agonist and antagonist muscles). Warm-up sessions increase body temperature, circulation, and muscle elasticity and prepare you psychologically for the workout.

For example, a good warm-up routine would be to jog 440 to 880 yards in five minutes. Jog at an easy pace then progressively run at a faster pace as you approach the final 220 yards. You can add a variety of footwork patterns and basic skills as you run to improve and maintain these skills.

Try build-ups and walk backs on the playing field. Even if your sport is confined to different playing areas, it is still worth your while to spend time in the early part of training doing this workout. Break the circuit of 120 yards of running and 120 yards of walking into four phases: 40 yards of gradual acceleration, 40 yards of maintained speed, 40 yards of gradual coast-down, and 120 yards of recovery (walking back). Perform 8 to 10 easy repetitions. Emphasize good running form while gradually increasing the speed of the run.

Another variation is to jump rope for three to six minutes. The time can be broken into rounds that emphasize various foot and hand rhythms.

Speed bag or shadow boxing for three to six minutes is another good warm-up. (Shadow boxing can be adapted to other sports, such as a basketball player defending an opponent.) Shadow boxing is an exercise in creative imagination. You are fighting an imaginary opponent and in the process have a sport-specific, meaningful way to warm up. Find those openings and use the skills to land the most effective punch. The time can be divided into rounds that emphasize various foot and hand combinations and rhythms.

A different warm-up routine is tennis ball reaction catching. Stand six feet away from a wall. Throw and catch a tennis ball at increasing speeds. Gradually move forward until you are able to reach a speed and distance that yields a 60 percent performance score. Maintain that position until you can perform at the 80 percent score level, then increase the difficulty. Complete 100 catches and record the following information: distance from the wall in feet at completion of 100 catches, speed (slow, medium, fast), number of catches out of 100 throws, and time to complete 100 catches. When you think you're hot stuff, have someone else throw the balls from behind you into a flat wall or corner.

Juggling for three to six minutes is another good warm-up. Use a variety of juggling techniques. Use two or three bags of various textures and weights along with more advanced techniques such as bouncing on a mini-trampoline or running as you juggle. When you get really good, use the balls from your sport. These methods fit nicely into a warm-up and provide an integrated way of training the brain, neuromuscular system, and visual elements (tracking and peripheral vision).

To warm up for balance, stand on one foot for 30 to 60 seconds. Increase difficulty by circling or drawing eights with the free leg. You can add advanced variations by changing the patterns to circles, squares, triangles, and so on.

Proper warm-up and stretching reduces the incidence of soft tissue injuries, mentally prepares an athlete, and aids performance. A general warm-up period will adequately prepare an athlete for the flexibility portion of the program.

Flexibility

Flexibility (stretching) exercises are often too closely associated with the warm-up. Consequently, some athletes make the common mistake of stretching cold muscles before beginning a workout, rather than first warming up the body with large-muscle activities such as walking or jogging for five to eight minutes or until perspiration is evident. At this point, body temperature has been elevated two to four degrees and muscles can be safely stretched. Keep in mind that you warm up to stretch, you do not stretch to warm up.

Some athletes need to stretch more than others. Lean body types with a good range of motion may need very little stretching, whereas stocky, more powerfully built athletes with limited ranges of motion need 5 to 10 minutes of flexibility exercises before making any radical moves such as bending over to touch the toes or explosive jumping or sprinting. Athletes of all ages and skill levels can benefit from stretching. Routines can be gentle, easy, relaxing, and safe, or they can be extremely vigorous.

A daily stretching routine will help increase range of motion, improve playing and sprinting performance by conserving energy and increasing fluid motion, aid muscle relaxation, aid sprinting form, and help you cool down at the end of your workout. An improvement in overall flexibility may improve speed by slightly increasing stride rate and decreasing energy expenditure and resistance during sprinting. Regular stretching also helps reduce the incidence of injuries that may occur in high-speed activities and sport competitions. Continuous exercise such as jogging, running, cycling, and aerobics tightens and shortens muscles. Tight muscles are more vulnerable to injury from the explosive movements common in sports. A brief warm-up followed by stretching will not only increase range of motion but will also provide some protection from common soft tissue injuries such as strains, sprains, and tears. Striving to maintain a full normal range of motion in each joint with adequate strength, endurance, and power throughout the range will reduce your chances of experiencing an exercise-induced injury.

Stretching exercises should be used to prepare the body for vigorous activity during the regular warm-up routine before each workout, to return muscles to a normal relaxed state during the cool-down, and to improve range of motion any time you can work exercise into your schedule.

If your flexibility test scores from the assessment in chapter 2 were poor, plan to stretch for a longer period of time before and after each workout, after sitting or standing for long periods, whenever you feel stiff, or even while engaged in passive activities such as watching TV or listening to music. Remember to first elevate your body temperature and produce some sweat by engaging in large muscle group activity before stretching.

When recovering from soft tissue injuries, focus on reducing pain and swelling, returning to normal strength, and achieving full nonrestricted range of motion. Unless regular stretching begins as soon as pain and swelling have been eliminated, loss of flexibility in the injured joint is almost certain.

A well-rounded flexibility program for speed improvement must devote attention to all the body's major joints: the neck, shoulders, back, and hips, as well as the knees and ankles. You can increase range of motion in each of these major joints in six to eight weeks by following one of the recommended stretching techniques.

Several approaches to stretching have been shown to safely increase range of motion (ROM): dynamic stretching (used at the beginning of each workout after the general warm-up period) and static or PNF stretching (used at the end of the workout during the cool-down period). For each exercise, concentrate on two phases of stretching: (1) *easy stretching* in which you move slowly into the stretch and apply mild tension with a steady, light pressure or execute a dynamic movement at slow speed and (2) *developmental stretching* in which you increase the intensity for an inch or less, easing off the stretch if the tension does not diminish, or increase the speed of the dynamic movement from low to medium to high.

Dynamic stretching exercises involve sport-specific movements such as high knees lifts, stationary arm swings, running in place and sprinting form drills such as butt kickers, quick feet, down-and-offs, pull throughs, wall slide, cycling, African Dance, and Drum Major (see chapter 12). This technique uses the range of joint movement during physical activity progressing from low to medium to high speed. Stretching movements are nearly identical to a specific activity such as jogging, sprinting, jumping or to movements in a sport and have the highest correlation to sport performance. Movements of a sport or activity are performed with the limbs moving to near full range of motion in the sport or activity. Five to six exercises should be completed immediately following the general warm-up session and involve 6 to 8 repetitions at each speed (low, medium, high).

Static stretching involves a slow move into the stretch before applying steady pressure until the point of discomfort without bouncing or jerking. Each static exercise should be completed slowly, beginning with a 10 to 15 second hold, adding 2 to 3 seconds each workout, until you can comfortably maintain the hold position at the extreme ROM for 30 to 45 seconds. Disregard the "no pain, no gain" mentality; improvement occurs without undue pain. Joint pressure should produce only mild discomfort. Too much pain and discomfort is a sign you are overloading soft tissue and risking injury. After experiencing mild discomfort with each stretch, relax the muscles being stretched before the next repetition. You will learn to judge each exercise by the "stretch and feel" method, easing off the push if pain becomes intense or gets worse as the exercise progresses. You can begin with the neck and progress down to the shoulders and chest, trunk and lower back, groin, hips, abdomen, and upper and lower legs. Use during the cool-down period at the end of the workout.

Proprioceptive neuromuscular facilitation (PNF) stretching is a two-person technique based on the contract-and-hold principle. PNF stretching requires a partner to apply steady pressure to a body area at the extreme range of motion until you feel a slight discomfort. When stretching the hamstrings, for example, lie on your back with one leg extended to 90 degrees or a comfortable stretch. Have your partner apply steady pressure as you attempt to raise your leg further overhead. Push against the resistance by contracting the muscle being stretched. This isometric hamstring contraction produces no leg movement because your partner will resist the force you apply during the push. After a 10-second push, relax your hamstrings while your partner applies pressure for an additional 5 seconds. Repeat two or three times.

The PNF method involves four phases: an initial easy stretch of the muscle, an isometric contraction with resistance from a partner, relaxation of 5 seconds, and a final passive stretch for 5 seconds. PNF stretching relaxes the muscle group being stretched, producing greater muscle length and improving flexibility. Disadvantages include the presence of some discomfort, a longer workout time, and the inability to stretch without a partner. PNF or static stretching is used at the end of the workout during the cool-down period.

For static or PNF stretching, choose at least one stretching exercise for each of the major muscle groups and apply exercises equally to both sides of the body. These exercises represent a sound general stretching routine for sprinting and most team sports. Approach this session with an attitude of relaxation.

✦ Hamstrings. Here are the two best ways to stretch the hamstrings at the back of the upper legs. First stand erect with both knees slightly bent. Bend over and touch the ground, holding your maximum stretch position. While in the maximum stretch position, you can slightly flex and extend each leg alternately. Second lie on your back. Sit up and reach for your toes with both knees slightly bent, holding your maximum stretch position. Keep both knees slightly bent in both exercises to remove the pressure from your lower back.

✦ Quadriceps. The quadriceps are the muscles in the front of the upper legs. To stretch the quads, stand on your left leg. Grasp your right ankle with your right hand and pull your heel toward your buttocks, holding your maximum stretch position. Repeat using your other leg.

✦ Hips. To stretch your hips, lie on your back and then relax and straighten both legs. Pull your left foot toward your chest and hold. Repeat using the right foot. Increased flexibility in the ankles, hips, and shoulders may help prevent understriding because of inflexibility.

✦ Groin. To stretch the groin area, assume a sitting position with the soles of your feet together. Place your hands around your feet and pull yourself forward.

✦ Calves. To stretch your calves, stand about two feet from a wall and lean forward in a stride position with the lead leg bent and the rear leg extended.

Move your hips forward and keep the heel of the straight leg on the ground until you feel a stretch in your calf.

✦ Achilles Tendon and Soleus. To stretch the Achilles tendon and the soleus, stand approximately two feet from a wall or fence in a stride position. Bend the back knee slightly, keep both heels on the ground, and lean forward. Increased range of motion in the ankle (extension) may favorably improve stride length.

Cool-Down

The justification for a cool-down period after any vigorous workout is quite simple. Blood returns to the heart through a system of veins; the blood is pushed along by heart contractions, and the milking action of the veins is assisted by muscle contractions during exercise. Veins contract, or squeeze, and move the blood forward against gravity while valves prevent the blood from backing up. If you stop exercising suddenly, this milking action also ceases, and blood return will drop quickly. This may cause blood pooling (blood remaining in the same area) in the legs, leading to deep breathing, which may in turn lower carbon dioxide levels and produce muscle cramps. At this point, blood pressure drops precipitously and causes functional problems. The body compensates for the unexpected drop in pressure by secreting as much as 100 times the normal amount of a hormone called norepinephrine. This high level of norepinephrine can cause cardiac problems for some individuals during the recovery phase of vigorous exercises such as a marathon or triathlon.

The final three to eight minutes of a workout should involve a period of slowly diminishing intensity through the use of a slow jog for three quarters of a mile to one mile at a pace of three to four minutes per quarter mile, each quarter mile slower than the previous one. The ideal cool-down should take place in the same environment as the workout (except in extremely hot or cold weather), last at least five minutes, and be followed by a brief stretching period. Stretching during the final phase of the cool-down period helps fatigued muscles return to normal resting length and a more relaxed state, reducing the chance of muscle soreness the following day.

The importance of foundation training cannot be overestimated. It is the bedrock, the foundation on which you build all other steps. The sport check scorecard has given you the basis for your individualized program. Periodization was given to help properly put all the parts of the program into a logical sequence. The testing program was designed to help you consider the demands of your sport and identify any limitations that need to be corrected.

Remember, there are no make-ups on the road to maximum development, no opportunities to get what you didn't get when you were supposed to get it! A later start on this road to development decreases the number of neural pathways developed, reduces the number of acquired skills, and ensures that you will not reach maximum potential in your sport. But don't stop now just because you started a bit late—keep on going. Don't worry if you've been a little lazy in the past. Our sports speed program will help you be the best you can be wherever you are. Keep this in mind as you move into strength and power training.

Chapter 4

STRENGTH AND POWER TRAINING

*F*unctional strength and power training aims to improve your ability to apply sufficient force to an opponent or object at the right time, at the required performance speed, and in the right direction. The key is to discover how much force is required at various times during the game and to learn to precisely apply that force. As functional strength and power increase, so will horsepower reserve (speed strength), which will allow you to play the game at a lower percent of capacity, with more available power for the more demanding adjustments that arise during the game. Certainly, a big benefit of a high horsepower automobile engine is its rapid acceleration. Similarly, a high-powered human body will reach a chosen speed more quickly than a lower-powered body. Improved functional strength and power can provide this advantage.

Before we discuss the purpose of the functional strength program, let's take a look at the basic elements that make up a game or competition to see what kind of program is required. Although these events may vary according to the situation and sport, most competitive sports have some sort of stimulus that requires a response.

Each one of us comes with built-in performance qualities that can be influenced by a functional strength program. Each of these qualities has a range of trainability. These qualities determine how fast we recognize and respond in athletic situations and therefore determine our level of success or failure in our chosen sports.

The primary purpose of a functional strength and power program is to develop the required force and tissue capacity for your sport. Tissue capacity includes the ability of body tissues to defend, build, repair, heal, regenerate, remodel, and regulate themselves. All functional changes bring structural changes in tissues and systems. These changes involve the whole organism.

Any builder knows that the materials used in construction must be able to sustain the loads in all stress ranges. The human body also has its limitations. These limitations were very evident when former Washington Redskins quarterback Joe Theismann was seriously injured in an NFL game. During a sack, functional demands were placed on his leg that exceeded the physiological limits of bone and soft tissue. As a result, something had to give—Joe's leg. Doctors, coaches, athletes, and fans should recognize that forces in sport can and do go beyond human tolerance. Often the forces exceed the tissue's capacity to protect the body, and injuries occur. Although there can be no guarantee that a high level of functional strength and power will provide protection from such injuries, it does provide some amount of basic insurance.

With proper training, the human body will take care of needed structural changes. Tissues will be strengthened as a natural consequence of functional strength and power training. You must also develop enough additional size, strength, and power reserve so you can perform at the very high playing speeds in your sport and still protect yourself from injury. Unquestionably, the most important injury prevention factor is to be an alert, highly skilled player with the ability to control the forces on the field. Proper use of the program described in this chapter will do the rest. Immediate and long-term benefits will be evident through improved performance, faster recovery time, reduction in injuries, and reduced healing time should an injury occur.

The ability to propel a stationary body into rapid movement and exert maximal force requires both strength and power (speed strength). An athlete may be quite strong yet lack explosive power and be incapable of sprinting a fast 40-yard or 40-meter dash. Speed and power training should involve movements that are similar to those in the sport (the principle of specificity).

Work and Power

The relationship of work and power can be illustrated by imagining yourself completing a simple task. The task is to move 100 10-pound weights onto a one-foot-high train in 10 seconds. The train will depart in 10 seconds; therefore, you get credit only for the weights on the train. In a similar manner, the foot of the sprinter has a window of time to apply force. Accordingly, it is important that you train to meet the many specific power output requirements in your sport.

Table 4.1 summarizes the power output of an athlete who moves 10 weights from the platform to the train in 10 seconds. Remember that in most explosive sports, there is about .1 to .3 second to apply additional force at the foot. The only way to increase speed of action is to accelerate (increase speed of work) the speed at which the 10-pound weights are moved.

This illustration tells us a great deal about what we must do to run or play at faster speeds. Many of the activities in this book have been designed to identify, correct, or improve the ability to apply more force at the foot during ground contact. In good sprinting, the time you have to make this adjustment is about .10 second. The timing required for generating more force at the foot is like the timing required for cracking a whip. The better the sequencing of the limbs of the body, the more effective or louder the pop of the whip or the faster we run and play.

The results given in table 4.1 show that the athlete was credited with only 10 percent of the power and work possible. Only the work and power recorded in the allotted time counted. Similarly, in sprint training, a sprinter's foot is in

Table 4.1   **Power Output**

Total lb. available	Total lb. in 10 sec.	Total work in 10 sec.	Total power in 10 sec.
1,000 lb.	10 × 10 lb. = 100 lb.	100 lb. × 1 ft. = 100 ft./lb.	100 ft./lb./ 10 sec. = 10 ft./lb./sec.
100%	10%	10%	10%

contact with the ground for about .09 to .11 second at a time. Any force that is not applied at the foot during this time is of no use in sprinting faster. Think of the many complicated tasks in your sport to see how important this principle is. Imagine the complexities of covering your opponent during the game. What if you need to move or cut left, which requires a planting of the right foot, but your right foot is still in the air? Add this delay time into the playing equation to see how far your opponent will be from you in the time it takes you to put your foot on the ground to apply appropriate countering force.

Acceleration or Mass?

Most team sports are played with multiple starts and stops and many directional changes. Under these circumstances, it is no surprise that average speeds used during competition are well below players' maximum sprinting speeds. It is interesting to note that all-pro running backs such as Tony Dorsett, Emmitt Smith, and Barry Sanders generate as much force as big linemen in short ranges. This fact dramatically illustrates that the amount of force generated is influenced by either a change in the player's mass (weight) or acceleration (quickness of movement).

If you have a choice, the best way to generate force is to increase acceleration. Obviously, these all-pro running backs are able to accelerate more rapidly than 300-pound linemen and, therefore, match the linemen's force output to make first downs in short yardage situations. The standoff between the giant linemen and smaller, quicker running backs can produce a structural problem for the running back because of his less protective body tissues. The smaller running back does give away a lot of protective tissue that could be used to absorb the forces of constant pounding. The best of both worlds is to become a big and fast running back like Hall of Famers Jim Brown and Earl Campbell.

Work Fast to Be Fast

Because the work fast to be fast principle is essential in all explosive sports, we recommend you make use of high power output exercises for mental and physical focus. Weights can be selectively used to train for explosive sports. It is important to recognize that there is a fine range of speeds and loads that must be adhered to in order to maximize transfer to your sport. Tissue strength will be gained over a wide range of high-intensity explosive lifts. One guideline is to use the threshold principle discussed in chapter 3. Remember that mental quickness is an essential element of physical quickness; you must *think* fast to be fast.

A number of training programs have been successful in bridging the gap between strength and power to improve speed strength and sprinting speed. Combinations of weight training, explosive power training, and various forms of traditional speed training (speed endurance, overspeed, sprint loading) significantly improve speed in short distances.

Many weight room exercises can be used to develop functional strength and power output. Inertial impulse exercises and Olympic lifts are the most important of these exercises.

Inertial Impulse

According to Albert (1995), "functional activities and sports activities have been shown to occur between 700 to 6,000 degrees per second for the upper and lower limbs." Therefore, performance measurements and training should fall in these same ranges. Unfortunately, few machines can step up to the plate and swing at those speeds. An exception is the Impulse Training Systems machine by EMA, Inc. (www.sportsscience.com) which is capable of hitting the conditioning and rehabilitation ball out of the traditional training ballpark.

Impulse training exercise machines are available at many rehabilitation centers. Impulse training machines have a nongravity, horizontal sliding loading mechanism for working the athlete. A handle and rope connection to the horizontal sliding mechanism allows the athlete to do a variety of rehabilitation and sport-specific actions. Scientific data can be collected from the exercising athlete by connecting an accelerometer or force transducer and oscilloscope to the rope handle device.

These machines provide a major breakthrough in training on-field power in the weight room. Although various inertial impulse training devices, such as the speed bag, have been used in the gym for other purposes (see chapter 5 for more practical suggestions), special inertial impulse machines are different in that they can be used for numerous body actions and with various loads and speeds, depending on the desired outcome. In fact, these machines provide the perfect illustration of the interrelationship between mass (weight) and acceleration (quickness).

To feel the impact of the Impulse Training System in a familiar skill setting, imagine putting 500 pounds in a wheelbarrow and then recording how fast you could get it moving and how quickly you could stop it. No doubt you would find that it takes a lot of time to start and stop the wheelbarrow. Suppose you took the weight out of the wheelbarrow and did the same experiment. Would you feel the difference? If you lined up some football dummies and tried to knock them down with the heavy and light wheelbarrows from one, two, and three feet away, what would the results be? Weight and quickness apply to performance in any sport. Even in noncontact sports, this principle can be used to improve sport performance and reduce the likelihood of injury.

Some of the benefits you can expect to gain from using impulse training include the duplication of and selected increase in on-field forces, functional strength and power gains that are transferable to competition in your sport, stronger tendons and ligaments, and a reduction in training time. Dr. Jim Counsilman, noted swim coach from Indiana University, coined the term for this type of training as "programmable acceleration." He believes programmable acceleration programs will form the basis of modern sports speed training programs in the near future. Although most facilities don't have the kind of equipment to apply a precise acceleration program, a small level of effectiveness can still be achieved by using barbells and dumbbells.

If you don't have access to special impulse training equipment, use any system that you can hit and that hits you back or that you can respond to as a training device, including all kinds of plyometrics, speed bags, boxing, and, yes, even a pool.

The pool provides the most universally available way to apply programmable acceleration techniques. Many of the major body movements can be exercised in the water by moving very short distances (inches to about a foot) with rapid starts and stops that mimic specific positions of the skill. You can do sets of 10, each set lasting 20 seconds. Practice either a limited starting position or a complete joint range of motion for the desired actions. Actions can be explosive or rehabilitative. Therefore, the complete exercise spectrum of training objective speeds can be included. For instance, a discus thrower can work the discus arm action with the throwing arm by quickly starting, stopping, and returning to the original starting position. Be creative by designing special exercises for your sport and applying them to your program.

Weight Throwing

Weight throwing is the most practical, yet under-systematized, method available for conditioning in team sports. Track and field throwers have used this method for many years. Plagenhoef's research (1971) showed that hammer throwing produces the highest moments (forces) in sport. Before specialization entered the athletic world and redirected conditioning programs, many football programs used track and field as a part of their out-of-season and preseason conditioning programs. In fact, Bob Ward's entry into the NFL was highly influenced by his background and training in track and field and football.

The Pud is a throwing device of varying weights that is thrown into an area about the size of a shot put area. Any level surface, ground, cement, or shot ring can be used. The standard Pud has a fixed handle attached to a weight that can be gripped with one or two hands (figure 4.1). However there are other similar devices that can be used for throwing.

Figure 4.1   A Pud throwing device.

Lance Deal, American record holder in the hammer, designed the Puds. They can be used in a variety of specific explosive power exercises. On Tracks (www.ontrack.com) carries the Puds in 14-, 21-, 28-, and 35-pound sizes.

A comprehensive program should include throwing in all the planes of the body through all the angles used in throwing. Remember to keep an equal number of left and right throws to keep the body balanced.

There are three stances: square with feet shoulder-width apart facing the throwing area; with feet shoulder-width apart, front foot closest to the throwing area; and rear facing as in the square stance.

Swing the weight back, turning the shoulders around and bending the legs on the back swing (figure 4.2). Take a number of swings with the weight before throwing it to develop good rhythm and timing. Try performing left and right one-handed throws to the side, left and right two-handed throws to the side (figure 4.3), two-handed throws over the head

Figure 4.2   Back swing when throwing the Pud.

Figure 4.3   Two-handed Pud throw to the side.

while facing away from the throwing area (extend your body up and back during the throw), and two-handed throws after swinging between your legs (extend your body up and back as you throw) (figure 4.4).

Include Pud throwing in your program after skill work and prior to weight lifting. Warm up prior to throwing hard. Start with the lightest weight and move up to the heaviest. Do 1 set of 4 throws with left and right or per each throwing action if you have all four weights (1 rep per weight). Of course, the nature of your workout will depend on the number of different weights available. On speed days, use lighter weights; heavier weights are used for strength building.

Figure 4.4 Two-handed Pud throw, swing between legs.

Olympic Lifts

Olympic lifts are the most commonly recommended and used exercises in sophisticated power and speed training programs. In a study of the heaviest successful lifts in the snatch and the clean and jerk for five Olympic gold medalists, Garhammer (1991) showed that "athletes trained in the Olympic style of weightlifting have an extremely high capacity to develop power, which is necessary for success in the sport." Since Olympic lifts require high power output, they have become popular exercises in sport conditioning programs. In addition, proper lifting teaches good fundamental body mechanics that may be adapted to many sports.

These exercises provide an excellent means of improving functional strength and power. Because Olympic lifts usually do not involve a trunk-twisting action when performed with a barbell, a one-hand dumbbell will yield greater benefits and complement the barbell exercises.

Free weight exercises are preferred over machines for two major reasons: The actual movement and muscle involvement for which you are training can be replicated more closely, and the three-phase response of the body to stressors (Selye's general adaptation syndrome) is enhanced.

Power exercises, such as Olympic lifts, focus on optimum starting speed and blinding quickness in movements from power positions and in recovery to catch the weight. They train the mind and body to develop peak force, they aid in increasing the amount of time peak force is applied, they develop force in a short period of time, and they emphasize good body position and movements that cross over into other sports.

CLEAN (BARBELL AND DUMBBELL)

The clean (figure 4.5) develops the large muscles of the body in an explosive action that requires the use of many joints and muscle groups in a coordinated movement. The use of dumbbells requires a twisting of the body and tends to enhance training benefits.

Assume a comfortable stance with feet spread about hip- to shoulder-width apart. Grasp the bar with an overhand grip at slightly wider than shoulder-width. You can use an overhand hooked strap. Bend your legs at the start of the lift, and use your legs to lift the weight first. Maintain a straight back and hold it tightly in that position as you bring the bar up, keeping the bar close to your body. Place your shoulders over the bar (8 to 12 centimeters). Rebend your legs after the bar clears the knees. Keep your arms straight; remember, this is a leg and back exercise. Jump vertically into the lift with your legs, pulling the bar as high as possible. Your arms will blend in after the leg and back action. Drive your elbows up. Drop your body quickly and catch the bar on your shoulders while bringing your elbows quickly under the bar.

Figure 4.5a

Figure 4.5b

Figure 4.5c

Near-maximum weight will require that you go into a deep knee bend to catch the bar; therefore, leg and back strength is essential for good lifting. Use the "1.3 times the clean" rule for estimating squatting strength (maximum clean in pounds times 1.3 equals squat weight). This estimate provides an excellent guide to ensure sufficient foundational leg and back strength.

JERK (BARBELL, DUMBBELL, AND MACHINE RACK)

The jerk (figure 4.6) develops the large muscle groups of the body with an explosive, total body, multijointed action.

Take the bar from the rack to work primarily on the jerking movement. Assume a comfortable stance with feet spread hip- to shoulder-width apart. Grasp the bar with palms facing up. Hands should be slightly wider than shoulder-width. Rest the bar primarily on your shoulders. Keep your back vertical and tight. Bend your legs with a quick dipping action. Experience will help you find the proper depth for a quick, explosive return. (A depth of 10 to 15 percent of the athlete's height is recommended.) Jump explosively into the bar, attempting to drive the bar as high as possible. The bar should move vertically overhead. The action of your shoulders and arms will blend into the explosive leg jumping action. Drop directly beneath the bar, catching it straight over your shoulders. In the catch phase, the legs can be kept shoulder-width apart or in stride position. Experiment to determine which foot to place forward. Both feet should be turned in. Straighten your arms vertically,

Figure 4.6a

Figure 4.6b

holding them and the rest of your body rigidly. Return to the erect position by moving the front foot back first with a slight jab step (this shortens the distance), and then step forward with your back foot.

SNATCH (BARBELL AND DUMBBELL)

The snatch (figure 4.7) develops the explosiveness of the muscle groups of the body in a coordinated multijointed action.

Assume a comfortable stance with feet spread about shoulder-width apart. Widen the clean grip so that at full extension the height of the bar will be lower and therefore require less vertical work. Experience will help you determine the optimal grip to use for a traditional lift. The close grip can be used as a variation. Bend your legs before lifting the bar and use them to get the weight off the ground. Your back should be held straight with arms medially rotated as far as possible to place your shoulders over the bar. Place your shoulders over the bar. Keep the bar close to your body. Rebend your legs after the bar clears the knees. Keep your arms straight to allow the legs and back to lift the bar as high as possible. Jump vertically into the lift with your legs, pulling the bar with your arms as high as possible. Your arms will fit in the action after the legs and back have done their part. Drive elbows up. Drop your body quickly, and catch the bar directly over your head and shoulders.

Keep in mind that leg and back strength is essential in all aspects of lifting, but it is extremely important in the recovery phase when lifting maximum weights.

Figure 4.7a

Figure 4.7b

Sample Power Output Program

The speedweek principles, covered in greater detail in chapter 13, use high-intensity work Monday through Wednesday when the body isn't as fatigued. A power exercise program using Olympic lifts should be performed on Monday and Wednesday after completing your overspeed and sports speed programs.

Your one repetition maximum (1RM) should be used as the basis for loading. To determine 1RM, find the maximum weight that you can lift in one repetition for each exercise. Table 4.2 shows six levels of workout intensity based on the percent of 1RM and the quality developed.

The sample program shown in table 4.3 indicates how Olympic lifts should be incorporated into a program to increase maximum strength. You can see from the numbers in the table that there are wide ranges in intensities, with loads increasing to or close to 1RM. Maximize rest between sets to minimize the effects of fatigue as a limiting factor. It is recommended that you vary lift emphasis on Monday and Wednesday. For instance, the clean can be at higher intensities and volumes on Monday, and the jerk can be at higher intensities

Table 4.2   **Rating Intensities of the 1RM for Exercise Prescription**

1RM (%)	Rating	Quality developed
90+	Very heavy	Strength
80 to 90	Heavy	Strength and strength endurance
70 to 80	Medium	Power and strength endurance
60 to 70	Medium light	Power and muscle endurance
50 to 60	Light	Power and muscle endurance
40 to 50	Easy	Threshold of training effect

Table 4.3   **Sample Program Using Olympic Lifts**

Monday	*Wednesday*
Warm-up	**Warm-up**
Cleans: 3 to 6 sets 3 to 5 repetitions per set 66 to 100% of 1RM 1.5 to 5 min. rest between sets	Snatches: 3 to 6 sets 3 to 5 repetitions per set 66 to 100% of 1RM 1.5 to 5 min. rest between sets
Jerks: 3 to 6 sets 3 to 5 repetitions per set 66 to 100% of 1RM 1.5 to 5 min. rest between sets	Cleans: 3 to 6 sets 3 to 5 repetitions per set 66 to 100% of 1RM 1.5 to 5 min. rest between sets

and volumes on Wednesday. The power component in this step will be of great use as you continue to step three, ballistics, in which time for work output decreases at a tremendous rate while loads on the body increase.

Functional Strength Program for the Serious Athlete

The components of the complete workout schedule remain the same during the preseason; however, intensity and duration increase during the second half. In phase A of the preseason, most exercises should start at approximately 50 percent of your maximum level as a general guide. The rate of increase should be variable, such as 8 to 10 percent per week if previous maximum levels are to be regained by the time you begin phase B.

Phase B is composed of many sets and repetitions at a high percentage of 1RM for each lift. An increased intensity in muscle endurance is also a definite objective sought during this period. The increase in workout intensity will require a comparable increase in the number of sets (at least five sets in most areas); consequently, the length of the ideal workout will increase from two to three hours. Table 4.4 outlines a standard program to help you get started.

Table 4.4   **Sample Functional Strength Program**

1. Warm-up, flexibility, body control: running or jumping techniques

    a. Jogging one-half mile or jumping rope (5 min.)
    b. Speed bags (boxing bags of various sizes, 15 min.)
    c. Running and jumping for flexibility (10 min.)

2. Power position exercises (40 min.)

    a. Snatch: power
    b. Snatch: split squat
    c. Clean and push jerk
    d. Pull

3. Legs and back (23 min.)—3 to 5 sets of 3 to 5 repetitions per set

    a. Deadlifts
    b. Squats: front
    c. Squats: back

4. Shoulders and arms (18 min.)—3 to 5 sets of 3 to 5 repetitions per set

    a. Incline
    b. Bench
    c. Curls

5. Abdominal muscles and neck (9 min.)

    a. Four-way neck: 1 set of 8 to 12 repetitions
    b. Rotary neck: 1 set of 6 repetitions each way
    c. Abdominal muscles: 3 sets of 25 repetitions per set

A minimum of two strength sessions weekly, preferably every other day, is needed to improve speed strength; one workout per week during the season will nearly maintain off-season gains. During the first two weeks of a newly started program, more recuperation time is needed. Using maximum and near-maximum weight also lengthens recovery time. Short (45 minutes or less), highly intense workouts allow athletes to train more often.

Table 4.5 shows a sample functional strength and power program for a beginner. Three sets of the leg press exercise would be performed, first with 60 percent of maximum for 10 repetitions, second at 65 percent of maximum for 8 repetitions, and third at 70 percent of maximum for 6 repetitions. The same procedure should be followed for each exercise.

A sample program for the athlete at the intermediate stage of strength development is shown in table 4.6. A workout would involve three sets of five to eight repetitions of each exercise, with the first set at 60 percent of maximum, the second set at 65 percent of maximum, and the third and final set at 70 percent of maximum.

The advanced program shown in table 4.7 is programmed for high intensity. Four sets are performed: the first set at 60 percent of maximum for five repetitions, the second set at 75 percent of maximum for three repetitions, the

Table 4.5   Sample Functional Strength and Power Program for Beginners

Exercise	RM	Monday	Wednesday	Friday
Warm-up: flexibility		**Before every workout**		
Legs and back:				
Leg press	____	L	M	H
Knee extension	____	L	M	H
Knee flexion	____	L	M	H
Toe raises	____	L	M	H
Shoulders and arms:				
Lat pull-down	____	M	H	L
Bench press	____	M	H	L
Press (seated)	____	H	M	L
Press (standing)	____	H	M	L
Curls (dumbbells)	____	M	H	L
Trunk and abdomen:				
Sit-ups (bent knee)	____	3 × 15	3 × 15	3 × 15
Neck:				
Partner four-way neck	____	3 × 8 to 12	3 × 8 to 12	3 × 8 to 12

Percent RM, sets, and repetitions:

  Light (L): 60% RM, 1 × 10; 65% RM, 1 × 8; 70% RM, 1 × 6

  Medium (M): 60% RM, 1 × 10; 70% RM, 1 × 8; 80% RM, 1 × 6

  Heavy (H): 60% RM, 1 × 10; 70% RM, 1 × 8; 75% RM, 1 × 6

Table 4.6   **Sample Functional Strength and Power Program for Intermediate Athletes**

Exercise	RM	Monday	Wednesday	Friday
Warm-up: flexibility		**Before every workout**		
Power: clean	___	H	M	L
Legs and back:				
Squat	___	L	M	H
Deadlift	___	M	H	L
Knee extension	___	M	H	L
Shoulders:				
Bench press	___	H	M	L
Press (seated, behind neck)	___	M	H	L
Rowing (bent over)	___	L	M	H
Trunk and abdomen:				
Sit-ups (medicine ball)	___	2 × 12	2 × 12	2 × 12
Sit-ups (crunches)	___	3 × 25	3 × 25	3 × 25
Trunk (hyperextension)	___	2 × 12	2 × 12	2 × 12
Neck:				
Partner four-way neck	___	3 × 8 to 12	3 × 8 to 12	3 × 8 to 12

Percent RM, sets, and repetitions:
  Light (L): 60% RM, 1 × 5 to 8; 65% RM, 1 × 5 to 8; 70% RM, 1 × 5 to 8
  Medium (M): 50% RM, 1 × 5 to 8; 70% RM, 1 × 5 to 8; 80% RM, 1 × 5
  Heavy (H): 60% RM, 1 × 5 to 8; 75% RM, 1 × 5; 85% RM, 1 × 5

third set at 85 percent of maximum for three repetitions, and the fourth set at 90 percent of maximum for two repetitions.

Explosive power in all directions is a critical quality to demonstrate as an athlete. In fact Counsilman stated that the Russian and East German coaches felt so strongly about explosive power that they monitored training sessions and stopped their athletes if their speeds decreased below the desired speed of movement. To apply this concept to your program, stop if your perceived speed of action decreases.

Advanced athletes can train this quality by performing the clean, jerk, or snatch one time at 70 percent on one of the speedweek sessions (Monday or Wednesday), by working with weights at fast speeds with 70 percent 1RM for 12 repetitions, and by working with weights at fast speeds with 50 to 60 percent 1RM for 16 to 20 repetitions. Table 4.8 lists performance standards for men in percent body weight for various feats of functional strength and power.

Table 4.7   Sample Functional Strength and Power Program for Advanced Athletes

Exercise	RM	Monday	Tuesday	Wednesday	Thursday	Friday
Power:						
Clean, power	___	M		H		
Snatch, power	___		M		H	
Jerk, rack	___	H		M		L
Legs and back:						
Pull, clean	___	M		L		H
Deadlift	___	H		M		
Squat	___	L		M		H
Squat, front	___					M
Shoulders, chest, and arms:	___					
Bench press	___	H		M		
Incline press	___		M		H	
Rowing	___	H		M		L
Flys, supine				L		M
Trunk and abdomen:						
Trunk (hyperextension)	___ ___			3 × 10 (60%)		3 × 10 (70%)
Sit-ups (bent knee)		3 × 25		3 × 25 (60%)		3 × 25 (70%)
Neck:						
Partner four-way neck	___	3 × 8 to 12		3 × 8 to 12		3 × 8 to 12

Percent RM, sets, and repetitions:

Light (L): 60% RM, 1 × 5; 65% RM, 1 × 5; 70% RM, 1 × 5

Medium (M): 60% RM, 1 × 5; 70% RM, 1 × 5; 80% RM, 1 × 5

Heavy (H): 60% RM, 1 × 5; 75% RM, 1 × 3; 85% RM, 1 × 3; 90% RM, 1 × 2

Table 4.8   Functional Strength Performance Standards

Level	Snatch	Clean	Clean and jerk	Power curl	Pull
Very poor	.50	.90	.90	.70	1.10
Poor	.70	1.10	1.10	.90	1.30
Average	.90	1.30	1.30	1.10	1.50
Good	1.10	1.50	1.50	1.30	1.70
Excellent	1.30	1.70	1.70	1.50	1.90

	Legs and back					
Level	135° 1/4 back squat	90° 1/2 back squat	Full 3/4 back squat	Front squat	Deadlift	Good morning
Very poor	1.70	1.50	1.30	1.20	1.30	.30
Poor	2.00	1.80	1.60	1.40	1.60	.40
Average	2.30	2.10	1.90	1.60	1.90	.50
Good	2.60	2.70	2.50	2.00	2.50	.70
Excellent	2.90	2.70	2.50	2.00	2.50	.70

	Arms and shoulders				
Level	Military	Incline	Bench	Dips (20 sec.)	Push-ups (20 sec.)
Very poor	.40	.50	.80	4 reps	11 reps
Poor	.60	.80	1.10	12 reps	19 reps
Average	.80	1.10	1.40	20 reps	27 reps
Good	1.00	1.40	1.70	28 reps	35 reps
Excellent	1.20	1.70	2.00	36 reps	43 reps

Notes: Numbers indicate percent of body weight; weight times the percent equals weight lifted.

Female athletes should use this table as well. For a more accurate interpretation of performance, use the category one level above your score. For example, a snatch using .90 would be a rating of good for the female athlete rather than average.

Shoulder and Arm Exercises

INCLINE PRESS (DUMBBELL AND BARBELL)

The incline press (figure 4.8) is an excellent exercise to develop the chest, shoulders, and arms. It closely simulates the working angles of the muscles in many sports.

With the bench in an incline position, place your hands on the bar at or slightly wider than shoulder-width. Hands spread wide work the shoulders and chest, whereas hands positioned closer together on the bar work the triceps more. Inhale as you bend your elbows and bring the bar to your chest. Exhale as you straighten your arms to the starting position.

Figure 4.8

BENCH PRESS (DUMBBELL AND BARBELL)

The bench press (figure 4.9) strengthens the shoulders and arms for optimal shoulder girdle protection. With the bench flat, position your hands at or slightly wider than shoulder-width. Inhale and lower the weight to your chest. Exhale as you straighten your arms to return to the starting position.

Figure 4.9

DUMBBELL ARM CURLS

Dumbbell curls (figure 4.10) develop arm strength to help maintain proper left to right muscle balance. For an alternate dumbbell curl, hold the dumbbells at your sides with palms facing your body. As you curl each arm forward, one at a time, rotate your palm upward. The curling arm moves down as the opposite arm moves up. Emphasize an even rhythm, and take one breath for each cycle of left and right arm curls. Also try this exercise by starting with your palms facing backward to work the biceps more as you rotate your palm during the curl.

Figure 4.10

LAT ROW (MACHINE, DUMBBELL, OR BARBELL)

The lat row (figure 4.11) strengthens the chest, back, shoulders, and arms. Execute the lat row using many different hand positions to isolate different muscles. Inhale as you pull the cable to your chest, making sure your trunk is vertical. Exhale as you return your arms to the starting position, following the same path as your pull. Completely extend your arms at the end of each repetition to stretch the lats.

Figure 4.11

LAT PULL-DOWN

The lat pull-down (figure 4.12) strengthens the chest, back, shoulders, and arms. As in the lat row, try a variety of grips and hand widths. Vary hand width and position on the bar (palms away, toward, or alternated). Inhale while pulling the bar down to the chest or to the shoulders, and exhale as you bring the bar up. Be sure to completely extend your arms at the top of each repetition to stretch the lats.

Figure 4.12

FLYS (SUPINE)

Flys (figure 4.13) are perfect for maintaining proper muscle balance of the chest, shoulders, and arms. The actions of this lift should cover the wide variety of shoulder movements. Lie on your back on a flat, incline, or decline bench. Hold the dumbbells over your body, arms extended with a slight bend at the elbow. Inhale as you lower the dumbbells to your sides, keeping your arms slightly bent until you reach your maximum range of motion. Exhale as you return to the starting position.

Figure 4.13a

Figure 4.13b

Abdominal and Neck Exercises

ABDOMINAL CRUNCHES

Although the abdominal muscles have a limited range of motion, they play a major role in proper breathing and supporting all actions of the trunk. Start on your back with your hands behind your head and your knees up. Curl your body, flexing the abdominal muscles and forcing out air as you curl (figure 4.14). Just clear your shoulders from the floor. Hold and exhale as you return to the floor. Use twisting actions in the curl to work all aspects of the trunk.

Figure 4.14

NECK STRENGTHENING

Many athletes fail to develop their necks adequately. This two-person exercise ensures that your neck will be ready for action. All areas—front, back, and side—should be strengthened. Lie on your back on a bench or assume a wrestler's floor position. Your partner places his hands in a position that gives you a good pushing surface to resist against without discomfort. Your partner applies even pressure with his hands as you push against the resistance (figure 4.15).

Figure 4.15

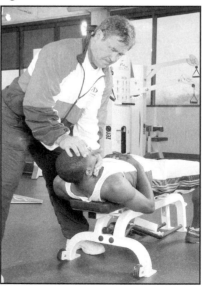

Leg and Back Exercises

DEADLIFT WITH ALTERNATE GRIP

For the deadlift with alternate grip (figure 4.16), assume a comfortable stance with your feet about shoulder-width apart. Bend your knees to grasp the bar and lift it from the floor, keeping your back straight. Hold the bar at your thighs before bending your knees to place the bar back on the floor.

Figure 4.16

TOE RAISES

Toe raises (figure 4.17) strengthen your calf muscles for powerful leg thrusts. Toe raises can be done on a machine, using a padded barbell, or with a partner sitting on your back. Repeat the exercise with your feet in the following three positions to develop all aspects of the calf: heels out, heels straight, and heels in.

Figure 4.17

FRONT AND BACK SQUAT

The front squat develops strength in the lower extremities and trunk. Take the bar from a weight rack, using a weight belt to support your back. Position the bar on your shoulders so it rests evenly on the deltoids. Spread your feet comfortably with toes slightly out. (Placing the toes in various positions will work different parts of the thighs.) Keep your neck and back straight and elbows lifted high throughout the lift. Inhale to support your trunk at the start, and bend your knees as far as you can until your upper thighs are parallel to the ground. Exhale as you return to standing. You can also place a thick board or weight under your heels. The added height will work the front part of your thighs more.

For the back squat (figure 4.18), position the bar on your shoulders behind your head and execute the same movements as the front squat.

Figure 4.18a

Figure 4.18b

Strengthening the Hamstring Muscle Group

Evaluating the hamstring/quadriceps strength ratio is more complicated than simply doing gross balance testing. Peak torque is not identical at opposing angles. Consequently, Grimby (1993) suggests that measurements be taken at the same joint angles and not at peak torque. Therefore, make sure you interpret any results from our testing as a gross indicator. Should problems arise, seek a more sophisticated testing assessment from your doctor.

The hamstring/quadriceps strength ratio test completed in chapter 2 provided you with a gross indication of the need for further testing on more sophisticated equipment that considers different joint angles. Most athletes, however, need additional training to increase the strength and power of the hamstring muscle group. Many experts feel that the hamstrings are a sprinter's weakest link. The leg curl and leg extension tests described in chapter 2 estimate the comparative strength of the quadriceps (front of upper leg) and hamstrings (back of upper leg). Only a few elite athletes are equally strong in both muscle groups (e.g., some champion sprinters, power lifters such as world champion Dr. "Squat" Fred Hatfield, and some defensive backs in football [backward sprinting develops the hamstrings]). In more than 25 years of sponsoring speed clinics and camps, we've seen only one athlete who had equal strength in both muscle groups; the large majority of athletes failed to meet our minimum standard (hamstring strength should equal 75 to 80 percent of quadriceps strength).

The power exercises (Olympic lifts) described previously are excellent hamstring exercises, as is the leg curl exercise. You also can lie on your back with your foot extended to a point several feet up on the wall. Pull down with a straight leg and hold that contraction for 8 to 10 seconds. Repeat the exercise three to five times. This "paw down" motion is similar to Ralph Mann's and Tom Tellez's form drills and closely simulates that phase of the sprinting action.

Hypergravity training (weighted suits, vests, or pants) can be added to the sprint drills shown in chapter 9 for extra loading of the lower extremities. Care should be taken in selecting the training loads that allow you to maintain good sprinting action.

Roller skates or in-line skates offer a unique method of training the muscle groups at the hip, knee, and ankle (gluteus, hamstrings, quadriceps, calf muscles) responsible for the driving force behind high levels of sprinting. Five areas of conditioning are recommended using skates:

✦ Range of motion in all possible directions of hip and leg movement. Legs should be moved in all directions. Hold onto a chair while completing 8 to 12 repetitions in all directions. Build up to three sets and emphasize flexibility.

✦ High-speed assisted drills using the Sprint Master or surgical tubing to focus on the sprinting action. The pull-through sprint drill shown in chapter 9 is one that can be done at high speed. Make sure that the speed is not excessive.

✦ Overspeed skate training. Hold on to a support and move the legs as fast as possible in a back and forth motion. Complete three to five sets of 8 to 12 repetitions with maximum rest (full recovery) between each set. When you have adjusted to the high-speed work, complete each set without holding on.

✦ Speed endurance exercises. Move back and forth at high speed for 10 to 30 seconds, working up to 30 to 60 seconds. You should gradually build up to 8 to 12 repetitions in sets of four, resting one and a half to three minutes between each set.

✦ Muscle endurance exercises for sprinting. Move the legs back and forth with a slight bend at the knee. The use of ankle weights or surgical tubing will provide the necessary loading. Complete three sets of 8 to 12 repetitions with as rapid a movement as possible with the load.

Special equipment also strengthen the hamstring muscle group as you perform specific movements of sprinting (see figure 4.19).

Specific programs, such as strength training involving heavy weight, near-maximal muscle contractions, low repetitions, and full recovery between sets, have been shown to produce greater increases in the cross-sectional area of fast-twitch fibers than slow-twitch fibers.

Figure 4.19   Strengthening the hamstrings using a special machine.

Shoulder and Arm Exercises for Throwers

The biomechanics laboratory at Centinela Hospital Medical Center in Inglewood, California, under the direction of medical director Dr. Frank Jobe, MD, has published a shoulder-strengthening program designed for baseball players, although anyone interested in strengthening the shoulders and arms can follow the program. Write to the Centinela Hospital Medical Center for an illustrated copy of this program or visit www.sportsscience.com. Essentially, the exercises prescribed cover every movement that the shoulders and arms can make. Multijointed pushing and pulling exercises recommended in our program will exercise the shoulders and arms as a unit, and the Jobe exercises will isolate the finer shoulder girdle and arm actions. A combination of both of these programs will produce the results you need for superbly conditioned shoulders and arms.

The following arm and shoulder girdle actions are specifically isolated in the Jobe dumbbell program: external and internal rotation; shoulder flexion, extension, and adduction; scapular adduction and abduction; horizontal flexion; arm flexion and extension; forearm supination and pronation; wrist flexion and extension; and ulnar deviation.

Strengthening the Knee

According to many experts in athletic training and rehabilitation, it is necessary to have strong legs from the ankle to the hip. There are 13 muscles that provide the tension to support the knee. All of them must be properly strengthened to give the knee maximum support throughout the total range of motion. The following knee functions should be included in your training program: flexion, extension, medial rotation, and stabilization.

The next chapter on ballistic and plyometic training builds on the functional strength and power developed in step two. Although all movements require the use of energy, chapter 5 describes body toughening factors and how to manage the explosive energy output (sending) and energy input (receiving). Consequently, training for high-energy movement is required. Overcoming the inertia of changing the directions of body movement and its impact on the tissues of the body needs to have a special place in your conditioning program.

BALLISTICS AND PLYOMETRICS

*B*allistics and plyometrics are important components of a holistic speed improvement program for team sport athletes. Both programs improve the explosive power of the upper and lower body and have a positive effect on starting speed, acceleration, and stride rate and length. These programs are key to improving high-speed starting, stopping, and cutting. The programs also prepare the body for the explosive delivery and reception of contact in sports such as football, basketball, lacrosse, rugby, and soccer.

Ballistics

Sports fans often enjoy events packed with incredible excitement, electricity, and action. Spectators can feel the high level of energy. High-powered actions play a major role in the outcome of all sporting events. Playing or sprinting at high speeds can provide much of the necessary short-term energy system development for most sports. There are three basic purposes of movement: to maintain equilibrium, to move an object, and to stop an object. The majority of sports include multidirectional movements, short starts and stops with bursts of speed, rapid changes in direction, explosive power delivery of an impact through contact with the ground or an opponent, instantaneous power reception at contact, and explosive power delivery to an object. Often these tasks occur at the same time and, in fact, should not be isolated from the total action at all.

The ability of body tissues to deliver, transmit, and absorb energy is fundamental to human performance and survival in athletic environments. Former Indiana University coach Dr. Counsilman used the sport of diving to illustrate the best way to manage energy. Have you ever done a belly flop when diving? How about a perfect dive? The difference in how the two dives feel tells you a lot about how the energy of the dive is managed. In the belly flop, body tissues have to manage all the energy of the dive in milliseconds and in a limited distance because of the water's incompressibility. The perfect dive, on the other hand, spreads the same energy out over a much longer time and distance. How can you apply this information to your sport?

All tissues are not able to manage energy at the same level. The ability ratings for energy absorption of the most important tissues may surprise you.

Their comparative ability to manage energy is shown in the energy-absorbing capabilities scale (figure 5.1).

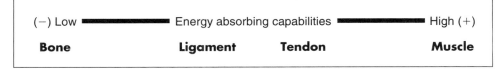

Figure 5.1 The energy-absorbing capabilities of bone, ligament, tendon, and muscle.

Maintaining Equilibrium: Flow

Before elaborating on energy management, let's examine the importance of joining, resisting, and yielding into a unified whole, commonly referred to as the flow state or the zone.

Technically, there are three categories of energy management:

1. Sending energy away from the body. This category includes all types of hitting, kicking, and throwing various implements, from footballs to medicine balls to assorted weights.

2. Receiving energy from outside sources. Forces that come into the body in the form of a ball or opposing players are listed in this category. Any form of catching develops the necessary sensitivity needed for receiving outside forces.

3. The zone, or flow state. Whatever this state is finally discovered to be, most athletes who claim they have been there report that it is an effortless state. Time and motion slow, and performance approaches the spiritual. All of these factors permit athletes to perform at levels closer to their maximum potential. It is important to recognize that there are degrees and levels of flow. Furthermore, each level or amount of time in the zone will bring a different degree of performance enhancement. The higher the level, the higher the quality of energy management.

Modern technology and practical methods, such as those in chapter 3, have enabled you to reduce play to a single performance curve by plotting every step you take during performance and identifying the actions taking place. To plot this curve, review a videotape of performance and make a sequential list of the skills used during each play (see chapter 3). This list is your performance notation on how you executed each play during the game or each step of the race or jump. No matter which method you use, all the elements of play can be recorded during a single play or movement in any sport. These patterns enable you to make a step-by-step evaluation of how you manage energy during performance. Study your responses to the starts, stops, contacts, and pressures of other players attempting to block, screen, or use you in some way.

Ballistics Training

Many programs fail to toughen the body in a systematic way during the off-season. Yes, the strength and power program (chapter 4) has a toughening effect, but additional methods are required to move the body to higher levels of toughness. Boxers have used medicine balls for many years. During the Landry era, the Dallas Cowboys used medicine balls to toughen their bodies. The balls also were used to sensitize the neuromuscular system to respond instantly to contact. Many present-day systems fail to recognize the importance of delivering and redirecting these outside forces to the athletes' advantage. We have worked with many outstanding players from high school, college, and professional teams. The majority of the players we worked with showed little skill in the sophisticated unity of resisting and yielding. Remember, this skill is not inherited; it must be taught. If you are searching for the edge against your competition, find a way to include this skill in training.

MEDICINE BALL TOUGHENING CATCHES

Most sports have some physical contact even if contact isn't part of the game. These drills provide a safe way to toughen the body. This drill develops receiving skills.

You will need medicine balls or sandbags weighing 2 to 25 pounds and a mini-trampoline. You can make a good sandbag from an inner tube of a car tire. Tie it off on one end and fill it with sand, and then tie it off again after you have reached the desired weight. You can perform this exercise on your own or with a partner or group. Perform 25 to 50 repetitions.

Figure 5.2

+ Individual: Throw the ball in the air or at the mini-trampoline and catch it with your body (figure 5.2). Make sure the ball contacts various body parts to get the maximum training effect. Do not catch the ball in a way that places undue stress on joints.

+ Partner or group: Any number of players can participate. Form a circle, standing three to four feet apart. Pass the ball in any direction. If you feel there aren't enough opportunities for catching and throwing, add more balls. Include unexpected elements by throwing the ball at various speeds or at different parts of the catcher's body. When catching the ball, absorb the shock with body movements and various body parts.

MEDICINE BALL THROWS AND TOUGHENING CATCHES

This drill develops power in all directions of movement. You will need medicine balls, sandbags, or weights weighing 2 to 25 pounds.

You can perform this exercise on your own or with a partner or group. Perform the following movements 8 to 10 times in each direction: seated throws, forward throws (underhand and overhand), backward throws (overhead), and side throws (left side and front, right side and front; left side and back, right side and back). When you perform these exercises with a partner or group, you achieve the benefits of the toughening drills by catching the balls.

OVERWEIGHT IMPLEMENT PROGRAMS FOR ALL THROWING ACTIONS

These exercises are appropriate for pitchers, quarterbacks, javelin throwers, or any athletes that need to improve throwing action. Use whatever weighted implement is appropriate for your sport: football, basketball, baseball, javelin, discus, or small medicine ball. Although the arm is the most visible segment in a throw, the superb timing of the total body action produces great feats in throwing. Slow-motion cameras capture the complexity and energy involved in a throw and demonstrate the importance of training the throwing action of the legs, hips, trunk, shoulders, and arms. Additional insurance is provided from functional strength and power training in the form of greater strength in supporting tissues of the joints, tendons, and ligaments.

Figure 5.3

The throwing sequence should progress from heavy to light. Start with the heavy ball for foundation and progress to lighter balls for throwing. The heavy ball strengthens the muscles and joints used in throwing, establishing a sound foundation. Lighter weights provide the high-speed throwing action needed to improve throwing skill. Throwing into a net (figure 5.3) will allow you to complete a high-intensity workout with more throws and less wasted time.

Escaping and Avoiding Tight Spots

Martial artist Dan Inosanto shared some proven methods to escape, avoid, or improve the application of ballistics and energy management in your sport. Inosanto recommends the following for all athletes:

+ Level changes (dropping from a high to a low stance)
+ Angle changes (moving from the direct line of the attacking player)
+ Sensitivity training (bringing awareness to the level of first touch)
+ Increasing energy of contact gradually, building to maximum effort
+ Being aware of natural movements and applying them to your advantage
+ Being constantly in slow phasic motion to make it easier to move and change direction
+ Lateral contact (when the attack comes from the side, making level changes and simultaneously moving to the line of least resistance)
+ Frontal attack (moving forward to the line of least resistance)
+ Moving in the direction from which the opponent (force) is coming to put maximum distance between you and your opponent (force) with a minimum amount of time and effort
+ Mastering techniques such as ducking, slipping, rolling, and footwork (step and slide with a push, sidestep, and short steps to maintain balance and quick changes in angle)
+ Moving from a crouched position upward and forward
+ Deceiving an opponent by giving an indication of forward motion to make the opponent commit his forward motion, then dropping back a half step and changing the angle to your advantage in forward motion
+ Linemen advantage: one hand hitting the opponent's shoulder while the other is pulling the opponent's other shoulder or arm
+ Both hands hitting the same shoulder of the opponent to change the angle
+ Both hands hitting the opposite shoulder of the opponent, then one hand hitting and pulling

This section has presented those principles and skills that answer the question "How does ballistics training improve playing speed?" It would be nice if all you had to do was line up and sprint as fast as you could to the finish tape, but this isn't always the case. Mary Decker Slaney was jostled and lost her balance in the 1984 Olympics and was put out of the race. Maybe if she had had ballistics training, she would have been able to recover and get back in the race. The next section in this book continues to move you closer to the higher reaches of playing speed.

Plyometrics

The word *plyometric* is derived from the Greek word *pleythyein*, meaning "to increase" or from the Greek roots *plio* and *metric*, meaning "more" and "measure." *Plyometrics* refers to exercises that enable a muscle to reach maximum strength in as short a time as possible. Plyometric exercises are important in sports requiring high levels of speed strength (ability to exert maximum force during high-speed activity) to complete movements such as starting, stopping, cutting, accelerating, sprinting, jumping, and throwing.

The term was first used in the United States in 1975 by Fred Wilt, former Olympic runner and women's track coach at Purdue University. Coach Wilt got the term from European track and field coaches who had already used plyometrics for more than a decade in the training of sprinters and athletes in jump events. Yuri Verkhoshansky, a coach in the Soviet Union, is credited as being one of the early pioneers and leading researchers of plyometric training. Although plyometrics were slow to be accepted in the United States, numerous articles, books, and videos produced in the 1980s and early 1990s have led to their widespread use in baseball, basketball, football, lacrosse, rugby, soccer, and other team and individual sports.

Although plyometrics take many different forms, activity revolves around jumping, hopping, and bounding movements for the lower body and swinging, quick action push-off, catching and throwing weighted objects (medicine balls, shots, sandbags), arm swings, and pulley throws for the upper body. The medicine ball throws presented in this section are similar to some of the ballistic exercises described previously; however, the emphasis is placed on loading the abdominal and arm muscles before the movement or toss rather than on catching the ball. Exercises that simulate specific movements in a particular sport or activity are chosen.

Plyometrics develop both strength and power in the muscles involved in sprinting. An athlete may have superior strength yet be unable to produce the needed power to sprint a fast 20- to 60-yard dash. The completion of some movements in sports, such as sprinting, involves less time than it takes for the muscle to develop a maximal contraction. For such actions, an athlete will use only 60 to 80 percent of her absolute strength. The key to plyometric training is to display strength as quickly and as forcefully as possible. Plyometric training has also been found to be an ideal program to develop explosiveness and improve quickness.

Plyometric exercises use gravity to store energy in the muscles before the athlete immediately releases the energy in the opposite direction. Plyometrics provide an important training program for team sport athletes since speed strength (exerting maximum force during high-speed movements) is required throughout each contest.

Plyometric training is used to improve speed strength, which is the application of maximum force during a high-speed activity such as sprinting. The unusual progress and success of Russian sprinter Valeri Borzov, 100-meter gold medal winner (10.14) in the 1972 Olympic Games, are partially attributed to the use of plyometric exercises in the six years before the games. Borzov progressed from a 100-meter time of 13.0 seconds at age 14 to 10.0 at age 20. Although you may not show such dramatic improvement, the hops, jumps, bounds, leaps, skips, ricochets, swings, and twists that make up plyometrics are an important part of a speed improvement program.

Plyometrics focus on the two key aspects of speed strength: starting strength, which is the ability to instantaneously recruit as many muscle fibers as possible, and explosive strength, which is the ability to keep the initial explosion of a muscle contraction going over a distance against some resistance. Starting strength is the key to sprinting a fast 20 to 100 yards, throwing or kicking a ball, and similar movements requiring little more than overcoming body resistance. Examples of explosive strength are football blocking, performing the shot put or hammer toss, Olympic weightlifting, power lifting, and other movements requiring considerable resistance. As Hatfield and Yessis (1986) point out, "The lighter the implement you have to move and the shorter the distance, the more your starting strength becomes important; the heavier the resistance and the longer the distance, the more important your explosive strength becomes."

The main objective of plyometric training is to improve an athlete's ability to generate maximum force in the shortest time. This objective is accomplished by first loading muscles to accumulate energy before unloading this energy in the opposite direction. Gravity is used to store energy in the muscles that is immediately released in an opposite reaction. In other words, plyometric exercises involve powerful muscular contractions in response to the rapid dynamic loading (stretching) of the involved muscles.

Most athletes already apply the basic concept of loading and unloading when they cock their wrists or ankles before throwing a baseball or football, hitting a baseball, shooting a basketball, kicking a soccer ball or football, swinging a golf club, or executing the forehand or backhand stroke in tennis. The rapid stretching (loading) of these muscles activates the muscle stretch reflex, which sends a powerful stimulus to the muscles that causes them to contract faster and with more power. In the previous actions, athletes rapidly stretch a muscle group then transfer the energy by immediately contracting that same group. A rapid deceleration of mass is followed by a rapid acceleration of mass in another direction. The loading or stretching action sometimes is called the yielding phase, and the reflex contraction of the muscles is called the overcoming phase. The objective is to obtain a maximum eccentric contraction (muscle develops tension while lengthening) to load the muscle, then switch this contraction to concentric (muscle develops tension while shortening), which produces the desired explosive movement. The faster a muscle is stretched with rapid eccentric loading, the more powerful the concentric contraction.

Rapid loading of the muscles (yielding phase) must occur just before the contraction phase of these same muscles. When you jump from an elevated platform to the ground, for example, your legs bend under the g-force (kinetic energy) and an immediate reactive jump occurs. How much your legs bend depends on the g-force and the stored energy that will be used to release the powerful contraction to jump. The yielding phase produces stored energy, which is released during the overcoming phase by a powerful contraction.

Does this sound complicated? It is really quite simple. To plan and use plyometrics properly for speed improvement and other quickness skills critical to your sport, just follow these guidelines:

✦ Remember that plyometrics are merely a type of resistance training to develop strength and power. Gravity is used to store energy in the muscles; the energy is then used immediately in an opposite reaction, causing the elastic properties of the muscle to produce kinetic energy.

✦ Exercises should correspond to the form, muscle work, and range of motion in your sport. The main goal is to rapidly apply overload force to the muscles to improve speed strength.

✦ Exercises should correspond to the correct direction of movement. Because the leg moves toward the rear in one phase of sprinting, for example, some plyometric movements should also be directed toward the rear.

✦ The rate of the stretch is strongly tied to the effectiveness of plyometric training; the higher the stretch rate, the greater the muscle tension and the more powerful the concentric contraction in the opposite direction.

✦ Exercises for sprinting speed improvement should explode at the beginning of the movement and allow inertia to move the limb through the remaining range of motion. In one phase of sprinting, for example, maximum effort is exerted at the point you begin to pull the thigh through and diminishes as the leg passes underneath the body.

✦ Although weights (vest, ankle spats) can be used to increase resistance, too much weight may increase strength without much effect on power. Too much weight increases the risk of injury and also makes it impossible to jump or sprint explosively, which defeats the purpose of the plyometric workout. Your body already provides considerable resistance. Adding a lot of weight is unnecessary. Light weight or body weight is recommended to develop quick force. Alternating light (1 to 2 percent of body weight, no more than 2 to 3 pounds) and heavier weight (5 to 6 percent of body weight, no more than 10 to 12 pounds) in the same plyometric exercise is also an excellent technique to experience the feeling of higher speed action.

✦ Whenever possible, a plyometric exercise should be performed at a speed faster than you are capable of producing without some assistance. The objective is to use plyometric exercises that result in down time (the time your feet are on the ground) that is less than the down time in sprinting. The faster a muscle is forced to lengthen, the greater the tension it exerts. Also, the closer the stretch of the muscle to the contraction, the more violent the contraction. When you are jumping from boxes or bleachers, avoid hesitating after ground contact; the goal is to be on the ground as little as possible by shortening the span between contact and takeoff. The use of box jumps to increase the loading phase and surgical tubing to decrease the resistance to be overcome in speed hops are examples of techniques that allow a more forceful load or a faster contraction speed. You are teaching your nervous system to experience the higher speed generated so it can duplicate it later in competition without any assistance from boxes or tubing.

✦ Make a strong effort to handle the forces of landing with as little flexion of the joints as possible. When jumping on a flat surface or off boxes, too much flexion of the legs on landing increases the time spent on the ground, absorbs most of the force, and allows little preloading or tensing. As soon as the balls of your feet touch the floor, rapidly flex your knees to your comfortable jumping position (never beyond right angles). This proper knee flexion position also prevents excessive ankle flexion, such as allowing your heels to touch the surface.

✦ Master proper form for each exercise. A key aspect of proper technique is assuming a knees- and thumbs-up position (knees bent just above a right angle, elbows to sides with hands in front of the body and thumbs facing upward) to help maintain balance and center the workload around your hips and legs. For upper-body exercise, stress proper follow-through. Emphasize the quality (proper form and speed) of each jump rather than the quantity of jumps.

✦ A highly explosive movement in sports does not occur automatically. You do not sprint at maximum speed, serve at 100-plus miles per hour in tennis, kick a ball 60-plus yards, or jump 25-plus feet without being psyched before the movement. It takes a concentrated mental effort to perform these actions.

✦ Adequate recovery is necessary between each high-intensity plyometric workout, with a minimum of 48 hours recommended. Alternating light-intensity and high-intensity workouts permits the use of additional workouts weekly if necessary.

Safety Precautions

Although plyometric training is not likely to result in injury, unsound or unsupervised programs could cause shin splints and knee, ankle, and lower back problems. These injuries are often a direct result of too many workouts per week, too many jumps per workout, incorrect form, jumping on hard surfaces, and using plyometrics at too early an age or without the necessary strength and conditioning base. To reduce the risk of injury, follow these guidelines:

✦ Because of greater susceptibility to injury before puberty, preadolescent boys and girls should avoid plyometrics, unless other factors indicate more advanced maturity.

+ Plyometrics should also be postponed for athletes who do not have a sufficient strength and conditioning base. Avoid lower-body plyometrics until you can leg press 2.0 to 2.5 times your body weight; avoid upper-body plyometrics until you can perform five consecutive clap push-ups. Athletes weighing more than 260 pounds should be capable of bench pressing their body weight; athletes weighing less than 160 pounds should be capable of bench pressing 1.5 times their body weight. Athletes falling between 160 and 260 should be able to meet gradations between these guidelines (160 to 184: 1.4; 185 to 209: 1.3; 210 to 234: 1.2; 235 to 259: 1.1).

+ Experts recommend that large athletes over 200 pounds, who may be more susceptible to injury, should avoid high-volume, high-intensity exercises. Very large football players such as interior linemen must also take extra precautions.

+ Athletes who do not respond well to the instructions of coaches are also at greater risk of injury and under- or overtraining.

+ Precede a plyometric workout with a general warm-up period consisting of walk-jog-stride-sprint cycles for one-half to three-quarters of a mile, followed by careful stretching exercises.

+ Use footwear with good ankle and arch support, lateral stability, and a wide, nonslip sole, such as a basketball or aerobic shoe. Running shoes with narrow soles and poor upper support can lead to ankle problems and are not recommended. Heel cups may be needed for those who are prone to heel bruises.

+ Plyometrics should be performed only on surfaces with good shock-absorbing properties, such as soft grassy areas, well-padded artificial turf, and wrestling mats. Never do plyometrics on asphalt or gymnasium floors.

+ Boxes should be sturdy and have a nonslip top.

+ Depth jumping from objects that are too high increases the risk of injury, particularly to larger athletes, and prevents the rapid switch from eccentric to concentric activity. The average recommended heights for depth jumps are .75 to .8 meter; athletes more than 220 pounds should use heights of .5 to .75 meter.

+ Plyometric training should be supervised at all times, the number of weekly sessions should not exceed two or three for a maximum of 15 to 20 minutes each session, and the total number of quality jumps per session should be carefully controlled.

Frequency, Volume, Intensity, Recovery, and Progression

Perform plyometric workouts no more than twice weekly during the off-season and preseason and once weekly during the season. Plyometric training is extremely strenuous; about 48 hours of rest is needed to fully recover. There-fore, plyometric exercises should be completed near the end of a workout. High-speed activity or physical contact work (such as scrimmage in soccer and football) after a plyometric workout may be performed at less than competition speed; plyometric training could disrupt timing and increase the probability of fatigue-related injuries.

Because of fatigue, avoid lower-body weight training on days when lower-body plyometrics are used. Doing both in one day negates the full effect of each program. You can perform upper-body plyometrics and lower-body weight training, or vice versa, on the same day. A sample workout might include a general warm-up (such as jogging), stretching (flexibility exercises), sprint-assisted training, anaerobic training, plyometrics, and a cool-down period, in that order.

To date, there is no magic number of jumps (foot or feet contacts with the surface) that produces the best results. Coaches at various levels differ in terms of the number of repetitions, sets, and total jumps in a single workout. Taking too few jumps is better than taking too many, however. Ideally, the number of jumps should not exceed 80 to 100 per session for beginners and athletes in early workouts, 100 to 120 per session for intermediate-level athletes, and 120 to 140 per session for advanced athletes who have completed four to six weeks of plyometric training.

The amount of stress placed on the muscles, the connective tissue, and the joints is referred to as intensity. Skipping movements provide minimum stress and are considered low-intensity exercises; box jumping, two-foot takeoff and landing exercises, high-speed movements, and using additional weight all in-crease the intensity of the workout. Your program should take place over a period of 8 to 10 weeks, involve no more than two sessions weekly (Monday and Friday or Tuesday and Saturday is ideal), and progress from low- to high-intensity exercises and low to high volume. Before beginning the program, each athlete should be evaluated and approved, sport-specific goals should be defined, and proper warm-up and technique should be mastered.

Remember that you are trying to improve speed strength, not speed endur-ance. Thus, adequate rest (recovery) between repetitions, sets, and workouts is required. For example, recovery for box jumping may take 5 to 10 seconds between repetitions and two to three minutes between sets. In repeated jumps where limited ground contact is stressed, there is no recovery period between repetitions; the athlete immediately unloads into the next repetition. Recovery between workouts is two to four days, depending on the sport and time of year. Two days is generally sufficient during the preseason; a period of three or four days is appropriate during the season. The key to a successful program is to do each explosive movement with perfect form.

Exercises should progress from low-intensity in-place exercises for beginners to medium-intensity and then high-intensity for advanced athletes. Table 5.1 outlines a 10-week off-season program that moves from low- to medium- to high-intensity exercises over 6 weeks. You can develop your own program by

Table 5.1   **Sample Off-Season Plyometric Program**

Week	Drills	Sets and repetitions	Rest between sets	Sessions per week
1 to 2	4 low-intensity drills	2 × 10	2 min.	2
3 to 4	2 low-intensity drills 2 medium-intensity drills	2 × 10	2 to 3 min.	2
5 to 6	4 medium-intensity drills	2 or 3 × 10	2 to 3 min.	2
7 to 8	2 medium-intensity drills 2 high-intensity drills	Medium: 2 or 3 × 10 High: 2 × 10	2 to 3 min. Box jumps: 10 to 15 sec. between repetitions	2
9 to 10	4 high-intensity drills	Non-box jumps: 2 or 3 × 10 Box jumps: 2 × 10	3 min.	2

Reprinted, by permission, from W.B. Allerheiligen, 1994, Speed Development and Plyometric Training. In *Essentials of Strength Training and Conditioning*, edited by T. Baechle (Champaign, IL: Human Kinetics), 323.

using this table and selecting your choices from the low-, medium-, and high-intensity exercises on pages 105 to 127. In 6 to 8 weeks, when high-intensity plyometric drills become the foundation, decrease the volume of exercise. A sample plyometric program to begin 8 weeks before the start of the competitive season is shown in table 5.2.

Table 5.2   **Eight-Week Plyometric Program for Speed Improvement**

Type	Exercises	Sets and repetitions	Rest	Progression
Low intensity Week 1	Squat jumps Double-leg ankle bounces Lateral cone jumps Drop and catch push-ups	3 × 6 to 10 3 × 6 to 10 2 × 6 to 10 4 × 6 to 10	2 min.	Add 1 repetition each workout
Low to medium intensity Week 2	Lateral cone jumps Split squat jumps Double-leg tucks Standing triple jumps Medicine ball throws (overhead backward and underhand forward) Clap push-ups	3 × 8 to 10 2 × 8 to 10 2 × 8 to 10 2 × 8 to 10 2 × 8 to 10 2 × 8 to 10	2 min.	Add 1 repetition each workout, up to a maximum of 10 repetitions

(continued)

Table 5.2 (continued)

Type	Exercises	Sets and repetitions	Rest	Progression
Medium to high intensity Weeks 3 and 4	Standing long jumps Alternate-leg bounds Double-leg hops Pike jumps Depth jumps Medicine ball throws (with Russian twist) Dumbbell arm swings	3 × 8 to 10 3 × 8 to 10 3 × 8 to 10 2 × 8 to 10 2 × 8 to 10 3 × 8 to 10 2 × 8 to 10	2 min.	Add 1 repetition each workout, up to a maximum of 10 repetitions Reduce weight each workout; maximum of 20 lb.
Medium to high intensity Weeks 5 and 6	Double-leg tucks Single-leg zigzag hops Double-leg vertical power jumps Running bounds Box jumps Dumbbell arm swings Medicine ball sit-ups	3 × 10 to 12 3 × 10 to 12 3 × 10 to 12 3 × 10 to 12 2 × 8 to 10 3 × 12 3 × 10 to 15	2 min.	Add 1 repetition each workout, up to a maximum of 10 repetitions
High intensity[a] Weeks 7 and 8	Alternate-leg bounds Running bounds Single-leg speed hops Double-leg speed hops Multiple box jumps Double-arm skipping Standing arm swings Dumbbell arm swings Contrast arm swings Side jump and sprint Decline hops Medicine ball sit-ups	2 × 12 to 8 2 × 12 to 8 2 × 12 to 8 2 × 12 to 8 2 × 12 to 8 2 × 12 to 8 2 × 12 to 8 2 × 12 to 8 2 × 12 to 8 5 × 3 2 × 12 to 8 3 × 15 to 20	60 to 90 sec.	Stress form and maximum explosion; decrease repetitions from 12 to 8 in two weeks Start with 2 lb., reduce to 1 lb. Contrast: Complete 12 with 2 lb., 12 with 1 lb., and 12 with no weight
Maintenance program	Alternate-leg bounds Running bounds Double-leg speed hops Side jump and sprints Dumbbell arm swings Contrast arm swings Medicine ball sit-ups	2 × 12 2 × 12 2 × 12 5 × 5 2 × 15 2 × 15 3 × 20	90 sec.	Stress form and quality on each repetition

Note: Cycle begins eight weeks before competition and assumes that the athlete has a solid conditioning foundation in strength training.

[a]High-intensity plyometrics now become the foundation of the program. Total volume (number of jumps) for the lower body has been reduced, sprint-specific jumps are emphasized, and a series of upper-body-form plyometric exercises have been added.

Plyometric Exercises and Drills

Many types of plyometric exercises are used in various sports. For playing speed improvement, we are primarily interested in a few basic jumps that involve limited ground contact time. A number of common plyometric drills result in a down time two to three times longer than in the sprinting action. Although some of these drills are important because the down time is similar to that during the start and acceleration phase of the 20-, 40-, and 60-yard dash, most high-intensity routines should involve high-speed jumps with short down times.

In the following exercises, L indicates low-intensity, M indicates medium-intensity, and H indicates high-intensity. Plyometric training and heavy strength training should not be performed on the same day unless lower-body strength training is combined with upper-body plyometric work or vice versa. Neither program should be used on two consecutive days; 36 to 48 hours of recovery time is recommended.

In-Place Jumps

SQUAT JUMP

Stand upright with hands behind your head. Drop to a half squat and immediately explode up as high as possible (figure 5.4). Repeat after landing, stressing maximum height.

Figure 5.4

DOUBLE-LEG ANKLE BOUNCE

With arms at your sides, jump up and forward using your ankles (figure 5.5). Immediately on landing, execute the next jump. Complete the desired number of repetitions.

Figure 5.5

SPLIT SQUAT JUMP

Assume lunge position with one leg extended forward and the other behind (figure 5.6a). Perform a vertical jump off the front leg, landing with the same leg forward (figure 5.6b). Repeat with the other leg forward.

Figure 5.6a

Figure 5.6b

LATERAL CONE JUMP

Standing to one side of a cone, jump laterally to the other side (figure 5.7). Immediately on landing, jump back to the starting position to complete one repetition.

Figure 5.7

Upper-Body Exercises

SINGLE-CLAP PUSH-UP

Assume a normal push-up position and lower your chest to the floor. Push your body up with an explosive action that allows you to clap your hands (figure 5.8) and catch yourself in the upright position. Repeat the movement immediately for the desired number of repetitions.

Figure 5.8

DROP AND CATCH PUSH-UP

Kneel on both knees with the upper body erect, as though standing on your knees (figure 5.9a). Place hands in front of your chest, palms down, and drop your upper body to the floor, catching your weight with both elbows bent in the bottom phase of the push-up position (figure 5.9b). Immediately push off with both hands to extend your arms and return to the upright position.

Figure 5.9a

Figure 5.9b

In-Place Jumps

PIKE JUMP

Assume an upright stance with both arms to your sides, feet shoulder-width apart. Execute a vertical jump, bringing both extended legs in front of your body, and reach out with both hands to touch your toes in a pike position (figure 5.10). On landing, immediately repeat.

Figure 5.10

DOUBLE-LEG TUCK JUMP

Assume an upright stance with both arms to your sides, feet shoulder-width apart. Execute a vertical jump, grasping both knees while in the air (figure 5.11). Release your knees before landing and immediately execute the next jump.

Figure 5.11

Standing Jumps

STANDING TRIPLE JUMP

Assume the standing broad jump position: arms to your sides, feet shoulder-width apart. Using a two-foot takeoff, jump forward as far as possible, landing on the right foot, then immediately jump and land on the left foot. Finally, jump once again and land on both feet. The standing triple jump is identical to the triple jump in track (hop, step, and jump), except for the use of a two-foot takeoff. The objective is to generate maximum speed and secure as great a distance as possible in each of the three phases.

STANDING LONG JUMP

Complete only the initial jump described in the standing triple jump using maximum arm swing. Strive for both vertical and horizontal distance.

SINGLE-LEG HOP

Assume a standing broad jump starting position with one leg slightly ahead of the other. Rock forward to your front foot and jump as far and high as possible, driving your lead knee up and out (figure 5.12). Land in the starting position on the same foot and continue jumping to complete the desired number of repetitions.

Figure 5.12

Short-Response Hops and Bounds

DOUBLE-LEG BOUND

From a standing broad jump position (half-squat stance, arms at sides, shoulders forward, back straight, and head up), thrust your arms forward as your knees and body straighten and your arms reach for the sky (figure 5.13).

Figure 5.13

Figure 5.14

DOUBLE- AND SINGLE-LEG ZIGZAG HOP

Place 10 cones 20 inches apart in a zigzag pattern. Jump with legs together in a forward diagonal direction over the first cone, keeping your shoulders facing straight ahead (figure 5.14). Immediately on landing, change direction with the next jump to move diagonally over the second cone. Continue until you have jumped over all 10 cones. Execute the single-leg zigzag hop in the same diagonal direction but using one leg at a time.

ALTERNATE-LEG BOUND

Place one foot slightly ahead of the other. Push off with your back leg, drive the lead knee up to your chest, and try to gain as much height and distance as possible (figure 5.15). Continue by immediately driving with the other leg on landing.

Figure 5.15

RUNNING BOUND

Run forward, jumping as high and far as possible with each step (figure 5.16). Emphasize height and high knee lift and land with your center of gravity under you.

Figure 5.16

LATERAL BOUND

Assume a half-squat stance about one step from the side of an angled box or grassy hill. Push off with the outside foot to propel yourself into the box. As soon as you land, drive off again in the opposite direction (figure 5.17), stressing lateral distance.

Figure 5.17

Ricochets

INCLINE RICOCHET

Stand facing the bottom of the bleacher steps with your feet together and arms to the sides. Rapidly jump upward to each step as fast as possible by attempting to be light on your feet.

DECLINE RICOCHET

From the top of a two- to four-degree grassy hill, take a series of short, rapid hopping movements down the hill. Concentrate on being light on your feet.

Skipping

This series of exercises is designed to improve rhythm, balance, and push-off during the sprinting action (Bell 2000).

SINGLE- AND DOUBLE-ARM SKIPPING

Extend one arm to shoulder level with your thumb up and the palm toward the midline of your body (figure 5.18a). Emphasize the rear leg push-off, a hard drive forward with the lead knee, and a low hip profile with limited up and down movement.

A variation is double-arm skipping (figure 5.18b). The motion is the same except both arms are used.

Figure 5.18a

Figure 5.18b

SKIPPING WITH ARMS EXTENDED AND CROSSED

Lift your arms to shoulder height and cross them in front of your body as you skip (figure 5.19).

Figure 5.19

SKIPPING WITH SHOULDER BLADE SQUEEZES

Lift your arms to shoulder height and cross them in front of your body, then bring your arms behind your body as far as possible in a long swing as you skip (figure 5.20).

Figure 5.20

BACKWARD SKIPPING

Skip backward. Your heels must come up on each backward drive and a reach-back must occur. This is an excellent drill for the hamstrings.

Upper Body

PUSH-UP WITH WEIGHTS

Assume a push-up position with arms fully extended, both hands on top of the weights (figure 5.21a). Quickly remove your hands, drop to the floor, and catch yourself with your elbows slightly flexed before allowing gravity to flex the arms farther until your chest nearly touches the floor (figure 5.21b). Rapidly extend your arms so your hands leave the floor high enough to again assume the position of your hands on top of the weights.

Figure 5.21a

Figure 5.21b

MEDICINE BALL SIT-UP

Sit on the floor with your knees flexed to a 90-degree angle (figure 5.22a). Have a partner toss a medicine ball directly to your chest. Catch the ball with arms flexed and allow the force to push your upper body back and to the floor (figure 5.22b). When your lower back touches the ground, do a sit-up and chest-pass the ball back to your partner.

Figure 5.22a

Figure 5.22b

MEDICINE BALL OVERHEAD BACKWARD THROW

With the medicine ball in both hands and elbows extended, bend lightly forward and then backward as you propel the ball over your head to a partner (figure 5.23).

Figure 5.23

MEDICINE BALL UNDERHAND FORWARD THROW

Face your partner with the medicine ball in both hands in front of your body. Bend over slightly before propelling the ball forward to your partner (figure 5.24).

Figure 5.24

MEDICINE BALL THROW WITH RUSSIAN TWIST

While sitting, hold the medicine ball over your head in both hands. Move the ball backward slightly before throwing an overhead pass forward to your partner as you twist your body to the right (figure 5.25). Repeat the throw, twisting your body to the left.

Figure 5.25

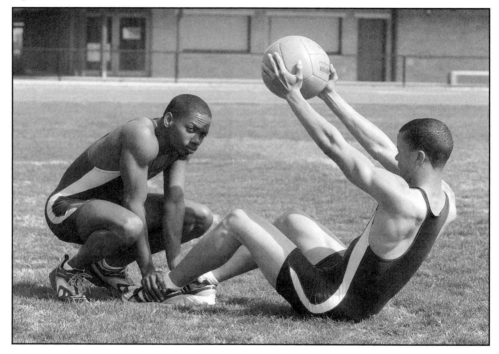

In-Place Jumps

DOUBLE- AND SINGLE-LEG VERTICAL POWER JUMP

Stand with feet shoulder-width apart and arms to your sides in preparation for a vertical jump. With a powerful upward thrust of both arms, jump as high as possible (figure 5.26a). On landing, immediately jump again with as little ground contact time as possible.

A variation is the single-leg vertical power jump (figure 5.26b). Complete the same action as the double-leg vertical power jump with a one-foot takeoff. Repeat with the other foot.

Figure 5.26a

Figure 5.26b

SINGLE-LEG TUCK JUMP

Stand upright with both arms to your sides and feet shoulder-width apart. Execute a vertical jump with a one-foot takeoff, grasping both knees in the air. Release your knees before landing on the same foot, and immediately execute the next jump. Repeat using the opposite leg.

SIDE JUMP AND SPRINT

Stand to one side of a bench or cone with feet together, pointing straight ahead. Jump back and forth over the bench or cone for 4 to 10 repetitions (figure 5.27). After landing on the last jump, sprint forward for 25 yards.

For a competitive angle, have two athletes begin at the same time. The first athlete to complete the specified number of jumps and reach the finish line is the winner. Two benches or cones can be set 100 yards apart. Athletes perform 4 to 10 jumps and sprint to the next bench or cone before repeating the jumps and sprinting again.

Figure 5.27

Short-Response Hops

DOUBLE- AND SINGLE-LEG SPEED HOP

From an upright position with back straight, shoulders forward, and head up, jump as high as possible, bringing your feet under your buttocks in a cycling motion at the height of the jump (figure 5.28). Jump again immediately after making contact with the ground.

A good variation is the single-leg speed hop. Assume the same beginning stance with one leg in a stationary flexed position. Concentrate on the height of the jump.

Figure 5.28

DECLINE HOP

Assume a quarter-squat position at the top of a grassy hill with a three- to four-degree slope. Continue hopping down the hill for speed as described for the double-leg hop. Repeat using the single-leg decline hop.

DEPTH JUMP

From an elevated box or grassy surface, drop to the ground (do not jump), landing with both feet together and knees bent in an attempt to "freeze" your body and absorb the shock (figure 5.29). Slowly return to the box and repeat for the desired number of repetitions.

Figure 5.29

SINGLE-LEG STRIDE JUMP

Stand to the side at one end of a box with your inside foot on top of the bench and arms at your sides. Drive your arms up as the leg on the bench pushes off to jump as high into the air as possible (figure 5.30). Continue jumping until you reach the other end of the bench.

Figure 5.30

BOX JUMPS

Step off a box that is within the recommended box heights for your weight and age. Immediately jump up and out after making contact with the ground (figure 5.31).

Figure 5.31

MULTIPLE BOX JUMPS

Set up five boxes of different heights three to five feet apart. Stand on the first box with your toes slightly extended over the edge. Step off the first box and, after making contact with the ground, jump up and out to land on the next highest box. Repeat the action for the remaining boxes, alternating low and high boxes.

Stationary Arm Swings

STANDING AND SITTING

Stand with both feet together and swing your arms with proper sprinting form (figure 5.32a): elbows bent at 90 degrees, relaxed open hands with palms facing inward, forward movement to the shoulders and then back to the hips without crossing the midline of the body. Emphasize vigorous, high-speed arm movement.

Figure 5.32a

A variation is the seated arm swing (figure 5.32b). Use the same motion as the standing arm swing except sit on the floor with your legs extended in front. Avoid bouncing off the floor.

Figure 5.32b

SPRINT ARM ACTION WITH WEIGHTS

Place a 1- to 10-pound dumbbell in each hand. Assume a stance with your upper body leaning only slightly forward, both arms bent at right angles in the correct sprinting position (left arm raised in front, elbow close to the body with the hand about shoulder height; right arm lowered, elbow close to the body with the hand no farther back than the right hip). Swing your arms from the shoulder joint and execute 10 to 15 explosive arm movements with the correct form described in chapter 12 (figure 5.33). On the upswing, your hand rises to a point just in front of your chin and just inside your shoulder. As your arm swings down, your elbow straightens slightly and your hand comes close to your thigh.

Figure 5.33

DUMBBELL ARM SWINGS

With a 5- to 25-pound dumbbell in each hand, assume a stance with feet apart, hands at your sides, shoulders and upper body tilted slightly forward, and head straight. Drive one arm upward to a point just above your shoulder as the other arm drives backward behind your body. Before each arm reaches maximum stretch, check the momentum and initiate movement in the opposite direction.

CONTRAST ARM SWINGS

From a standing position, complete vigorous arm swings with a 5-pound weight in each hand. Repeat using a l-pound weight in each hand. Finally, release the weights and complete one set without resistance.

Chapter 6

SPORT LOADING

You might take the position that any kind of training is a form of sport loading. If you increase acceleration, the amount of force the body has to manage increases, thereby providing increased loading on the body. Jumping higher and farther in competition or practice produces a higher functional loading with specific positive benefits.

We define sport loading as the systematic adding of weight to the body in any form (uniform, vest, pants, or suit) or to the implements used in sports (bats, balls, and so on). This method is not new. Many athletes through the years have used it, by accident in many cases and by design in others. Interestingly, coaches of sports that involve carrying additional weight in the form of protective gear haven't placed a great emphasis on adding uniform weight to the body during training or testing and evaluating players. The majority of the loading has been applied by using partners or field equipment such as sleds.

Sport loading is designed to improve explosive concentric movements such as sprinting speed. A relatively light resistance that does not drastically alter sprinting form produces the best results.

Imagine the kind of sport loading program David and Goliath might have used. Can you design a program for them? David had to rely on attributes such as quickness and precision of mind, body, and spirit. Shepherds commonly used a sling as a weapon to protect their flocks from predators. The sling perfectly matched David's qualifications and the situation. Goliath, on the other hand, selected a long and heavy sword and shield. These weapons were perfectly suited to his physical attributes. However, you must follow other principles to achieve victory on the battlefield or in a game. Consider the situation and terrain along with your own capabilities. Reliance on favorite weapons, plays, players, or moves may be of little value in the ever-changing circumstances taking place on the field. David's quickness, speed, and accuracy were the deciding factors in the victory over Goliath's size and crushing close-range strength. David won because he chose a fighting style that fit both his qualifications and the demands of the situation. You must learn to do the same thing in your sport. Resolve, as David did, to be flexible, open, and unrestrained by traditional thinking and common methods. Try to find other creative solutions to getting the job done better.

Many teams in the NFL have their own version of the David and Goliath story. Most teams favor players who are Goliaths. Take the offensive line, for instance, where excessive size and strength are overvalued. The trend toward increasing size is evident in the shift from 250-pound players to 260-pound players to players over 300 pounds (figure 6.1). Passing and running strategy is often based on the idea that bigger is better, and allowances are not made for smaller players. Consequently, all defensive strategists have to do is find the proper size and performance mix that counters the size and performance qualities of the offensive line. Then the pendulum will swing back to more agile, explosive offensive linemen to keep up with defensive performance. Lawrence Taylor and other defensive linemen created havoc in the offensive backfields in the NFL. Obviously, some NFL staffs see the performance benefits of good body mechanics, quickness, explosion, and playing speed over size.

The NBA also has its version of David and Goliath. In a land of seven-foot giants live few successful relatively short players, such as Mugsy Bogues and Spud Webb. These short players are even short to the rest of us. These contrasting players add some excitement and enthusiasm to the game. Coaches and franchises are to be commended for their vision and openness to innovative ways of getting the job done.

Your program needs to match the demands you will face on the field. The concepts of sport loading in this chapter will help you devise a personal program that is perfectly adapted to your needs and playing situation. Each element of a practice session contributes different amounts to performance. Greater stress should be placed on sport loading, form training, speed endurance training, and sprint-assisted training because more sport-specific skills are done in these programs. Nearly 100 percent of the work done in these training programs has a good chance of improving sport performance. The other programs work on building the best car for the race (your body), but these programs work on you, the driver (the nervous system that directs all the action). Sport loading along with strength training, speed endurance training, plyometrics, and overspeed training produce the greatest changes in the exercised fast-twitch muscle fibers.

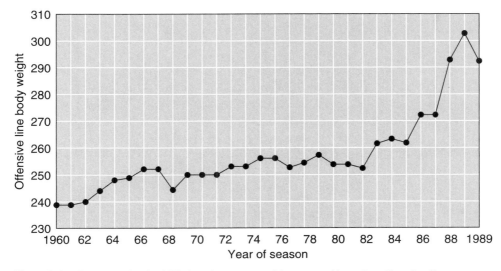

Figure 6.1 The trend in the NFL has been toward larger and heavier offensive linemen.

Although you may not have access to all the technical equipment found at many colleges or professional facilities, you can still develop an outstanding sport loading program. You will need to find alternative methods of sport loading training that involve little or no equipment. A number of sport loading techniques yield effective results. Athletes of all ages can use the methods that follow to attain benefits from sport loading.

Weighted Body Suits, Vests, and Shorts

Why weight resistance training? It's important to understand conceptually the purpose and benefits of integrating weight resistance in the form of clothing into your training regimen.

Stan Plagenhoef conceptualized a weighted strap system to fit around various body segments—a weighted body suit. Each strap is placed at specific biomechanical segment points. This system is the best way to load an athlete because the method distributes the load over each body segment. Ce'bo, a company from England, manufactures and markets a body suit design (Ce'bo Bodykit™) that is available to the general public. In the literature promoting the Ce'bo Bodykit, the company states that the suit is "a weighted exercise garment that increases the gravitational pull on the body of the wearer while exercising." The suit includes four sections: upper body, arms, upper legs, and lower legs. This allows you to distribute the weight over your body to attain more precise loading. To our knowledge, this suit is not constructed to match an athlete's biomechanical characteristics. However, keep a close watch on the advances in this technology because they will result in a more effective training device for your sport loading program.

Materials and designs used in constructing weight vests are improving. More durable, light, tight-fitting vests that allow the user to easily change weights offer greater control and variation. A weighted vest should become the foundation piece of equipment for a sport loading program. This vest can be safely used by male and female athletes of all ages and adapted to practically any sport.

Research by Bosco and associates (1985) indicated that the proper use of sport loading improves power output and aids performance in sprinting. An average improvement of 10 centimeters in vertical jumping ability was also measured after three weeks of training. A repeat study of Bosco's design for female subjects at Brigham Young University (BYU) showed similar positive effects on vertical jumping ability, with an average gain of 5 centimeters for the athletes. The study used a weekly increase in the vest loads of 8 percent of body weight the first week, 10 percent the second week, and 12 percent the third week. Female athletes wore the vests during the day and for practice sessions. BYU researchers also suggested that the vest could influence other aspects of power output. For many, the benefits are not so clear. Many athletes worry that wearing a weighted vest or shorts may hurt the lower back, knees, and ankles. The other concern is restricting the form, function, and range of movement while performing their sport. This can happen if too much weight is used or the weighted vest or shorts fit poorly. This section is designed to educate you on how to train and what equipment performs most effectively and safely.

So, let's exercise the science behind weight resistance training. Currently, most athletes engage in weight resistance training. Lifting weights is the most recognizable form of resistance training, and we all understand the benefits of increasing strength and power. Athletes achieve significant gains in performance by applying weight resistance to specific sport movements. By simply and wisely using weighted vests and shorts, you will strengthen the muscles associated with performing the movements in your sport. By training this way, you're directly converting and generating strength gains into the neuromuscular movement patterns performed in your sport. Weighted vests and shorts act as the catalyst for this conversion. As long as you follow the guidelines set forth in this book, you will achieve safe, steady, and noticeable results.

Choose a vest that can be incrementally loaded, such as the SmartVest® by Training Zone Concepts, Inc. In addition, it is desirable to be able to increase the weight on the vest in half-pound or one-pound increments (figure 6.2). Table 6.1 summarizes the major purposes and weight ranges of the three vests in the SmartVest system. Vest I with heavy weights is used primarily to improve basic strength. Vest II provides an opportunity to develop speed endurance (see chapter 7), and Vest III uses lighter weights so you can perform at higher rates of speed to improve quickness and power.

A sample sport loading program using Vest I is shown in table 6.2. The program progresses from heavy weights (20 pounds) to lighter weights (6 pounds) over a 10-week period; you slowly progress to high-speed training with a weight that permits rapid, explosive turnover in sprinting.

You can easily use the vest during various parts of the practice session in your sport. In general, avoid using a vest during highly technical aspects that require considerable precision. The majority of precision practice should be done in a training zone that uses the same high-speed work levels expected during competition because this kind of session is best for improving skills. Load depends

Photo courtesy of Todd Nadeau

Figure 6.2 Choose a vest that can be incrementally loaded.

Table 6.1   Sports Speed Vest and Body Suit Programs

Vest	Name	General purpose	Weight range[a]
Vest I	Basic training vest	Strength endurance	1 to 20 lb. maximum
Vest II	Speed endurance vest	Strength endurance	1 to 16 lb. maximum
Vest III	Speed vest	Quickness, speed, power	1 to 8 lb. maximum

[a]For the body suit, use comparable weights.

Table 6.2   Sport Loading Program for Hypergravity Vest and Body Suit Training

Week	Repetitions	Vest	Distance	Rest	Progression
1	3 to 5	I 20 lb.[a]	120 yd.	Walk back HR > 120	40 yd. building to 75% speed gradually 40 yd. at 75% speed 40 yd. easing off
2	4 to 6	I 18 lb.	120 yd.	Walk back HR > 120	40 yd. building to 75% speed gradually 40 yd. at 75% speed 40 yd. easing off
3	6 to 8 3 to 5	I 20 lb. I 16 lb.	20 yd. 120 yd.	Full recovery Walk back HR > 120	Power starts at 85% 40 yd. building to 80% speed gradually 40 yd. at 80% speed 40 yd. easing off Complete two sets
4	6 to 8 3 to 5	I 18 lb. I 14 lb.	20 yd. 120 yd.	Full recovery Walk back HR > 120	Power starts at 90% 40 yd. building to 85% speed gradually 40 yd. at 85% speed 40 yd. easing off Complete two sets
5	6 to 8 3 to 5	I 16 lb. I 12 lb.	20 yd. 120 yd.	Full recovery Walk back HR > 120	Power starts at 95% 40 yd. building to 88% speed gradually 40 yd. at 88% speed 40 yd. easing off Complete three sets

Week	Repetitions	Vest	Distance	Rest	Progression
6	6 to 8 3 to 5	I 14 lb. I 10 lb.	20 yd. 120 yd.	Full recovery Walk back HR > 120	Power starts at 95% 40 yd. building to 90% speed gradually 40 yd. at 90% speed 40 yd. easing off Complete three sets
7	6 to 8 3 to 5	I 12 lb. I 8 lb.	20 yd. 120 yd.	Full recovery Walk back HR > 120	Power starts at 95% 40 yd. building to 90% speed gradually 40 yd. at 90% speed 40 yd. easing off Complete three sets
8	6 to 8 3 to 5	I 10 lb. I 6 lb.	20 yd. 120 yd.	Full recovery Walk back HR > 120	Power starts at 95% 40 yd. building to 95% speed gradually 40 yd. at 95% speed 40 yd. easing off Complete three sets
9	6 to 8 3 to 5	I 8 lb. I 6 lb.	20 yd. 120 yd.	Full recovery Walk back HR > 120	Power starts at 95% 40 yd. building to 95% speed gradually 40 yd. at 95% speed 40 yd. easing off Complete three sets
10	6 to 8 3 to 5	I 6 lb. I 6 lb.	20 yd. 120 yd.	Full recovery Walk back HR > 120	Power starts at 95% 40 yd. building to 98% speed gradually 40 yd. at 98% speed 40 yd. easing off Complete three sets

Note: Vests I and II can be used for all loads; Vest III can be used for loads of 8 pounds or less.

[a]For the body suit, use comparable weights.

on the objectives set for the practice period. If the vest is used intelligently, skill development and conditioning will occur simultaneously. Coaches can handicap elite players during training sessions to stimulate competition and force more talented players to work harder. Table 6.3 lists some practice elements and suggests vest loads and durations for each of them.

Table 6.4 gives six training zones and suggested loads and durations for organizing a training program. Be aware that Vest II and III can be used for all Vest I weights. The big advantage in using Vest I and II is that they are designed to fit better and allow greater freedom of movement.

Table 6.3   **Sport-Specific Training Using a Weighted Vest and Body Suit**

Practice period	Suggested load and duration
Warm-up and drills	Vest I, II, III; 1 to 20 lb.[a] for 10 to 15 min.
Scrimmage sessions	Speed vest; 1 to 4 lb. until the end of scrimmage
Drills	Speed vest; 1 to 8 lb. throughout practice
Conditioning sessions at the end of practice	Vest I, II, III; 1 to 20 lb. for 15 to 30 min.

[a]For the body suit, use comparable weights.

Table 6.4   **Sport-Specific Training Zones Using a Weighted Vest and Body Suit**

Practice period	Distance (m)	Suggested load and duration
Starting zone	0 to 20	Vest I, II, III; 1 to 20 lb.[a] for 15 to 30 min.
Acceleration zone	0 to 30	Vest I, II, III; 1 to 20 lb. for 15 to 30 min.
Flying zone	20 to 40	Speed vest; 1 to 4 lb. for 15 to 30 min.
90 percent zone	100 to 300	Speed vest; 1 to 4 lb. for 15 to 30 min.
Speed endurance zone	30 to 200	Speed vest; 1 to 8 lb. for 15 to 30 min.
Aerobic zone	400	Speed vest; 1 to 8 lb. for 30 to 60 min.

[a]For the body suit, use comparable weights.

Because more is not always better, it's important that athletes understand at some level the science behind training. Being aware of the cause and effect training has on performance is the guiding light to what is and isn't working in a training program. When you study sport, you recognize the complex interplay between the mind and movement, of which little is understood. What we do know is that how well you think and move within your game will define your level of success. You need to be mentally sharp and athletically talented to develop a complete game. So, let's discuss how to take the mystery out of this form of resistance training by using weighted vests and shorts to reach your peak performance zone.

Integrating Weighted Suits, Vests, and Shorts Into a Training Program

The first step toward using weighted garments in a training program is to master the mechanics. For 20 to 30 minutes at the beginning of your training session, focus your mind on executing the movement mechanics required to complete a specific skill in your sport (e.g., a basketball player performing a crossover dribble into a two-step jump shot or a volleyball player going up to block an opponent's shot).

The second step is skill drill mastery. First, slow the movements down and focus your mind on the rhythm (flow) and speed (power) necessary to most effectively execute the movements within the skill. As you build confidence, increase intensity to gamelike conditions. Remember, the goal is for the mind to automate these skills so you no longer need to focus on them. This frees the mind to focus on other aspects of the game. Skill command is defined by response time, or how long it takes for you to react to a sport trigger. This is the stimulus response theory; as you play against better athletes, the amount of time you need to respond will shrink.

In the third step, strengthening and reinforcing movement, the weighted vest and shorts are used. By adding weight in one- to two-pound increments, you're able to accelerate the strengthening and mastery of these movements. This is critical because the body tends to move toward old patterns of movement; the old saying that a person will always move toward his strengths and away from his weaknesses holds true. The weighted vest and shorts are designed to accelerate the mastery of these new movements. They are an excellent training tool for the strengthening, integrating, and automating of new movement patterns.

Now that you understand the purpose of weight resistance training with the weighted vest and shorts, we will discuss where to get them, how to train with them, and what to expect in terms of results.

Vest information is available by contacting Training Zone Concepts, Inc., through the Internet at www.sportsscience.com. SmartVest products are the best on the market. The key features are a distraction-free fit, adjustable half- and one-pound weights, and a men's and women's model. By simply giving them your height, weight, and true waist size you will receive a guaranteed body glove fit. The SmartVest is sold with 12 pounds and the shorts with 8 pounds.

Let's more clearly define weight resistance training and how to work it into your training schedule. Resistance is created through the process of gradually adding weight to the body while sport training. The key is having a weighted suit (SmartVest) that creates a compression fit, allowing the body to experience the weight as its own. In practical terms, after you start training you forget you have it on other than you are working harder. Because of this fit, you can use the SmartVest or shorts during all aspects of training. You can wear them as part of your daily wear; while weightlifting; during conditioning for speed, agility, and quickness; while performing plyometric exercises for explosive and vertical power; while cross-training (running, biking, climbing stairs); while practicing sport-specific skill drills; or while playing scrimmage or pickup games in your sport.

Training Variables

You can do anything while wearing the SmartVest and shorts. The key to getting maximum results is to manipulate the training variables. The following guidelines will help you understand how to utilize overload training to maximize performance results.

✦ Progression and amount of weight. The rule is to master the mechanics of movement before adding weight. The strategy of adding weight depends on what training phase (off-season, preseason, or in-season) you are in. In the off-season, begin with 2.5 percent of your body weight. For example, a 160-pound football player would start with 4 pounds in the vest or shorts. Usually, every two to three weeks the athlete is ready to add weight. We recommend adding 2 pounds for the vest and 1 pound for the shorts. While performing high-speed movements, you shouldn't drop below 5 percent of your maximum speed. Most athletes will fall below this level when the weight load reaches 5 to 7.5 percent of body weight, depending on level of strength and conditioning. For any type of movement training, the athlete should not exceed 10 percent body weight. Again, progression is a process of gradually adding weight—this is a safe, effective means of building strength and speed.

✦ Tapering. When tapering, the athlete starts with a heavy load (12 to 15 percent of body weight) and performs the drills at 75 percent of maximum speed. The key is to determine a target date to peak (e.g., a tournament at the end of the season). Tapering is a gradual process of decreasing the amount of weight while increasing speed intensity. The goal is to stop weight load training one to two weeks before the target date. An athlete wants to gradually add weight in the off- and preseason, with the intent to begin tapering at the start of the season to peak for the playoffs.

✦ Volume, duration, and intensity. Volume means the number of drills, duration is how long, and intensity is the degree of maximum effort while performing the drill. In the off- and preseason, we recommend that 60 to 75 percent of drills be performed with the vest or shorts; during the season, 20 to 40 percent. Duration is longer in the off- and preseason, then gradually shortened as you move into the season.

✦ Contrast training. Contrast training can be performed within a set or during a practice session. For example, if performing four sets of a drill, wear the weighted vest or shorts for two or three of the sets. During a particular session, the athlete would wear the weighted vest or shorts 30 to 70 percent of the practice session.

✦ Creativity. Sport psychologists understand the impact the mind has on training. Be creative with training. This book and the guidelines outlined in this chapter provide you with the knowledge and fundamental concepts of training. Our goal is to empower you to create challenging training programs. Taking this approach will generate excitement in your training regimen. Remember to listen to your body; results will always guide your training direction.

Now that you understand training variables and overload training, let's explore what areas and strategies to focus on that will build strength, speed, and quickness in your sport. Phase I is a broad-based approach to making you more athletic. The goal is to work on technique, body posture and control, and overall speed, quickness, agility, and vertical power. Acceleration and maximum speed are the performance goals for phase I.

Training Acceleration

To generate quick explosive starts or changes in direction, you need to focus on acceleration. In most sports, the first step (start or on the move) is crucial for creating an edge against an opponent. The largest gains are realized in training by dedicating 15 to 30 minutes to training starts, finding the acceleration zone, and generating acceleration bursts.

Starts

Your first two steps generate power and direction; in most sports, these two steps determine success. The key is to design drills that simulate the stance and footwork used in your sport. Depending on strength level, loading recommendations begin with 2 pounds and add 2 pounds every two weeks with a maximum of 8 to 10 pounds for the vest. For the shorts, start with 1 pound on each thigh, then add 1 pound to each thigh every two weeks to a maximum of 4 pounds.

CLOCK DRILL

Get into an athletic stance and visualize around you the numbers on a clock. When your coach or training partner calls out a number, explode in that direction. The key is to stay low and extend your lead foot in the direction of the number on the clock. Depending on your sport, take two or three steps and finish with a sport-specific move such as shooting a jump shot, making a stick stop, catching a football pass, squaring up to tackle, or blocking or digging in volleyball. Be creative within your sport.

MIRROR REACTION DRILL

Measure 10 yards. Place a cone at each end and one in the middle. Two players face each other over the middle cone. One is the leader and the other is responsible for mimicking the leader's movements. Players can sprint, shuffle laterally, backpedal, or jump vertically. The leader can change directions between the three cones at any time. Perform the drill for 30 seconds, gradually increasing the duration over time.

Acceleration Zone

The acceleration zone occurs after the start and builds toward maximum speed. In the acceleration zone, a tremendous amount of force is generated. From 20 to 60 yards is considered the range in which an athlete climbs to maximum speed. Drills need to focus on sport-specific movements. Weight load will begin with 2.5 percent of body weight and gradually climb to 10 percent.

10-YARD FLYING SERIES

Start in an athletic stance. For the first 10 yards, either sprint, shuffle, or backpedal at 75 percent speed. After 10 yards, explode into a full sprint, trying to reach maximum speed. You can vary the distance for the full sprint from 10 to 30 yards.

200-YARD BURSTS

Begin with a glide stride (75 percent maximum speed with hips down, ready to change directions) for 10 yards. Burst for 15 yards, glide for 15 yards, burst for 20 yards, glide for 20 yards, burst for 25 yards, glide for 20 yards, burst for 30 yards, glide for 20 yards, and burst for 25 yards. This covers a 200-yard stretch.

CLOCK DRILL WITH GLIDE

The clock drill is performed in an open area. Glide stride for 10 yards. When your partner calls out a number, burst for 15 to 30 yards in that direction. Repeat six times.

Acceleration Bursts

The acceleration burst occurs in the 25- to 50-yard range in which an athlete moves toward maximum speed. Athletes in all sports come to some point when they need to throw it into high gear. Training needs to reflect these moments. Weight load begins at 2.5 percent body weight and gradually climbs to 10 percent.

25-YARD FLYING SERIES

Glide stride for 25 yards then burst for 25 yards. You will progress from 25- to 30- to 35- to 40- to 45- to 50-yard sprints, while maintaining a 25-yard glide stride. Do a mixture of these for 10 to 20 minutes, depending on strength and season.

ZIGZAG SERIES

Glide stride for 20 yards at a 45-degree angle, then burst at a 90-degree angle for 25 to 30 to 35 to 40 to 45 to 50 yards. Perform the drill at right and left angles. Do a mixture of these for 10 to 20 minutes, depending on strength and season.

It is important to incorporate other movements—the backpedal, lateral shuffle, vertical jump, and change of direction—into your drills. Be creative in developing a daily training regimen.

Training Maximum Speed

The purpose of maximum speed training is to reach maximum speed as quickly as possible and sustain maximum speed as long as possible. Speed is a by-product of the force generated from striking the ground and then powering off the same leg in a running cycle. The leg cycle is contingent upon leg extension, or stride length, and stride frequency—how fast the leg moves through a complete cycle.

Stride frequency is a limiting factor in running faster. Running mechanics need to be polished through practice to master and maximize each component of sprinting. A major percentage of maximum speed is reached by 20 to 30 yards. From around 60 to 70 yards (the point of maximum speed) to about 300 yards, speed endurance (anaerobic/O_2 zone) comes into play as an absolute essential for running faster over extended distances.

Examine the distances and movements that are typical to your sport, and design drills to maximize speed. Begin with two pounds in the vest and one pound on each thigh in the shorts. Every two weeks, increase by two pounds in the vest and one pound on each thigh of the shorts.

In the flying speed zone, the athlete is training to maximize speed in the 20- to 100-yard range. Most team sports do not require an athlete to travel farther than 100 yards, though there are exceptions.

COUNTDOWN SPEED DRILL

Begin all speed drills 20 yards before the starting line so that when you cross the starting line you will be near top speed. Begin with one or two 100-yard dashes, then do two or three 80-yard dashes, three or four 60-yard dashes, four or five 40-yard dashes, and end with five or six 20-yard dashes. Increase the number as you become stronger.

CHANGE OF DIRECTION SPEED

Glide stride for 20 yards with cones at 20, 30, 40, and 50 yards. Change direction by powering off the outside leg toward the cone.

Football players often have to run 10 to 40 yards every play. By the third or fourth quarter, conditioning begins to play a factor. The athlete who fatigues will play poorly and place himself at greater risk of injury. This is why it's necessary to train speed endurance. You need to perform drills designed to build speed endurance if you want to feel strong as you enter the fourth quarter in a football game—often this is when games are won or lost. The speed endurance range is 30 to 200 yards.

SPEED REPEATS

Begin with 10 repetitions for 30 yards with 30 to 45 seconds of rest between repetitions. Progressively increase the distance by 10 yards when you are able to average 90 to 95 percent of your best time for 30 yards.

Reduce repetitions to 8 for distances of 70 to 100 yards. Rest for 30 to 45 seconds between repetitions. If speed drops to about 80 percent of your best time for 30 yards, rest until your heart rate reaches 120 beats per minute before the next repetition.

Decrease the number of repetitions to 6 for 110 to 140 yards, 5 for 150 to 180 yards, and 4 for 190 to 220 yards. Rest until your heart rate reaches 120 beats per minute between repetitions.

300-YARD SHUTTLE

The 300-yard shuttle can be performed several ways. You can measure out 25 yards and sprint back and forth 12 times, measure 50 yards and sprint back and forth 6 times, measure 75 yards and sprint back and forth 4 times, or measure 100 yards and sprint back and forth 3 times. The key to this drill is time. Keep track of your times and push yourself to improve your time every two weeks. Every other training session, perform the 300-yard shuttle.

Uphill sprinting and running up stairs are excellent ways to build power. In uphill sprinting, it's important to start with no weight and gradually add two pounds every two weeks until you reach 5 percent of your body weight (see table 6.7 [page 144] for details on incline grades and distances). With stairs, focus on high knees and quick reaction off the ground. Use the same weight load recommendation as for uphill sprinting.

For overspeed training, you are looking for a decline (see table 6.7 for recommendations). Begin with two pounds of weight and add two pounds every two weeks until you reach 5 percent of your body weight.

Agility is the ability to change directions quickly or explosively on command or in reaction to a stimulus. Agility is the process of accelerating then decelerating to a quick stop, either performing a two-legged stick stop or a one-legged outside foot plant, then reaccelerating to top speed. Team sports require a high level of agility for a variety of different movements. Therefore, it's important to design drills that simulate change of direction movements in your sport.

Plyometric training is an excellent way to improve vertical and horizontal jumps. Most sports require an athlete to explode off the ground (dunking or blocking shots in basketball, catching a high pass in football, killing a shot in volleyball). Be creative in designing drills that simulate plyometric movements in your sport. Begin with no weight and gradually add two pounds every couple of weeks up to 5 percent of your body weight.

Table 6.5 illustrates a sample broad-based workout that would be performed three or four days a week. The intent of this program is to progressively prepare the mind and body for peak performance. After warming up, the athlete moves through a series of stretches. The focus shifts to the fundamentals of movement and basic footwork. Finally, the athlete performs intense explosive movements that simulate gamelike intensity. This series is a great training routine to perform before practicing or playing a game of pickup. It's designed to get the body and mind ready for peak performance. The drills are designed to cover movement mechanics, flexibility, speed, quickness, agility, and vertical jumps. This format lets you add and subtract drills. Tracking the amount of weight you use helps you determine the effect you receive from using various loads.

Harnesses, Parachutes, and Weighted Sleds

The two-person harness is an affordable and effective tool for working on running techniques and sprinting. Two athletes of similar body weight and power use the same harness (figure 6.3). One athlete provides the resistance, and the other provides the power.

Table 6.5   **Movement Training Series: Turn Up the Heat**

Distance	Sets	Repetitions	Exercises
Full court	1	2	Warm-up: jog, backpedal, carioca, shuffle, high knees
	1	1	Functional flexibility: lunges, shuffle squats, inchworm, push-ups, sit-ups, complete stretching program
Full court	1	3	Form running: A-march, B-march, quick steps
Full court	3	1	Stride form drill (change of direction), zigzag drill (stick and stop)
Half court	3	1	Shuffle drill, shuffle-sprint cone drill
	3	1	20-yd. agility drill (shuffle-sprint and sprint-sprint)
Foul line	1	1	Complete-the-square drill (3 right and 3 left)
Half court	1	2	Jump series drills: two-foot takeoff (one step, hops, shuffle, diagonal hops); one-foot takeoff (one step, quick jump, bounding)
	1	20	Wall taps
Sidelines	1	1	1.5 sprint; 3.0 sprint/shuffle (sideline to sideline)
			Total time to complete: Weight load:

Using harnesses works best during basic training. Remember, the emphasis at this level is to perform at or near game playing speed. Speed levels should be close to 90 percent of your maximum speed.

Parachutes of various sizes provide some degree of resistance; however, the additional benefits that can be gained from other methods outweigh the cost and inconvenience associated with the use of parachutes. Younger athletes tend to enjoy parachutes as a sport loading technique. If you choose this method, follow the guidelines shown in table 6.6.

Both expensive and inexpensive weighted sleds are available. Metal and plastic models allow quick and easy weight changes. For little cost, you can use a spare tire with a rope and

Figure 6.3 One athlete is the resistance, the other is the power.

weighted belt. Regardless of the device you choose, make sure you use a load that allows proper form and high-speed sprinting. Too much weight will cause you to lose form and will prevent explosive movements. Time yourself over various starting and sprinting distances of 5 to 40 yards using both a stationary and a flying start.

Uphill Sprinting, Stadium Stair Sprinting, and Sand Running

Most parts of the country provide suitable terrain for sprinting uphill. Although a wide range of grades can be used, it is recommended that the degree of incline allows you to run with good starting and sprinting form.

When Bob Ward designed the incline/decline course for the Dallas Cowboys in the 1980s, he included the best features for uphill training. The angles and distances were selected from extensive research, consultation with many experts from around the world, and practical coaching experience. These angles and distances are shown in table 6.7.

If you can find similar angles and distances, apply them as shown in the Uphill use column. In general, steep angles (8.0 degrees) can be used for starts and acceleration loading, and angles of 1.0, 2.5, or 3.0 degrees can be used for

Table 6.6   **Sport Loading Program Using Hill Sprinting, Stadium Stairs, Harnesses, Sand Running, Parachutes, or Weighted Sleds**

Week	Repetitions	Pulling distance[a]	Rest	Progression
1	3 to 5	15 yd.	Walk back[b] HR > 120	Use power starts at 75% speed for hill sprinting, sand running, and stadium sprinting or with no weight on the sled. Complete two sets.
2	3 to 5	20 yd.	Walk back HR > 120	Repeat at maximum speed.
3	6 to 8 3 to 5	25 yd. 30 yd.	Full recovery Walk back HR > 120	Repeat power starts at maximum speed. Use power starts at 75% speed for hill sprinting, sand running, and stadium sprinting or with no weight on the sled. Complete two sets.
4	7 to 9 3 to 5	 40 yd.	Full recovery Walk back HR > 120	Use power starts at 90%. Repeat power starts and power sprints. Add weight to the sled that allows you to sprint with good form. Complete two sets.
5	7 to 9	50 yd.	Full recovery	Repeat workout. Add more weight. Complete three sets.
6 to 9	7 to 9	60 yd.	Full recovery	Repeat workout. Add more weight each week. Complete three sets. Include one final run to exhaustion by continuing your sprint for as long as possible. Record the distance and try to improve it each week.

[a]Actual distance you are pulling the sled or sprinting uphill or up stadium steps.

[b]No walk back if you are using a weighted sled.

starts and speed endurance. A 10- to 30-yard incline of 8 to 10 degrees should be covered in 2.5 to 3.5 seconds, followed by a near full-speed sprint of 20 to 80 yards at the same incline. These values have proven to be very effective for sprint loading programs at the Dallas Cowboys' training facility. Attempt to come as close as possible to these guidelines, although precise values are not absolutely necessary.

Stadium stairs or other stairs can be used in the same manner as uphill sprinting. Try to locate stairs that have the same approximate angles of incline. Make sure the steps provide a safe environment for training.

Table 6.7   **Dallas Cowboys Incline/Decline Course**

Total distance (yd.)	Distance (yd.)	Distance (m)	Featured angles	Uphill use
0.00	0.00	0.00	Start	
27.25	27.25	25.00	Flat	Recovery
33.81	6.56	6.00	8.0-degree angle	Starts
34.90	1.09	1.00	Flat	Recovery
67.70	32.80	30.00	3.5-degree angle	Acceleration
89.57	21.87	20.00	Flat	Recovery
122.37	32.80	30.00	3.0-degree angle	Acceleration
131.12	8.75	8.00	Flat	Recovery
196.72	65.60	60.00	2.5-degree angle	Speed endurance
278.72	82.00	75.00	1.0-degree angle	Speed endurance
328.72	50.00	46.00	Sand running	Body control Speed endurance

Sand running is an excellent way to stress the total body, especially the lower extremities. The foot, knee, and hip muscle-joint systems are required to adjust to the unstable sandy surface. This adjustment develops and toughens the body's ability to handle unexpected stability changes. Very few activities that you can include in your program work all joint actions as sand running can. It's almost a form of wrestling for the lower extremities.

Herschel Walker said that his father had him running over plowed fields in Georgia when he was a youngster. While running in a sand session with the Cowboys, Walker looked as if he were running on top of the sand while most of the other players labored or dug deep holes in the sand. His early training must have given him that kind of control.

When to Use Sport Loading

The ideal point to include sport loading training in your program is at the latter part of Wednesday's workout or later during a speedweek. There are two training objectives to consider.

The power start and explosive close-range movement phase (phase I acceleration) helps you overcome inertia to get started in any of your sport tasks. This is extremely important in sports that deal in close ranges. Phase II acceleration marks the end of the majority of your ability to run faster. This leveling in speed has been noted by many other researchers during maximum and near-maximum speed runs.

Unique studies conducted on the Dallas Cowboys (Ward 1987) showed that maximum acceleration takes place very close to the start (one to three feet) and rapidly diminishes to zero or to very low amounts somewhere around 50 to 60 yards. The drop-off rate is a good indicator of your running skill and conditioning level. The timeline of an athlete's run shows that his ability to accelerate and apply power continues for about six to eight seconds from the start in the case of all-out sprinting. Further, it has been demonstrated that world-class sprinters can accelerate slightly even in the last few yards to the finish. This slight increase could mean the difference between winning or losing.

In most sports, usable force (essentially acceleration) is attained within 15 yards (.6 to 1.5 seconds). Therefore, you should train multidirectional peak power by playing games such as handball, basketball, badminton, and racquetball. Doing 10 to 15 starts that cover 0 to 20 yards will help train straight-ahead aspects.

The power sprint phase trains you to develop power at high speeds. The speed curves of sprinters show that deliverable power drops off as they move faster. The best way to train high-speed power is to do sprint loading work from a flying start, using the vest or incline sprints at maximum or near-maximum levels. Perform 6 to 10 repetitions of 10 to 80 yards with weights or resistance that does not reduce performance speed by more than 1 to 5 percent. Adding weight to a vest, for example, of no more than 1 to 5 percent of body weight should put you in this range.

A sample sprint loading program for hill sprinting, stadium stair sprinting, and weighted sleds is shown in table 6.6 (page 143). A sample sport loading program for hypergravity vest training is shown in table 6.2 (page 132).

All the work you have done so far has prepared you to sprint faster and play faster in your sport. The next chapter will show you the methods used by world-class performers in all sports to accomplish their outstanding feats. These methods will help you improve playing speed, improve playing speed endurance, and develop world-class sprinting form and speed.

Chapter 7

SPEED ENDURANCE

S peed endurance training will not help you take a faster or longer step. It will, however, prevent you from slowing down late in the game, at the end of a long sprint, or after sprinting several times with little rest in between. You have seen many examples of poor speed endurance in different sports. A halfback is tackled from behind by a slower player. A sprinter is passed in the final 10 meters of a race. A baseball player runs out of steam and is tagged out at home. A basketball or soccer player is beaten to the ball by a slower athlete. All these are examples of poor speed endurance, which causes a player either to slow down or to fail to accelerate as fast as normal because of fatigue.

In most sports, a player is expected to make repeated bursts of speed. Ideally, the fourth or fifth sprint is run as fast as the first. This is often not the case because of poor speed endurance. By becoming well conditioned for speed endurance, you will gain several advantages in your sport: You will be able to make repeated short sprints at the same speed with minimum rest, you will be able to reach maximum speed more quickly, and you will be able to hold maximum speed for a longer distance before slowing down.

High levels of speed endurance provide a fresh start on each short sprint. Speed endurance training is a vital phase for athletes in team sports such as football, basketball, soccer, field hockey, and baseball. It is the phase that can give you the edge.

Speed endurance is easy to improve. You only need to sprint short distances two or three times per week and keep a record of how many repetitions you sprinted, how far you sprinted, and how much recovery time you took between each repetition. The rest is easy. In each workout, you simply increase the sprint distance and decrease the recovery time between each repetition. In six to eight weeks, your speed endurance scores will get better.

Speed Endurance Training

Designing a speed endurance training program requires a basic understanding of the anaerobic and aerobic energy systems and the typical performance actions completed in a team sport during competition. The actual program is specific to each team sport and is based on the typical distance an athlete sprints, the intensity of each sprint (three-quarter speed, all-out effort), the average rest or recovery period between repetitions of each sprint during competition, the recovery action (walking, jogging, standing), and the number of sprints that occur during competition. Once you understand the anaerobic and aerobic energy systems and the performance requirements of your sport, it is a simple task to prepare an effective speed endurance program.

Anaerobic Energy System

The anaerobic energy system, which allows you to complete repeated all-out sprints and other maximum effort muscular action, consists of two energy pathways: the ATP-CP (creatine phosphate) system and the ATP-LA (lactic acid) energy source.

The ATP-CP system requires no oxygen to supply five to eight seconds of maximum effort energy. In fact, you could hold your breath for this short time period without affecting energy supply or performance. Phosphate substances and amino acids in the muscles are metabolized to produce cellular energy. This system provides the fuel for the first 60 to 80 meters of an all-out sprint and complements the ATP (adenosine triphosphate) energy already present in the muscles. The CP energy system can be fully recharged after two to three minutes of rest.

The ATP-LA system also requires no oxygen. When anaerobic energy is needed beyond the supply of the CP system, working muscles release pyruvic acid, which is converted to lactic acid. These two by-products are metabolized to produce ATP, allowing energy output to continue for up to 60 seconds without oxygen. Continued maximum effort exercise beyond this point will produce more lactic acid than can be metabolized, resulting in rapid fatigue until exercise cannot continue. At this point, approximately one hour is needed to fully remove lactic acid from the system. Light activity at 40 to 50 percent of maximum can reduce the recovery time somewhat.

Lactic acid energy is what allows you to continue to exert near-maximum effort once the CP energy is exhausted (after about 60 to 80 meters). This permits a sprinter to complete a powerful striding effort for the final 20 to 40 meters of a 100-meter dash, when an athlete tries to hold his current speed or gently build up if he is not at maximum. It also allows team sport athletes to sprint longer distances, recover faster, and execute repeated sprints throughout the game with little or no slowing due to fatigue.

Aerobic Energy System

Although short sprints rely mainly on CP and lactic energy sources, athletes with a high $\dot{V}O_2$max (maximum oxygen uptake) obtain a higher anaerobic threshold (intensity point at which lactic acid begins to accumulate). This delay in the onset of lactic acid accumulation in the blood may allow a higher work output before fatigue begins to develop, permitting form and speed to be maintained at the end of longer sprints. Anaerobic work also produces pyruvic acid, which is later converted to lactic acid. Since these two by-products are eventually removed aerobically during the rest period, a high aerobic capacity will expedite recovery from repeated short sprints both during competition and during speed endurance training sessions.

Athletes who participate in sports that have a higher aerobic component—basketball, soccer, lacrosse, rugby, and field hockey—have a more critical need for aerobic fitness than athletes who compete in baseball, softball, and football.

It is important to keep in mind that the anaerobic and aerobic processes function continuously and at the same time. Anaerobic energy is used at the beginning of any type of exercise and during exercise of high intensity such as all-out sprints. If exercise demands are beyond your maximum oxygen uptake capability, anaerobic metabolism must supply the additional energy.

Table 7.1 displays the percent contribution of the anaerobic and aerobic systems based on the number of seconds in an all-out maximum effort. In an all-out sprint of 0 to 5 seconds, for example, 96 percent of the energy is provided by anaerobic metabolism. The longer exercise continues (30, 60, 90 seconds), the more the body relies on aerobic metabolism. Football, baseball, and softball fall into the 0- to 5-second category. Soccer, basketball, field hockey, rugby, and lacrosse are more likely to be in the 5- to 10-second range and therefore require a slightly different training approach.

Table 7.2 lists the predominant energy systems and the approximate percent requirement of the anaerobic and aerobic energy sources in several sports. These percentages were used to design the team sport speed endurance programs.

Aerobic fitness is vital in sports such as lacrosse that demand a lot of constant running.

Table 7.1 — Contributions of Anaerobic and Aerobic Mechanisms to Maximum Sustained Efforts

	Duration of effort (sec.)			
	0 to 5	30	60	90
Exercise intensity (% of maximum power output)	100	55	35	31
Contribution of anaerobic mechanisms (%)	96	75	50	35
Contribution of aerobic mechanisms (%)	4	25	50	65

Conley, M. 2000. Bioenergetics of Exercise and Training. In *Essentials of Strength Training and Conditioning* (2nd ed.), edited by T.R. Baechle and R.W. Earle. Champaign, IL: Human Kinetics. Page 87. Used by permission.

Table 7.2 — Predominant Energy Systems Used in Sports

	Emphasis per energy system (%)		
	Anaerobic		Aerobic
Sport	ATP-CP and -LA	LA-O_2	O_2
Baseball	80	20	0
Basketball	85	15	0
Field hockey	60	20	20
Football	90	10	0
Ice hockey			
Forwards, defensemen	80	20	0
Goalies	95	5	0
Lacrosse			
Goalies, defensemen, attackers	80	20	0
Midfielders, man-down situations	60	20	20
Soccer			
Goalies, wings, strikers	80	20	0
Halfbacks, linkmen	60	20	20
Tennis	70	20	10
Track and field			
40 to 220 yd.	99	1	0
440 yd.	80	15	5
Mile	20	55	25

Speed Endurance Training Programs

The eight-week speed endurance training program in table 7.3 is designed to train both the ATP-CP system and the ATP-LA system, since both systems play a major role in the ability to continually sprint at maximum speed for 5 to 8 seconds (ATP-CP) and up to 60 seconds (ATP-LA). The program combines the three main speed endurance programs presented in this section—pickup sprints, hollow sprints, and interval sprint training—and is based on the estimated percent of anaerobic and aerobic involvement shown in table 7.4. The improvement of each energy system occurs by manipulating training variables: frequency of training, number of repetitions, intensity of each repetition, distance covered or time required to complete each repetition, and recovery time and action between each repetition. The program is designed to improve the speed endurance of athletes in baseball, basketball, field hockey, football, lacrosse, rugby, and soccer.

The maintenance workout is based on the average distance sprinted in various sports. Sprint 12 to 15 repetitions at the distance specified for your sport. Rest the number of seconds indicated between each repetition. End the workout with two 300-meter sprints using a two-minute rest period between repetitions.

A 5- to 30-Second Running Program

This program, developed by Dr. Gene Coleman, the strength and conditioning coach for the Houston Astros, has been shown to effectively help maintain aerobic and anaerobic fitness during a professional baseball season. Running is done on a baseball field. Players run around the field in a clockwise direction. The coach stands behind second base. There are four steps in the program:

1. Players run for 3 minutes at a constant speed, usually between a 9- and 10-minute mile pace.

2. At the coach's signal, players sprint for 5 seconds at 80 to 85 percent of maximum speed. This is the anaerobic part of the run.

3. Without stopping, players resume aerobic running for 3 minutes. The pace is increased to 10 to 15 seconds faster than the initial 3-minute run.

4. On the coach's signal, players sprint for 10 seconds.

Steps one to four are repeated, with sprint time increasing by 5 seconds and the speed of the 3-minute aerobic run increasing by 10 to 15 seconds until players are sprinting for 30 seconds.

When starting the program, limit the total time to 15 to 16 minutes. Gradually increase the time until the total run takes 30 minutes. Do the

Week	Workout	Routine and distance	Repetitions	Rest interval
1	1	Jog 15 yd., stride 15 yd. (3/4 speed), jog 15 yd., walk 15 yd.	5	No rest between repetitions; walk is the recovery phase and end of 1 repetition
1	2	Same	7	Same
1	3	Jog 20 yd., stride 20 yd. (9/10 speed), jog 20 yd., walk 20 yd.	5	Same
2	4	Same	7	Same
2	5	Jog 15 yd., stride 15 yd. (3/4 speed), sprint 15 yd. (maximum speed), walk 15 yd.	5	Same
2	6	Same	7	Same
3	7	Jog 20 yd., stride 20 yd., sprint 20 yd., walk 20 yd.	7	Same
3	8	Same	9	Same
3	9	Jog 25 yd., stride 25 yd., sprint 25 yd., walk 25 yd.	7	Same
4	10	Sprint 15 yd., jog 15 yd., sprint 15 yd., walk 15 yd. Distance hop to exhaustion	7 / 1 each leg	Walk is the recovery phase and end of 1 repetition
4	11	Sprint 20 yd., jog 20 yd., sprint 20 yd., walk 20 yd.	7	Same
4	12	Sprint 20 yd., jog 10 yd., sprint 20 yd., walk 20 yd. Bench jump to exhaustion	9 / 2	Same / 1 min.
5	13	Sprint 25 yd., jog 25 yd., sprint 25 yd., walk 25 yd.	9	Same
5	14	Sprint 20 yd.	10	Walk 10 to 30 sec., depending on sport
		300-yd. sprint	1	3 to 4 min.
		Run in place to exhaustion	2	1 min.
5	15	Sprint 30 yd.	10	Walk 10 to 30 sec.
6	16	Sprint 40 yd.	8	Same
		300-yd. sprint	2	3 min.
		Distance hop to exhaustion	1 each leg	1 min.

(continued)

Table 7.3 (continued)

Week	Workout	Routine and distance	Repetitions	Rest interval
6	17	Sprint 40 yd. 440-yd. sprint	10 1	Walk 10 to 30 sec.
6	18	Sprint 20 yd., jog 20 yd., sprint 20 yd., walk 20 yd. 440-yd. sprint Bench jump to exhaustion	12 2 1	Walk is the recovery phase and end of 1 repetition 4 to 5 min.
7	19	Sprint 20 yd., jog 20 yd., sprint 20 yd., walk 20 yd. 300-yd. sprint	15 3	Walk is the recovery phase and end of 1 repetition 2.5 min.
7	20	On a 400-meter track, sprint 50 yd., jog for 10 to 12 sec., sprint 50 yd., jog for 10 to 12 sec., and so on. Sprint in place with high knee lift to exhaustion	20 sprints 2	Jog is the rest period 1 min.
8	21	440-yd. sprint	4	4 to 5 min.
8	22	On a 400-m track, sprint 50 yd., jog for 10 to 12 sec., sprint 50 yd., jog for 10 to 12 sec., and so on Bench jump to exhaustion	25 sprints 4	Jog is the rest period 1 min.

Notes: Cycle begins eight weeks from competition.

Program assumes the athlete has a good aerobic fitness foundation.

Sport	Distance sprinted (yd.)	Rest between sprints (sec.)
Baseball, softball	30	30 to 60
Basketball	30	5 to 20
Football	10 to 40	25 to 30 (huddle time)
Soccer, lacrosse, rugby, hockey	10 to 40	5 to 15
Tennis	5 to 10	3 to 5 (same point) 20 to 30 (between points) 60 (between games)

Note: Alter the distance sprinted and rest between sprints to make the eight-week speed endurance program specific to your sport.

Table 7.4   **Training Methods and Estimated Effect on Energy Systems**

		Anaerobic		Aerobic
Training method	Definition	ATP-CP and -LA (%)	LA-O_2 (%)	O_2 (%)
Pickup sprints	Gradual increases in speed from jogging to striding to sprinting in 25- to 120-yd. segments	90	5	5
Hollow sprints	Two sprints interrupted by "hollow" periods of jogging or walking	85	10	5
Interval sprints	Alternate sprints of 20 to 300 yd. followed by jogging and walking for recovery	80	10	10
Jogging	Continuous running at a slow pace over a distance of 2 or more miles	0	0	100
Sprint-assisted training	Repeated sprints at maximum speed aided by towing, downhill, or treadmill with complete recovery between each repetition	90	6	4

run twice per week in the preseason and once per week during the season. Limit relievers and starting players to 15 to 16 total minutes during the season. High school players should work until sprints reach 20 seconds. College players and pros can work until sprints reach 30 to 45 seconds.

Pickup sprints involve a gradual increase from a jog to a striding pace, then to a maximum effort sprint. A 1:1 ratio of the distance and recovery walk that follows each repetition is recommended. For example, jog 25 yards, stride for 25, sprint for 25, and end with a 25-yard walk. The walk or slow jog should allow some recovery before the next repetition. This jog-stride-sprint-recovery cycle tends to develop speed endurance and reduce the chance of muscle injury in cold weather. The cycle is an example of early-season training. The exact number of repetitions depends on conditioning level. As you improve, lengthen the distance, with late-season pickup sprints reaching segments of 50 yards or more.

New Zealand athletes use a routine similar to pickup sprints that involves a series of four 50-meter sprints at near-maximum speed (6 to 7 seconds) per

400-meter lap, jogging for 10 to 12 seconds after each sprint and completing the 400-meter run in 64 to 76 seconds. Athletes have performed as many as 50 sprints with little reduction in speed on any repetition.

Hollow sprints involve the performance of two sprints interrupted by a hollow period of recovery that includes walking or jogging. One repetition may include a 40-yard sprint, 40-yard jog, 50-yard sprint, and 40-yard walk for recovery. Similar segments of 80, 120, 150, 220, and 300 yards might be used.

Interval sprint training is also easily adapted to improve each metabolic system (two anaerobic pathways and the aerobic system). Since more work can be performed at high intensity when repetitions and sets are interrupted by recovery techniques (walking, jogging, complete rest) than through continuous exercise, interval sprint training effectively improves the energy system that predominates in a specific sport. The intensity of exercise, duration of exercise, and rest interval can be altered to achieve maximum results. Wind sprints, alternates, and other similar programs are commonly used by coaches in most team sports. These approaches often differ from interval sprint training because they may possess little formal structure and only a limited attempt to control the variables responsible for producing systematic increases in intensity.

The key variables to be controlled are frequency of training sessions, length and intensity of each repetition, and length and intensity of the rest interval.

Adequate rest is necessary before repeating an exercise if the body is to fully recover and benefit from the previous workout. Most athletes train daily, alternate light and heavy workout days, and take at least one day of rest at the end of the week and just before competition during the season. For team sport athletes, two or three speed endurance sessions per week is sufficient.

The number and length of repetitions vary from one team sport to another and depend on the average distance sprinted and the number of times sprints occur. It is not unreasonable for an athlete to complete 10 to 50 repetitions of a distance interspersed with walk-jog recovery. The intensity of training (speed of each repetition) is more important than the length of the workout. After an initial two weeks of progressing from one-half speed sprints to three-quarter to nine-tenths speed for untrained athletes, repetitions are completed at maximum speed, except for the initial two or three used as part of a warm-up routine. To train both anaerobic pathways, the time of each sprinting repetition and maximum effort exercise will range from 5 to 10 seconds, to 15 to 30 seconds, to 1 to 3 minutes, and occasionally, in excess of 3 minutes.

Training Tips

As Vince Lombardi once said, "Fatigue makes cowards of us all." Speed is hindered by fatigue, and fatigue keeps athletes from exerting maximum effort. Your speed endurance program is certain to delay fatigue during competition and allow you to exert maximum effort for a longer period of time.

Repetitions of maximum effort sprinting for 30 to 60 seconds should be a part of everyone's speed endurance program. At least one maximum effort exercise to complete exhaustion should be included at the end of each speed endurance workout. All-out sprints that cover approximately the same or greater distances than those normally sprinted in your sport should be used. A 1-minute maximum effort sprint followed by 3 to 5 minutes of rest before repeating the effort improves speed endurance. Repetitive 400-meter runs in 60 to 75 seconds followed by 3- to 5-minute rest periods are also effective.

Although complete recovery does not occur during the rest interval, partial return to preexercise levels does take place. The recovery interval between repetitions is based on the estimated time of recovery between sprints during competition in your sport. Sprints take place at maximum speed for distances of up to 120 yards and at near-maximum speed for longer distances.

Maximum effort training is an excellent method of improving speed endurance by completely exhausting the athlete in all-out efforts at the end of a training session. Only the best mentally and physically conditioned athletes will be capable of using this type of training. Maximum effort training is one of the few good methods of equalizing exercise effort among athletes at different conditioning levels. It offers training geared to the athlete, with each person working against her own previous distance or time record, each coping with her own stress and psychological barriers, until finally only complete physical exhaustion causes cessation of exercise.

The maximum effort program in table 7.5 should be used no more than one or two times weekly at the end of the workout. Records should be kept and periodic testing used to determine individual progress.

The speed endurance training programs discussed in this chapter permit the selection of the specific energy systems critical to different team sports. Most team sports require energy use similar to repeated high-intensity sprints interspersed with walking, jogging, or complete rest. The combination of pickup sprints, hollow sprints, and interval sprint training can easily duplicate competitive conditions to engage athletes in sport-specific speed endurance training. This type of training, in conjunction with a solid aerobic foundation, will prepare athletes for all levels of team sport competition.

The majority of speed endurance work for football, basketball, soccer, baseball, field hockey, rugby, and lacrosse should involve segments of 20- to 80-yard sprints or 5- to 10-second all-out sprints, with a recovery interval slightly less than the time that occurs between sprints during competition. Longer intermediate distances (100, 150, 200, 250, 300 yards) requiring a 15- to 30-second sprint are also important in the training of the ATP-LA system. Runs of 400 to 1,200 yards and maximum effort training are used occasionally as the final one to three repetitions of a workout.

Table 7.5   Maximum Effort Training

Program	Training action
Basic	
All-out sprint	Sprint up and back the length of an athletic field until you are no longer able to continue. Record the distance.
Distance hop	Perform a one-legged hop at maximum speed until you are no longer able to continue. Record the distance and time. Repeat with the other leg.
Squat jumps	Perform a maximum number of squat jumps for 90 sec., falling to a right angle only and avoiding the full squat position. Slowly increase the time limit as progress occurs.
Concentration I	Supplement the basic workout with these two concentrations to add variety to the lower torso muscles involved in the sprinting action.
Running in place	Lift knees to waist level and sprint in place to exhaustion. Record the time.
Treadmill pacing	Set the treadmill for 15 mph and run until you are no longer able to continue.
300-yd. run	Record your time in a 300-yd. sprint.
Two-legged hop	Record the distance covered in 45 sec. Slowly increase the time limit.
Concentration II	
440-yd. dash+	Surprise runners at the finish of the 440-yd. dash with the command to continue sprinting as far as possible.
Bench jump	Stand parallel to a bench. Jump to the other side with a two-foot takeoff; immediately jump back to the starting position. Repeat the action until you are no longer able to continue. Record the total number of jumps.
Isometric charge	With the legs moving continuously and shoulders and hands placed against an immovable object (sled, wall, post), drive forward until you are no longer able to continue.

You can check your speed endurance training progress by retesting yourself with the NASE repeated 20-, 30-, or 40-yard distances, depending on your sport. Complete 10 consecutive dashes at one of these distances using a 10- to 30-second rest interval between each repetition (choose the rest interval from table 7.3, page 151, for your sport) and compare the drop-off. Assume the three- or four-point stance at the starting line and have a coach or friend time you. After your first dash, slowly walk forward 10 yards and begin your second timed sprint when the appropriate number of seconds has elapsed. Repeat until you have completed 10 timed dashes with a rest period similar to what occurs in your sport. Ideally, none of the timed distances should be more than .3 second off your best effort.

Chapter 8

RECOVERY AND NUTRITION

*R*ecovery is the ability to return to some previous or higher level of performance. How well you do this will determine how well you are able to perform. Two major factors play a role in how well you recover: your current level of fitness and the accumulation of stress from the game and your daily environment. Certainly, the outcomes of future competition will depend on how well you cope with the sum stress.

Behind the scenes lurks the grueling side of sport. All that glitters on game day has been paid for at a great price. Some common stressors for an athlete include the daily accumulation of stress, the athlete's talent compared to an opponent's, injuries, stadium conditions, game site (home or away), travel (crossing time zones, going coast to coast, flying in a plane), importance of the game, game intensity, game length, and weather conditions.

This chapter describes important principles in the art and science of recovery and how to use them to achieve new heights in performance. Be aware of the times when psychological pressures of competition and winning arise. Irrational decisions can follow. The important principles in this chapter provide a basis for increasing recovery in a training program. These principles will help you make the right decisions and allow you to continue toward your goal.

Scientific evidence shows that recovery can be predictable. If recovery is to be predictable and successful, proven principles must be used at the right time and in the right order in the recovery plan. We have only so much adaptation energy capacity (the gas tank can hold only so much) to turn workouts into higher levels of performance.

All athletes strive to achieve positive training effects that translate into higher levels of performance. Table 8.1 relates training methods to the documented positive effects that science has identified. We have often observed athletes commit errors due to over- or underwork. Strange as it may seem, both produce the same result—submaximal performance. The principles in this chapter will ensure that you are sufficiently prepared for competition and are able to recover sufficiently in order to avoid staleness, the bonk, and mediocre performances. These conditions result from overtraining and improper adherence to the principles of recovery. If you are overtrained, this chapter will help you quickly return to a balanced physiological state.

Table 8.1 — Documented Positive Effects of Different Types of Training

Feature (marker)	Endurance		Strength				
	Aerobic	Anaerobic	Power	Speed	Max	End	Sustained output
Adrenaline		↑	↑	↑	↑		
Bone mass and density (osteopenia)	↑	↑↑	↑	↑↑	↑↑		↑
Blood pressure (rest)	↓						↓
Blood volume	↑					↑	↑
Buffer capacity	NC	↑	↑	↑	↑		NC
Capillary density	↑				NC	↑	↑
Cardiac output	↑						↑ NC
Cardiac performance	↑						↑
Stroke volume	↑						↑ NC
Kinase		NC					
Glucose uptake	↑						↑
Heart rate (rest)	↓						↓
Heart volume	↑	↑		↑		NC ↑	↑
Heart recovery							
Hemoglobin Pseudoanemia Iron deficiency							
Immune function							
Mitochondria number and volume	↑				↓	NC	↑
Muscle glycogen	↑	↑		↑		↑	↑
Muscle hypertrophy		↑↑	↑↑	↑	↑↑	↑	

Feature (marker)	Endurance		Strength				
	Aerobic	Anaerobic	Power	Speed	Max	End	Sustained output
Muscle phosphocreatine		↑		↑	↑		
Oxidative enzyme activity	↑				↓		↑
Plasma sodium							
Plasma volume	↑						
Precision of skill							
Strength		↑	↑	↑	↑	↑	
Stress hormones	↓						↓
Tendon/ligament strength	↑	↑↑	↑↑	↑↑	↑↑		↑
Urinary indices[1,2] Color Specific gravity Osmolality							
Thermal (onset of sweat)	↑						↑
Thermal (temperature regulation)	↑						↑
Urinary creatinine							
$\dot{V}O_2$max	↑						↑
↓$\dot{V}O_2$max/ standard							

[1]Shirreffs, S.M., and R.J. Maughan. 1998. Urine osmolality and conductivity as indices of hydration status in athletes in the heat. *Med Sci Sport Exer* 30: 1598-1602.

[2]Armstrong, L.E., C.M. Maresh, J.W. Castellani, M.F. Bergeron, R.W. Kenefick, K.E. LaGasse, and D. Riebe. 1994. Urinary indices of hydration status. *Int J Sport Nutr* 4: 265-279.

Monitoring Training Response

A change in fitness level will produce a lower heart rate at a standard workload. Likewise, a tired condition (poor recovery state) will cause an increase in heart rate, and a well-rested condition will be associated with a lower heart rate. A good test to determine the quality of your recovery is a sub-max bike test. Modify your workout if your heart rate is three or four beats per minute higher than your average heart rate standard.

For the sub-max bike test, select a workload that produces 120 beats per minute during the fourth and fifth minutes. The best time to take the test is in the morning before breakfast after using the toilet. Use the same workload and pedal rate (70 to 90) on all tests. Time yourself on the bike for five minutes. Take your heart rate at the fourth and fifth minutes. To find your heart rate score, take the average (fourth-minute HR plus fifth-minute HR divided by two; figure 8.1).

Maintain a healthy and functional body weight. It is possible to become too lean. For every sport, there is a zone of body fat percentage in which athletes will perform at an optimum level. If you are following the hormonal control diet (see page 175) and find that your body fat percentage is dropping below a desired level, add more monounsaturated fat to your diet to increase caloric intake and maintain your desired percent of body fat. If your body fat increases beyond a desired level, decrease the amount of added monounsaturated fat while maintaining the same protein-to-carbohydrate ratio.

The other Holy Grail for athletes is adding new muscle mass. Athletes are led to believe that they must consume mega doses of extra protein to achieve that goal. In reality, the extra amount of required protein to build new muscle is surprisingly small. To build one pound of new muscle per month is a noble

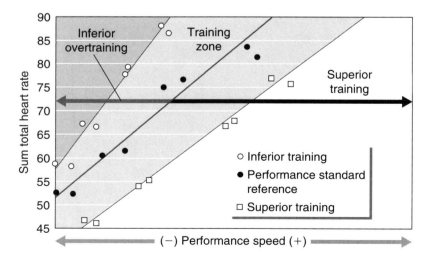

Figure 8.1   Athletic training response.

goal. About 70 percent of the weight of muscle is water. This means that each pound (454 grams) of new muscle developed each month contains only 136 grams of extra protein. There are about 30 days in a month, so extra protein beyond the amount required to maintain your existing muscle mass is something like five extra grams of protein per day. Of course, you still want to maintain the correct ratio of protein to carbohydrate, so you will need to adjust your carbohydrate portion to account for this extra protein.

The release of growth hormone from the pituitary gland coupled with testosterone transforms this extra protein into new muscle mass. You can't affect either hormone directly through diet, but you can use diet to set the appropriate microenvironment for the maximum release of growth hormone. The primary stimulus for the release of growth hormone is anaerobic training, such as speed training. Not surprisingly, insulin can have an adverse hormonal consequence on muscle mass development because it tends to block the release of growth hormone. Without adequate levels of growth hormone, maximum muscle building is impossible. Maximum new muscle development requires a hormonal control program to maintain insulin in a tight zone (neither too high nor too low), coupled with a well-designed resistive training program. Growth hormone is also released during deep sleep just before REM sleep. Therefore, a small hormonally balanced snack before going to bed can set the hormonal environment for maximum sleep-induced release of growth hormone for tissue repair after maximum effort and exhaustion.

Remember muscle mass gain and excess body fat loss are both governed by hormonal events as are training and performance. Diet remains the primary tool to control this cycle. You have to eat, so you might as well eat smart. Intelligence and emotional maturity often determine the winner. Newly developing knowledge is putting an additional premium on mental preparation and intelligence for diet during training and before competition. These qualities can influence who gets the gold and who gets the silver.

Overreaching and Overtraining

More so than the average person, athletes have uncommon goals and drives that stretch their limits. Many athletes maximize performances as a result of these extreme circumstances. An athlete's body must be able to operate at near-maximum output over and over. Consequently, overreaching and overtraining are concerns for highly motivated athletes. The numerous occurrences of overtraining emphasize that there is a constant struggle in an exercising athlete. The battle for recovery and superadaptation is between building, repairing, remodeling (anabolic processes), and tearing down (catabolic processes).

Not only is it necessary to have a plan, it also is important to know the hazards that can slow you down and detour you from the most direct route to your goals. Be aware of the signs that scientists have identified to determine if the right amount of training is being applied and received. The two most obvious and simple signs of proper adaptation are how you perform in practice and competition and how you feel in general. Subjective feelings of the athlete are one of the most reliable indicators (Uusitalo 2001).

In addition, other objective and subjective markers or signs can be used to determine if proper adaptation training is being achieved. Remember, any deviation from normal could be an indicator of improper training. Track these indicators on a chart to establish a normal level and show progress in recovery: quality of appetite, quality and amount of sleep, resting heart rate, increased heart rate, lying-to-standing heart rate changes, percent body fat, total testosterone concentration, ratio of total testosterone to cortisol, ratio of free testosterone to cortisol, ratio of total testosterone to sex hormone-binding globulin, serum testosterone, serum cortisol, sex hormone-binding globulin, infections and diminished immune function, T-cells, $\dot{V}O_2$max, blood pressure, muscle soreness, muscle glycogen, lactate, creatine kinase, cortisol concentration, sympathetic tone (nocturnal and resting catecholamines), sympathetic stress, tissue breakdown (e.g., loss of lean mass), and androgen.

Other factors that play a role in recovery fall into four basic categories: work (intensity, frequency, and duration); rest (quality and amount of rest or sleep); nutrition (diet or calorie reduction); and mental pressures (daily pressures, academic demands). Each of these categories has elements that can influence the quality of performance. In fact, we have the ability to modify these factors to positively or negatively affect performance.

Building a Recovery Strategy

Some time ago, Canadian physiologist Hans Selye developed the adaptation theory, which has been used by many coaches to guide training programs. Selye's theory laid out the scientific basis—the principles—for achieving maximum performance and avoiding overtraining. Two highly successful sport scientists helped spread the value of the principles of adaptation theory: Jim Counsilman, the famous Indiana University swimming coach, and noted Russian researcher Nikolai Volkov. Athletes of either sex and any age in many sport training programs can benefit from the application of adaptation theory.

The three stages of Selye's adaptation theory are the alarm stage (+ initial load reduces performance levels; too much can be lethal), the resistance stage (+ compensation and supercompensation occur), and the exhaustion stage (- there is a limit to man's adaptive capacity). Figure 8.2 shows the peak performance adaptation model.

The work of these scientists spawned the use of periodization in many sport training programs. Periodization splits the training plan into yearly, monthly, weekly, and daily cycles. According to Costa (1994), the Bulgarians added some interesting findings to the mix that further refine training regimes based on how the body responds to vigorous workouts. How to apply periodization to general and foundational training was covered in chapter 3 and will be specifically applied in chapter 13. These chapters are practical examples of how adaptation theory has been applied to training.

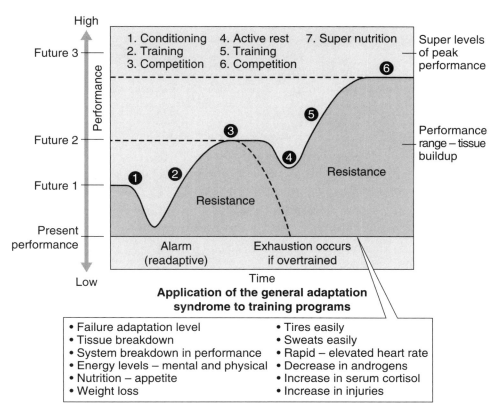

Figure 8.2 The peak performance adaptation model.

The key to a highly organized plan, or to a loosely structured plan, is that it must adhere to the principles of adaptation to be successful. The guiding rules of maximum recovery and maximum performance should be based on these adaptation theory principles.

Questions to Ask

In evaluating what it takes to recover from a workout, take into account work intensity, frequency, and duration; short- and long-term rest; and nutrition (immediate and extended replenishment of energy). It is common knowledge that exercise can lead to fatigue. Studies have shown that the main contributor to fatigue is depletion of the body's energy stores in the liver and muscles; water deficiency can make it worse. Failure to properly balance these factors will surely end in disaster or, at best, mediocre performance. Further, understand that recovery should not be thought of as independent of all other elements involved in the training process.

This idea is vividly presented in the book *The New Science of Swimming* by Counsilman and Counsilman (1994), in which the authors pose a number of questions about recovery. We have taken the liberty to add other critical questions to the ones the authors presented. The questions focus on the relationships that exist between work, rest, nutrition, and performance. Asking the right questions about recovery will enable you to direct your attention to the critical areas that need to be explored. The following questions will direct your thinking when formulating recovery principles to help you avoid staleness, the bonk, and mediocre performances between workouts and training cycles:

+ How hard should an athlete work?
+ How much fatigue should an athlete condition himself to endure in order to build maximum endurance (or other resources)?
+ Should an athlete work hard then rest when she becomes fatigued in order to be refreshed for the next practice?
+ Should an athlete impose another workload, one that is so great she will not recover completely from one practice to the next?
+ Should an athlete always be slightly fatigued?
+ Is it possible to optimally recover in a fatigued state?
+ What are the rates of energy replenishment? Of glycogen replenishment?
+ How much time does it take for the body to recharge itself?
+ What steps can be taken to guarantee that maximum recovery will take place after acute or extended bouts of exercise?

Just as sports speed training is more complicated than simply doing drills, running wind sprints, or lifting weights, the recovery process is far more complicated than just adhering to a few simple considerations. Recovery requires complex solutions. In the past, recovery recommendations have focused on a limited number of the critical concerns required for maximum recovery between workouts. However, the cells, the biochemically run units of the body, must be properly maintained and supplied with an adequate amount of all the essential elements that are practical, healthy, and legal. Therefore, today's recovery programs should include a full range of these essential elements to ensure maximum recovery from workouts.

Comprehensive Sports Training Model

Volkov (1975) stated that in order to achieve changes in performance, intense training must be repeated numerous times with appropriate rest periods between training loads. He went on to emphasize the importance of repeating the load (workout) after the correct amount of rest (short- or long-term recovery). If the next load (workout) is applied before complete restoration takes place, it will only increase the liklihood of unfavorable changes. If this happens often enough it will lead to overtraining. Therefore, athletes need to use a system that lets them manage the essential elements of the training program. Kondraske and Ward (1999) developed the comprehensive sports training model to manage all of the essential elements of the training program to ensure maximum attainment of training goals and avoid overtraining (figures 8.3 and 8.4).

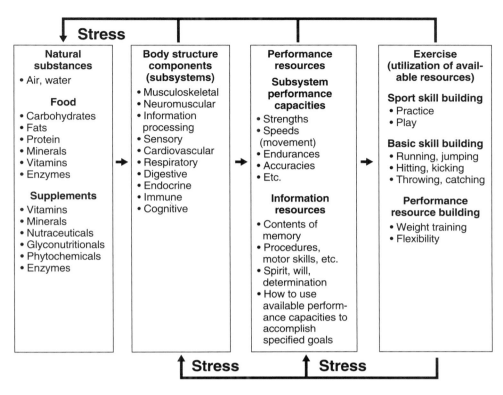

Figure 8.3 Basic relationships between nutrition, body structure, performance, and exercise form the basis of the comprehensive sports training model. Kondraske and Ward (1999).

Chronobiology

Chronobiology is the science of body rhythms. Physiological cycles keep the body operating efficiently. When an athlete gets in tune with these cycles, recovery, building, repairing, remodeling, and better performance follow. The science of chronobiology plays a crucial role in the training process. The appropriate times relative to training and competitive priorities must be used to produce optimal adaptation to physical loads. Table 8.2 illustrates how to manage many complicated elements using the principles of chronobiology.

Recovery Principles

To establish recovery principles, first find out where you are and where you need to be. A quality program requires the following assessments at appropriate times during the training year: clinical examination by a physician, assessment of sport goals, size, body composition, calculation of optimum performance body weight, calculation of weight loss necessary to reach optimum body weight, diet assessment including a seven-day dietary recall to calculate average daily intake, biochemical assessment, assessment of supplementation

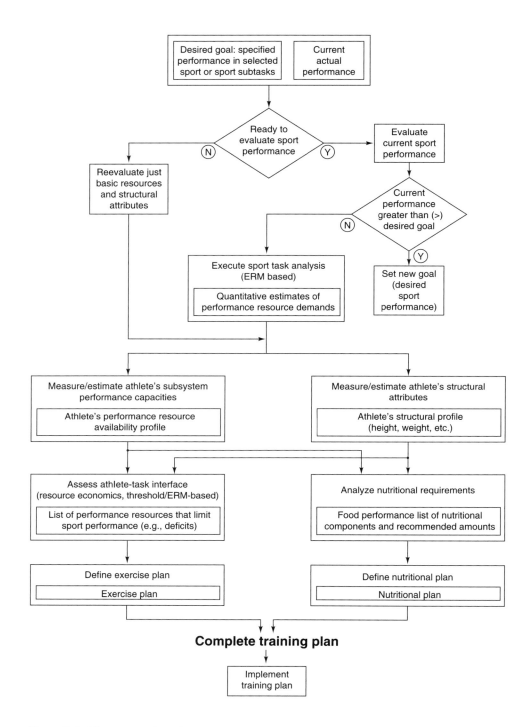

Figure 8.4 The comprehensive sports training model uses quantitative links across hierarchical performance levels provided by the elemental resource model, periodic performance and structural measurements for a specific athlete, and nutritional analyses to arrive at a complete training plan.

Table 8.2   **Chronobiology of Daily Recovery**

Time marker	Meals and snacks*	Fluids	Supplements	Other activities	Duration
Wake-up		2 glasses water	Enzymes	Meditation, HR check	Sleep 8 to 10 h.
A.M. (before noon)		2 glasses water		Bike	
Preworkout	~ 100 C bars	Water, recovery 100 to 200 C, electrolyte plus during and after	Anabolic, BCAA, antioxidants	Visualization, electrostimulation, warm-up	30 to 45 min.
Workout (A.M.)					1 h.
Postworkout			Immediately anabolic drink, joint support, omega oils	Cool-down, cold shower, lactate retention	
Before breakfast		Water	Empty stomach, probiotics		
Breakfast	Protein 35%, carbs 46%, fat 19%	Water	Vitamins and minerals, omega oils, enzymes		
After breakfast					
Snack (A.M.)	~ 100 C bars				
Before lunch		Water	Empty stomach		
Lunch	Protein 35%, carbs 46%, fat 19%	Water	Vitamins and enzymes		
After lunch					
Before rest			BCAA		
Rest					Active
After rest					
Before nap			BCAA		
Nap					60 min.

(continued)

167

Table 8.2

(continued)

Time marker	Meals and snacks*	Fluids	Supplements	Other activities	Duration
After nap					
P.M. (afternoon)		2 glasses water			
Preworkout	~ 100 C bars	Recovery 100 to 200 C, electrolyte plus during and after	Anabolic, BCAA	Visualization, electrostimulation, warm-up	
Workout (P.M.)			Anabolic drink, BCAA, antioxidants, omega oils	Cool-down, cold shower	
Snack (P.M.)	~ 100 C bars				
Before dinner		Water	Empty stomach		
Dinner	Protein 35%, carbs 46%, fat 19%	Water	Vitamins and enzymes		
After dinner					
Preworkout	~ 100 C bars	Water	Anabolic, BCAA	Visualization, electrostimulation, warm-up	
Workout (evening)		Recovery 100 to 200 C, electrolyte plus during and after			1 h.
Postworkout			Anabolic drink, antioxidants, omega oils	Cool-down, cold shower	
Before bedtime		Recovery 100 to 200 C	Anabolic	Massage	
Bedtime		Water	Protein, minerals	Meditation, flotation	8 to 10 h.
Bedtime (wake-up)			Enzymes		
After bedtime			Joint support		

* Meals and snacks are balanced to be 40% carbohydrate, 30% protein, and 30% fat for the daily diet.

program, monitoring of weight loss and fluid intake, and resolution of any special concerns the athlete has. Monitoring and assessing these areas is vital for ensuring the athlete's continued good health and sport performance. Consider the many recent deaths of young athletes and even professional athletes during workouts in extremely hot conditions. These factors contribute to the athlete's overall health and ability to train and compete at a high level. Take nutrition, for example. The diets of many athletes today are inadequate. Many exist on fast foods that are high in saturated fats.

Second, you need to get, use, and teach the facts. In their research, Wolinsky and Driskell (2001) found that athletes score low on nutrition knowledge and practices, one of the critical elements required for acceptable levels of performance and recovery.

Third, design a scientifically based workout program. Are workouts based on the assessments you took and what your sport requires? Your program has to be properly cycled between work, rest, and nutrition if the best results are to be attained. Reread chapter 3 to review the science of putting together a proper program. Know the energy systems and how they apply to your sport. Tables 8.3 and 8.4 put the energy systems' capacities in perspective. A careful study of the tables shows where the majority of energy must come from and how much is available.

Taper (reduce training) leading up to major competitions to achieve super-compensation. Anderson (2000) reported that type II muscle fibers doubled after three months of detraining. However, most team sports don't lend themselves to such periods of detraining. It may be possible to lighten workloads and gain some of the same benefits. More research is needed to verify that similar changes can be made within the shorter time frames in which team sports operate. How you use this information is up to the artistic talent of the creative coach.

Nutrition

A good diet means balancing protein, carbohydrate, and fat to optimize the production of glucagon, insulin, and eicosanoids. The better you balance your diet, the better the resulting hormonal response. The better the hormonal response, the better your physical performance. Although you should try to maintain a consistent diet (and therefore a consistent hormonal environment), there are three distinct critical hormonal windows for maximizing performance.

The first window is 30 to 45 minutes before exercise or competition. In this preexercise period, you should begin the hormonal changes that allow you to lower insulin and therefore tap into stored body fat more effectively. The number of calories consumed should be small (less than 100), so as not to divert any significant amount of energy toward digestion, but should provide enough protein and carbohydrate to begin changing hormonal levels before exercise. An example of a useful snack might be one ounce of turkey breast and half a piece of fruit.

Table 8.3

Major Energy Stores in the Human Body With Appropriate Total Caloric Value

Energy source	Major form of storage	Total body calories	Total body kJ	Distance covered
ATP	Tissues	1	4.2	17.5 yd.
PC	Tissues	4	16.8	70 yd.
Carbohydrate	Serum glucose	20	84	350 yd.
	Liver glycogen	75	315	4 mi.
	Muscle glycogen	2,500	10,500	15 mi.
Fat	Serum free fatty acids	7	29.4	123 yd.
	Serum triglycerides	75	315	1,320 yd.
	Muscle triglycerides	2,500	10,500	25 mi.
	Adipose tissue triglycerides	80,000	336,000	800 mi.
Protein	Muscle protein	30,000	126,000	300 mi.

Williams, M. 1995. *Nutrition for fitness and sport.* Brown & Benchmark: Dubuque. p. 77-78.

Table 8.4

Contribution of Anaerobic and Aerobic Energy Sources During Different Periods of Maximal Work

Time	Anaerobic (%)	Aerobic (%)
10 sec.	85	15
1 min.	70	30
2 min.	50	50
4 min.	15	85
10 min.	30	70
30 min.	5	95
60 min.	2	98
130 min.	1	99

Williams, M. 1995. *Nutrition for fitness and sport.* Brown & Benchmark: Dubuque. p. 78.

An athlete should eat a snack 30 to 60 minutes before a workout. A prepractice snack increases energy at the end of practice. Make sure that the snack is nutrient dense. Apply this snack selection advice to all of your snacks.

Plan meals to coincide with practices and games. The only differences in diet on game day compared to a normal day are the following:

+ Eat your last meal at least three to four hours before the game.
+ Eat a small hormone-balancing snack, such as two hard-boiled egg whites and half a piece of fruit, a snack less than 100 calories, about 30 to 45 minutes before the game.
+ Eat another hormone-balancing snack of 100 calories at halftime.

The second hormonal window occurs immediately after exercise. Again, have a small snack of approximately 100 calories 15 to 30 minutes after exercise to set the appropriate hormonal balance between insulin and glucagon for the maximum release of growth hormone.

The final window occurs in the two-hour time period after exercise. In this time frame, you want to eat a fairly large meal (but still maintain the appropriate hormonal balance) to replenish muscle glycogen levels more effectively.

Athletes need sufficient metabolic substrate at the right time. The more intense the training of an athlete, the greater the requirement for nutrient replacement. Kondraske and Ward (1999) covered the subject of nutrition and substrate availability in a Technical Report at the University of Texas at Arlington. They indicate that

> the role that nutritional and dietary supplements play in maximizing human performance is in its infancy. The concept here is that if we know the level of performance resources required (from the sport task analysis) and also know the athlete's performance resource availability profile and structural information, we have the information required to compute the nutritional requirements to support the necessary "growth" and maintenance. It is argued that the science exists to support development of computer-based models that provide reasonable estimates of many important nutritional components. For example, [figure 8.5] shows a well-known relationship (based on the so-called Michaelis-Menten equation) between substrate concentration and rate or velocity at which enzymatic reactions occur. This curve also shows that cellular synthesis reactions occur at higher rates (up to some maximum) as substrate (i.e., nutrient) concentrations increase. In humans, such reactions are common and the substrate is frequently a nutritional component (McAnalley 1998). It is not surprising to expect the rate at which biochemical reactions occur to be related to (i.e., limit) certain aspects of performance of neuromuscular and information processing subsystems. This connection is illustrated in [figure 8.5]. Thus high substrate concentrations (i.e., greater availability of nutritional components that serve as substrates) are linked to increased subsystem performance capacities. These biochemical reactions are not only operational in regard to sports performance but in recovery from all aspects of fatigue (acute, intermediate and long-term), sickness and injury.

Athletes need to take in enough calories every day. Size and activity level play a big part in the amount of calories needed. Athletes such as football linemen

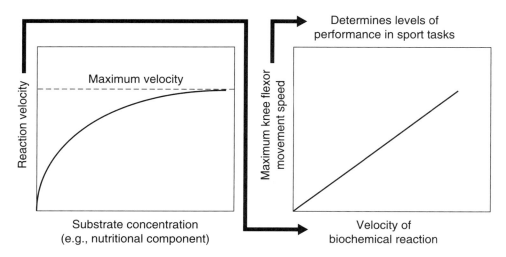

Figure 8.5   An example of the link between nutritional components and subsystem performance capacities, drawing on established concepts in biochemistry and physiology. Kondraske and Ward (1999).

and power lifters may require four to six meals per day (60 to 80 kcal/kg/day) to receive the proper amount of calories. Macronutrient (carbohydrates, proteins, and fats) recommendations vary, depending on the sport and individual differences (table 8.5). The generally accepted ranges are 50 to 60 percent carbohydrate, 15 to 20 percent protein, and 20 to 30 percent fat.

Breakfast is an important meal for an athlete. Breakfast stores energy for afternoon practices. It takes four hours to digest and store carbohydrate in muscle and liver. This makes breakfast the most important meal for an athlete who has afternoon workouts.

Oxygen is required to convert food into a useable source of energy. Therefore athletes need to make sure they have sufficient oxygen transport. One liter of oxygen is equivalent to 5 kcal (20.92 kJ). Optimizing the body's ability to deliver oxygen without interfering with other performance factors is very important. All energy systems are working in concert at all times. Even in intermittent anaerobic sports the aerobic system plays an essential role during the game and in acute and prolonged recovery. Further, there is an additional need for oxygen because of the close relationship that exists between energy metabolism and oxygen consumption.

Carbohydrates

Plan to consume about one-third more carbohydrates than protein at each meal. This amount equals about four grams of carbohydrates for every three grams of protein. Remember that carbohydrates stimulate insulin, but too much insulin is detrimental to performance. The ratio of protein to carbohydrate is critical to maintain the correct amount of insulin.

Table 8.5 **Estimated Energy Needs of Various Sports**

Sport	Caloric needs	Average daily needs
Basketball	300	2,200
Dancing	1,000	1,500
Gymnastics	1,400	1,400
Football	2,100	4,000 to 5,000
Running (men)	1,000	4,400
Running (women)	500	2,397
Swimming	500	2,900
Cycling (Tour de France)	4,000	6,700
Triathlon	1,500 to 2,000	4,095
Wrestling	200 to 1,000	Varies with weight class
Weightlifting	2,800 to 4,600	3,200 to 4,700
Sled dog racing (Iditarod)[a]		12,000

[a]Dee Dee Jonrowe, Iditarod musher; interview with Dr. Bob Ward, 1996 Iditarod.

Short, S.H., and Short, W.R. 1983. Four year study of university athlete's dietary intake. *J Am Diet Assoc* 82:632.

Adequate carbohydrate needs to be taken immediately after exercise. According to Shirreffs (2000), muscle has an affinity for carbohydrate immediately after exercise, with the greatest amount of resynthesis occurring during the first two hours. Leutholtz and Kreider (2001) found that replenishment of glycogen could be 7.5 to 15 times faster after prolonged endurance bouts if adequate carbohydrate is consumed.

Not all carbohydrates are the same when it comes to insulin. Complex or starchy carbohydrates such as pasta, grains, cereals, and breads tend to stimulate insulin to greater degrees than fruit and vegetable sources. Because fruits and vegetables have more fiber, they have a lower glycemic index. A lower glycemic index means that the carbohydrate enters the bloodstream more slowly, with a resulting decreased insulin response.

Therefore, the bulk of your carbohydrates should come from fruits and vegetables. Treat grains, cereals, breads, and pasta as condiments, not the main source of carbohydrates. Fruits and vegetables are low-density carbohydrates; pastas, starches, and grains are high-density. You have to eat a lot of fruits and vegetables to adversely affect insulin levels. On the other hand, it is very easy to overconsume high-density carbohydrates and induce an adverse insulin response.

Good sources of 46 grams of low-density, low-glycemic carbohydrate might be two pieces of fruit and a cup of steamed vegetables, three cups of steamed vegetables and a piece of fruit, or one cup of pasta and half a piece of fruit. As you can see, you have to eat a lot of fruits and vegetables to get your carbohydrate needs.

Protein

No athlete should ever consume more protein than needed, but to consume less is equivalent to protein malnutrition. Recent research has indicated that protein requirements, especially for athletes, are much higher than previously thought (tables 8.6 and 8.7).

If you are active (up to one hour of exercise per day, five times per week), you need .7 grams of protein per pound of weight. If you are very active (one to two hours of exercise per day, five times per week), you need .8 grams of protein per pound of weight. If you are performing heavy weight training or doing two workouts a day, five times per week, you need .9 grams of protein per pound of weight.

To calculate daily protein requirement, multiply lean body mass by the appropriate gram protein requirements for your activity level. For example, if you are doing the speed training outlined in this book, you will probably require about .8 grams of protein per pound of weight. If you weigh 160 pounds and have 12 percent body fat, you will require about 130 grams of protein per day.

You can divide that 130 grams of protein into three meals and two snacks per day. For our sample 160-pound athlete, this requirement could be met in three meals each consisting of 35 grams of protein and two snacks of 10 grams of protein each. Keep in mind that the human body can't metabolize more than 45 grams of protein at any one meal; if you eat more than that amount of protein at a meal, the excess gets converted into fat.

Excellent sources of low-fat protein include skinless chicken and turkey, very lean cuts of red meat, fish, egg whites, tofu, protein powder, and soybean products. You can find 35 grams of protein in a five-ounce chicken breast, five ounces of sliced turkey, eight ounces of fish, 10 egg whites, or two soybean hamburger patties.

Fat

Fat is an exceptionally powerful hormonal modulator for an athlete if fat intake is primarily of the monounsaturated variety. Add extra monounsaturated fat to each meal. Good sources of monounsaturated fat are olive oil, macadamia nuts, almonds, cashews, pistachios, avocados, and olives. Monounsaturated fat acts as a control rod in a nuclear reactor: It slows the rate of entry of carbohydrates (whatever their source) into the bloodstream, thereby reducing the extent of the insulin response. Fat also interacts with receptors in the stomach to send other hormonal signals to the brain to govern satiety so that you are not constantly hungry. In addition, fat supplies the building blocks for the most

Table 8.6 **Carbohydrate, Protein, and Fat Requirements**

System	Carbohydrate	Protein	Fat
Range	50 to 60%	15 to 20%	20 to 30%
Daily recommended value	60	10	30
Zone	40	30	30
Rod and Mark	30	40	30
Profile I	70	20	10
Profile II	35	45	20
Profile III	50	40	10
Simonsen 1991	10 g/kg^{-1}		
Lemon 1995 Endurance Strength		1.2 to 1.4 g/kg^{-1}/d^{-1} 1.4 to 1.8 g/kg^{-1}/d^{-1}	
Williams 1995 Weight gain		1.5 to 1.75 g/kg^{-1}/d^{-1}	
Spruce and Ticheneal 2001 Body builders		1.4 to 2.0 g/kg^{-1}/d^{-1}	

Simonsen, J.C., et al. 1991. Dietary carbohydrate, muscle glycogen, and power output during rowing training. *J Appl Physiol* 70:1500-1505.

Lemon, P.W.R. 1995. Do athletes need more dietary protein and amino acids? *Int J Sport Nutr* 5:S39-S61.

Williams, M. 1995. *Nutrition for sport and fitness.* Brown & Benchmark: Dubuque. p. 158.

Spruce, N., and Ticheneal, A. 2001. *An evaluation of popular fitness-enhancing supplements.* Calabasas, CA: Evergreen Communications. p. 50-51.

powerful hormone system for an athlete: eicosanoids. Table 8.8 shows the fat requirements for a 160-pound athlete.

Total Menu

The content of your diet influences the release and production of cell regulatory hormones. Table 8.8 includes fat requirements to show a balanced diet for a hypothetical 160-pound athlete. The balanced composition of this diet maximizes hormone responses that ultimately foster maximal athletic performance. Depending on your weight and physical activity level, you can construct an individualized hormonal-control menu.

The optimal hormonal control diet suggested for the 160-pound athlete in table 8.8 advocates less carbohydrate than has typically been recommended. If you understand the importance of controlling insulin, the reduction in carbo-

Table 8.7   **Necessary Protein Intake**

Category	Level	
	g/lb LBW[a]	g/kg BWT[b]
Basic requirements[c]		1.2 to 1.8 g/kg^{-1}/d^{-1}
BCAA		3 to 6 g/d pre- and postworkout
BCAA to aid performance		5 to 20 g pre-, during, and postworkout
Growing athlete		1.3 to 2.0
Endurance athlete		2.0
Body builder		1.4 to 2.0
Extreme	1.0 to 1.5	1.5 adult, strength training
Heavy	0.9 to 1.3	0.9 to 1.3 adult, active
Moderately heavy	0.8	0.8 current RDA
Moderate	0.7	
Light	0.6	
Sedentary	0.5	

[a]Hatfield, F., and Gastelu, D. 1997. Dynamic nutrition for maximum performance. Garden City Park, NY: Avery Publishing Group. p. 44-47.

[b]Spruce, N., and Ticheneal A. 2001. An evaluation of popular fitness-enhancing supplements. Calabasas, CA: Evergreen Communications. p. 50-51.

[c]Maughan, R. (ed.). 2000. Nutrition and exercise. Malden, MA: Blackwell Science. p. 146-145.

Table 8.8   **Diet Requirements for a 160-Pound Athlete**

Meal	Protein (g)	Carbohydrate (g)	Fat (g)
Breakfast	35	46	16
Lunch	35	46	16
Snack	10	14	3
Dinner	35	46	16
Snack	10	14	3
Total	125	166	54

hydrate makes perfect sense. The table also suggests consuming more protein than you probably have been consuming. Many elite athletes tend to be protein-deficient for their level of activity. Finally, even with the extra fat, this is still a low-fat diet in terms of total grams of fat, according to U.S. government guidelines. Table 8.9 breaks down the requirements into actual meals.

Table 8.9 **Typical Meals for a 160-Pound Athlete**

Meal	Food
Breakfast	5-inch omelet (1 whole egg and 4 egg whites, 2 oz. nonfat cheese, 2 tsp. olive oil) 1/2 cantaloupe 1 piece toast
Lunch	6 oz. tuna fish with 2 tsp. mayonnaise 1 orange 1 apple 2 cups steamed vegetables
Snack	2 oz. sliced turkey 1 piece fruit
Dinner	5 oz. chicken breast 4 cups steamed vegetables 1 piece fruit
Snack	2 oz. cottage cheese or 1 oz. sliced turkey 1/2 piece fruit

Although this diet is less than 2,000 calories, it would be difficult to consume all the food if the carbohydrate portion is mainly fruits and vegetables. Furthermore, any extra calories required for training would need to come from body fat. As a result, the athlete doesn't need to consume excessive calories to maintain high physical performance. If you need more calories, add them as extra monounsaturated fats since this type of fat has no effect on insulin. As you can see from these meals, grains, starches, and breads are not the major component of a hormonal control diet. Remember to introduce any change in your eating habits at least one week before competition to give your body adequate time to adapt to the changes.

All snacks or meals eaten within the three critical hormonal windows should have the same ratio of protein to carbohydrate to generate the optimal hormone response. Other meals eaten during the day should also have a similar protein-to-carbohydrate balance to maintain a consistent hormonal status within the body. To achieve maximum results, treat eating as an integral part of the training process. The appropriate balance assures that protein, the nutrient athletes neglect most, is sufficient.

Hydration

The most important nutrient for any athlete is water. Athletes should regard water as an indispensible resource. The fact that 75 to 85 percent of the body is water proves how vitally important it is for cellular life. Water's role in forming a gel in cells makes life possible. Dehydration is probably the greatest factor to adversely affect performance. Practical experience and scientific studies support the following recommendations.

The body most efficiently absorbs water at temperatures of 40 to 50 degrees Fahrenheit. Drink at least eight 10-ounce servings of water per day. During exercise, drink water every 15 to 20 minutes. Plain water provides the most effective results. Carbohydrate sports drinks have the effect of increasing insulin, and as discussed previously, excessive insulin formation is the worst hormonal enemy of any endurance or strength performance athlete.

It's important for athletes to maintain good water and electrolyte balance. Drink adequate amounts of water and supply the proper balance of electrolytes. Dehydration will occur if fluid intake doesn't match fluid lost.

Supplementation

Establish and maintain a normal acid-base level. Increasing the body's alkaline reserve before exercise by taking sodium bicarbonate or sodium citrate has been shown to significantly improve anaerobic performance.

Wisely evaluate commonly used nutritional aids. Oranges, which are frequently supplied after youth practices, contain 94 percent carbohydrate, 6 percent protein, and no fat and supply 64 calories. Sucrose is a commonly used aid, as is coffee. According to Williams (1995), moderate use of coffee poses few health hazards to those that tolerate caffeine. Scientists recommend two or three 6-ounce cups of coffee per day, which is equivalent to 200 to 300 mg of caffeine. Possible beneficial effects of drinking coffee include a significant increase in endurance and high-intensity effort, alertness, and clearer thinking. Tea is 100 percent carbohydrate and supplies 88 calories. A 12-ounce cola is 100 percent carbohydrate and supplies 164 calories.

Although it is wise to include certain dietary supplements, a serious athlete should avoid drugs and alcohol. Drugs, other than those prescribed by a doctor for medical reasons, are not acceptable in the athletic world. Alcohol, which provides 7 kcal/ml, initially has a stimulating effect but then becomes a depressant. Physiologically, alcohol has not been shown to produce any ergogenic effects on short- or long-term exercise.

Fluid is essential for maximum absorption of nutrients. Therefore, drink water when taking supplements. Water is the best choice when taking supplements or mixing drinks because milk or other beverages may interfere with proper absorption, either by coating the digestive tract or reacting with the product being taken. Fluid temperature is a critical element. Heat can destroy or interfere with products being taken. Amino acids can be destroyed by heat.

Take amino acids on an empty stomach. Food proteins are in direct competition with amino acids. Additionally, the presence of food causes digestive acids to be secreted that can destroy amino acids. Spreading amino acid consumption throughout the day will reduce amino acid competition and increase the likelihood of greater absorption. Include vitamins when taking amino acids. Vitamins are involved in the transport and metabolism of amino acids.

The normal diet has shortages in micro- and macronutrients. The chain of events starts with the soil and progresses through planting, watering and fertilizing, harvesting, storing, delivering, purchasing, and cooking, all adding up to a negative. A summary of the studies cited by Ward and Ward (1997) found that a cross section of foods eaten in a normal diet will not provide adequate vitamins and minerals, that faulty diets along with not getting enough vitamins and minerals are factors that contribute to many diseases, and that animal studies positively relate higher RDA amounts of vitamin and mineral intake to increased longevity.

Therefore it is important to supplement your diet. These supplements have a reasonable scientific basis for use in supporting health, fitness, and athletic performance: multivitamins and minerals; antioxidant complex vitamins (A, C, and E); creatine; the branch chain amino acids (BCAA) leucine, isoleucine, and valine; echinacea (herb), which enhances immune function; glucosamine for joint support; and Performance Optimizer System® (POS, nutritional system produced by AdvoCare®)—POS 1 (supports postworkout recovery, muscle regeneration, and hormone support), POS 2 (supports total body performance and recovery with special focus on muscle growth and minimization of muscle damage), POS 3 (supports rehydration, immune system, electrolyte uptake, and replacement; supplies carbohydrates, antioxidants, and energy system facilitators), POS 4 (supports performance, energy capacity, and building, repairing, and remodeling of muscle tissue), and POS 5 (supports performance, recovery from workouts, and muscle growth; promotes loss of fat).

The branch chain amino acids (BCAA) leucine, isoleucine, and valine are important in glutamine synthesis and can serve as a source of fuel. However, tissue cells can convert all proteins into Krebs cycle intermediates.

Creatine supplementation can improve structure and function. Creatine has improved performance in explosive sports by facilitating the regeneration of ATP, reducing lactic acid in the cells, and increasing muscle mass. Short-term power output closely parallels the recovery curve for creatine phosphate resynthesis after dynamic and isometric exercise. Therefore, creatine may have benefits for all sports but is especially important for anaerobic athletes. Other studies have indicated the following benefits of creatine: improved performance capacity, increased training volume, increased intramuscular creatine stores, increased phosphocreatine stores, and greater gains in strength and muscle mass. These findings suggest that athletes can endure greater training volumes and will have greater adaptation to exercise.

It's important to take supplements that reduce oxidative stress. Oxygen is a two-edged sword: On the one hand it plays a role in energy production in the mitochondria; on the other hand 2 to 5 percent of the oxygen forms free radicals such as superoxide, hydrogen peroxide, and hydroxyl radicals. Stress from exercise and the environment produces these free radicals (highly reactive molecules or molecular fragments that contain at least one unpaired electron in their outer orbitals, or valence shells; McArdle, Katch, and Katch 1996). Free radicals can damage or destroy the body's cells. Consequently, they interfere with normal cell function and affect the rate at which we age.

Subduhi and associates (2001) state that more than 60 diseases can be traced back to free radicals. The sum of all the negatives has a big effect on athletic performance.

The defense against free radicals is to remove their environment sources and to take supplements that are known to control them. A good way to nutritionally combat free radicals is to take an array of antioxidant scavengers such as the enzymes catalase, glutathione peroxidase, and superoxide dismutase; vitamins A, C, and E; and beta-carotene, a precursor to vitamin A.

Along with understanding why to take supplements and which supplements to take, it is important to understand the mechanisms by which ergogenic aids act. Aids such as caffeine, choline, amphetamines, and alcohol initially act as a central or peripheral stimulant to the nervous system. Carbohydrate, creatine, carnitine, and chromium increase the storage or availability of a limiting substrate. Glucose and medium-chain triglycerides act as a supplemental fuel source. Sodium bicarbonate, citrate, pangamic acid, and phosphate reduce or neutralize performance-inhibiting metabolic by-products. High-glycemic carbohydrates and water facilitate recovery.

Recovery Support

Rapid recovery from the effects of a hard workout or the accumulation of many workouts and additional stresses may require the use of other technologies. Athletic training has been a necessary part of sports for a long time. The oasis of recovery has grown to include such modalities as flotation tanks, hyperbaric chambers, and various other high-tech pieces of equipment in some advanced programs. To stay ahead or just to stay even, it is necessary to keep an open mind about new ways of improving recovery.

For example, chiropractic care can assist in recovery. Chiropractic and sports medicine could actually be classified as close cousins. They both essentially deal with and focus on optimum performance. In chiropractic, the belief is quite simply that the body has an innate intelligence to heal itself. Removing various interferences such as fixations or subluxations that can impede normal nerve flow and restrict normal biomechanics gives the body the ability to operate at its optimum potential. By introducing nutrition and various soft tissue techniques, we can help the body reach its maximum capabilities.

Sports medicine basically deals with the science of athletic performance. It not only encompasses training techniques and supplementation that can expand the body's physical limitations and capabilities, but it also concerns itself with injury prevention and rehabilitation.

Chiropractic and sports medicine have become even more intertwined in recent years. Most professional sports teams now either employ a chiropractor on staff or have one the athletes can work with. The chiropractor's knowledge of biomechanics as well as nutrition and healing can make him an important member of any team. For example, Dr. Jeffrey Spencer, MA, DC, CCSP, was a member of the medical team for Lance Armstrong and the U.S. Postal Team. It was his job to ensure that the cyclists were not only mechanically sound in their movement patterns but also nutritionally sound.

Several specific soft tissue techniques have also been designed by chiropractors and used widely in the athletic community. Active Release Technique (ART®) is a unique and highly effective approach to dealing with soft tissue injuries. Dr. Michael Leahy, a chiropractor based in Colorado Springs, developed ART. He has worked with various professional and Olympic athletes throughout the world. In fact, the technique has been so effective that Ironman organizers have requested the presence of ART practitioners at all of their events.

Besides focusing on achieving normal mechanics and movement patterns for a particular joint, rehab and support of that joint are a critical part of the sport chiropractor's job. One such technique developed by Tim Brown, a chiropractor in Newport Beach, is called specific proprioceptive response taping (SPRT). The objective of SPRT is to dynamically support injured soft tissue structures with taping materials applied to the skin in anatomically correct locations. Providing specific compression, approximation, support, and balance is of paramount importance for proprioceptive stimulation. The intent of this technique is to limit contraindicated symptoms from provoking movement of the injured tissue and to encourage nonpathological movements that enhance the physiological pump and diminish adverse compensatory reaction to the injury while providing protection via enhanced kinesthetic awareness feedback.

These are just a few examples of how chiropractic has provided the athletic community with recovery techniques that help get the athlete back to maximum efficiency. The increasing demand for chiropractic care by athletes, teams, and organizations is a reflection of the important role it has played in sport. The use of chiropractic will more than likely continue to grow in the future as the benefits are realized and documented. This is already evident by the establishment of various organizations such as the American Board of Chiropractic Sports Physicians. The group conducts symposiums throughout the year designed to keep doctors up to date on the latest research and findings in sports medicine. The board includes chiropractors, physical therapists, and medical and orthopedic doctors in its membership.

To find a chiropractor, especially one who is sport-minded and schooled in the soft tissue technique ART, contact www.activerelease.com. If you have any specific questions on chiropractic, you can contact Dr. Sam Symmank at www.sportsscience.com.

Sport massage can enhance performance and speed workout and injury recovery. The following information on myofascial sports massage was provided by Gary L. Buhler, RMT, MTI, of the North Texas Massage Institute, 1310 S. Stemmons Frwy., Lewisville, TX 75067; (214) 808-3315; crisbuhler26@msn.com or www.sportsscience.com.

An essential element of overall body condition is proper muscle health. Therefore, an assessment by a qualified myofascial sports massage therapist can be of significant value. A thorough examination will reveal the athlete's present condition. The examination will reveal the effects of any prior muscle and joint injuries and an assessment can be made as to how these injuries can affect present and future performance. A determination can be made as to what level of recovery in performance can be expected.

When an athlete experiences an injury, it triggers a chain of events that must be handled with care and caution. Muscle strains, sprains, spasms, tears, and corrective surgeries can lead to the development of adhesions and/or scar tissue. A return to active duty before proper muscle healing takes place can lead to joint pain, pain with loss of range of motion, pain at rest, or pain during activity. These conditions can be a factor in repetitive stress injury and general deterioration of muscle function. Overall performance may begin to fall off. Certain movements become difficult or impossible to perform. Muscle strength imbalance and compensation in other muscle groups begin to appear with new pain developing in other areas of the body.

There is no such thing as an anatomically perfect person. Sometimes gene deficiency can cause or contribute to muscle imbalances. Sports massage therapy can begin to address these muscle imbalances and return apparent lost range of motion or restore inherent muscle strength.

Scar tissue and adhesions from previous injuries and surgery can significantly restrict proper muscle function. Scar tissue is quite rigid and will cause varying degrees of range of motion loss. Myofascial sports massage therapy performed by a properly trained massage therapist can begin to mobilize surrounding muscle and corrective tissues. Blood flow will increase to the affected areas and begin breaking down developed adhesions and softening scar tissue. This specialized therapy needs to be done on an ongoing basis. Scar tissue is permanent and needs regular and consistent manipulation to restore vital range of motion.

Myofascial sports therapy can lead to shorter recovery time from injury or workouts. Increasing blood flow alone goes a long way toward quicker recovery times. A recovering athlete often experiences extreme muscle soreness or fatigue between workouts. Muscle by-product buildup is usually at fault. The overtrained athlete will experience a toxin buildup in his muscles. This can be a dangerous condition. With this buildup comes the beginning formation of adhesions, a potential for future muscle breakdown and injury. Myofascial sports massage can help reduce this buildup and help restore peak performance conditions.

Specialized sports massage therapy should be performed daily. An athlete will benefit greatly by having his muscles warmed up prior to daily training and specifically on game day. Posttraining massage will increase muscle recovery by reducing muscle by-product buildup. When athletes follow this program they will begin to see an increase in overall peak performance.

Every athlete will benefit from weekly corrective muscle therapy. This will allow the therapist to address existing muscle problems and catch hidden trouble areas before they become problematic. An additional benefit to the athlete is an increased overall sense of well-being. Regular massage therapy will make him sharper on game day.

Cryotherapy (ice), thermotherapy (sauna, steam baths, spa), and hydrotherapy (either hot or cold) can be used to accelerate recovery. Charlie Francis (1992), a Canadian sprint coach, maximizes the use of all regenerative techniques. He gives the following four reasons for using regenerative techniques as a major part of his training program:

+ Continuous management of muscle tension and muscle spasm
+ Accelerated removal of the effects of fatigue
+ Rapid restoration of body energy systems and energy substrate
+ Improved ability to renew physical activity without wasting the energy of the athlete

Rest and Relaxation

An athlete needs sufficient sleep, naps, and rest between practices. Adequate sleep is essential for an athlete in training. During 8 to 10 hours of sound sleep, the body builds, repairs, and remodels itself. Hormone levels increase during sleep to orchestrate the recovery process. If you don't get an adequate amount of sleep, your recovery will not be sufficient, and over time, lack of sleep will reduce performance.

In order to get a good night's sleep, the environment must be free of distracting stimuli. Develop patterns that support falling asleep. Consistent environmental conditions of the sleeping room, bedtime, and duration of sleep are three very important elements that you can control. Another important factor under your control is the positive effects of moderate exercise and fitness level on sleep.

Rest between workouts or the proper spacing of workouts is necessary to achieve improvement. It takes approximately 24 to 48 hours to remove the by-products of exercise and replenish energy stores in the muscles and liver.

Stress control is also important. Control stress to achieve superadaptation. According to Seiver (1996), light and sound stimulation can be used to manage stress. When the athlete adds preparation and competition stressors to societal stressors, it creates a greater need to focus on recovery. Consequently, not including mental recovery would exclude a major contributor to achieving the superadapted state. The more you push the pedal to the metal, the higher the RPMs and the more time you will spend in the red zone. Red zone workouts require red zone recovery. Otherwise, optimal control over stress associated with peak performance and distractibility, impulsiveness, hyperactivity, anxiety, and inadequate recovery will result in poor performance.

It is valuable to employ relaxation techniques in a recovery program. High arousal can draw on energy levels, and relaxation techniques that keep athletes in the zone conserve energy.

Chapter 9

SPRINT-ASSISTED TRAINING

Sprint-assisted training is one of the most demanding phases of a sports speed improvement program. This phase is also the most fun. You will experience the feeling of raw power and be amazed at the results as you sprint at high speeds, often as fast or faster than NFL halfbacks, MLB leading base stealers, or pro soccer and NBA speedsters.

Neuromuscular Training

World-class sprinters have a stride rate of about 4.5 (females) to 5 (males) steps per second. Women sprint the 100-meter dash about .6 to .8 second slower than males mainly because of slower stride rates and differences in strength and power. Children take faster steps than adults. As height and leg length increase, stride rate decreases.

There is no real advantage to having short or long legs. Long legs do allow a longer stride but a slower stride rate. Short legs result in a faster stride rate and shorter strides. It takes a lot more strength, power, and energy to move long legs through the complete cycle in sprinting than it does shorter legs. Studies show that the ability to take fast steps is not so common in young athletes. Among 13- to 14-year-old students, only 15 had high stride rates. Only 10 youngsters in 100 had a very short down time (the support phase when one foot is contacting the ground).

The main purpose of sprint-assisted training is to increase stride rate by forcing you to perform at a much higher level than you are capable of without assistance. Sprint-assisted training produces this effect on the neuromuscular system by getting the nervous and muscular systems used to higher contraction rates. A neurosurgeon speaking at the national convention of the National Association of Speed and Explosion (NASE) put it in layman's terms: "After several weeks of sprint-assisted training, the nervous system allows you to continue these higher rates without any help. As a result, you can now take those faster and longer steps without any assistance."

Although this statement is only theory, research shows that the number of steps taken per second and stride length will improve after four to eight weeks of sprint-assisted training. This improvement is attributed to neuromuscular adaptation to the forced higher speeds and longer steps (the neuron recruitment level increases) and, after several months of continued training, to conversion of the intermediate fast-twitch red fibers (type IIa) to fast-twitch white fibers (type IIb). Researchers at Lisle confirm the value of sprint-assisted training (Jakalski 2000):

> At Lisle we have done quite a bit of research on the effects of sprint-assisted training and are convinced that two things occur when athletes are sprint-assisted. First the towing procedure lights up the central nervous system, bringing into play great numbers of neurons. Second it makes the legs more responsive to ground reaction. By lighting up the central nervous system, I mean the towing alters the timing of the nervous system to the effector muscles. In other words, towing creates some anticipatory firing, and this kind of firing enhances intramuscular coordination. In terms of ground reaction response, we theorize that the increase in horizontal momentum resulting from towing alters the capacity of joint stabilization at the ankle and knee, thereby allowing for a greater transmission of force. (p. 95)

The proportion of fast-twitch muscle fibers can be increased by sprint-assisted and speed-strength training. Intermediate fast-twitch red fibers (type IIa) can be converted to fast-twitch white fibers (type IIb). The end result is an increase in stride rate and speed over short distances.

Electronic timing has shown that sprinters who perform repeated 30- and 60-meter fly or block starts after two or three repetitions of 30- to 60-meter assisted sprints run their unassisted sprints noticeably faster. This enhanced performance window remains open for a short time only; levels drop back to normal in 5 to 10 minutes. Using two or three towing repetitions as a warm-up immediately before the 40-yard dash test may improve times for some team sport athletes. It is well worth the effort to test this phenomena to see if it enhances your 40-yard dash time.

Guidelines for Sprint-Assisted Training

To receive maximum results, use sprint-assisted training correctly. Adhere to these guidelines for each of the four sprint-assisted training methods discussed in this chapter:

✦ Obtain a solid conditioning base of speed endurance training and weight training before beginning a sprint-assisted program.

✦ Warm up thoroughly before any type of sprint-assisted training. Begin every workout with a general warm-up routine to increase core temperature. Use the large muscle groups first with a slow jog for 400 to 800 meters, followed by a faster jog and three-quarter-speed striding for an additional 400 meters or more. When you are perspiring freely, stop and complete the stretching routine presented in chapter 3 for 8 to 10 minutes. You are now ready for the walk-jog-stride-sprint cycle (walk 15 steps, slow jog 15 steps, stride 15 steps at three-quarter speed, and sprint 15 steps); continue this cycle for 400 meters or until you feel prepared to execute your all-out sprint-assisted training sprints.

✦ Sprint-assisted training is an advanced program designed for athletes who have a stable motor pattern of correct sprinting technique. Form errors by those with poor sprinting mechanics are likely to be exaggerated by sprint-assisted training. Take sprint-assisted training seriously, and pay attention to the specific suggestions for each method to avoid muscle or equipment-related injuries that may occur from horseplay or carelessness.

✦ Perform sprint-assisted training only on a soft grassy area. Inspect the surface for broken glass and other objects.

✦ Apply the concept of "work fast to be fast." Since fast-twitch muscle fibers have a high firing threshold, training must include work at high intensity levels.

✦ Expect to experience muscle soreness one or two days after your first sprint-assisted training session. Sprint-assisted training is demanding and will recruit motor units and muscle fibers that you are not accustomed to using. Even if you have been involved in some form of sprint training for several weeks, you can still expect to experience considerable soreness. This soreness is an excellent sign that sprint-assisted training is going beyond your normal training routine.

✦ Use sprint-assisted training at the beginning of your workout, immediately after your general warm-up and stretching. You can take long ultra-fast strides only when you are free from fatigue. Avoid any type of sprint-assisted training after you are fatigued from drills, calisthenics, scrimmages, speed endurance training, weight training, or plyometrics.

✦ Remember, you are trying to take faster and longer steps than ever before, not improve your conditioning level for short sprints (see the speed endurance discussion in chapter 7). Take advantage of the entire rest period specified between each repetition, and make certain you are fully recovered before completing the next sprint-assisted training sprint.

✦ Emphasize quality form in all repetitions. If you are sprinting out of control, the pull must be reduced on subsequent repetitions to allow you to complete the run with perfect form. For maximum results, it is important to stay within the 10 percent zone on all repetitions. The most effective training of the neuromuscular system for speed improvement occurs when your sprint-assisted training program forces you to run no more than 10 percent faster than your unaided maximum speed. If you can run an unassisted 40-yard dash in 4.8 seconds, your sprint-assisted towing time must be in the 4.56 (5 percent) to

4.32 (10 percent) range. Faster pulls produce longer ground-contact time due to a braking action to avoid stumbling or falling, forming habits that have a negative impact on forward movement and are difficult to correct.

✦ After sprinting with the assistance of a pull or decline, try to maintain the high speed for another 10 meters without assistance.

✦ Be patient and progress slowly from one-half- to three-quarter- to maximum-speed runs over a period of two to three weeks.

Types of Sprint-Assisted Training

The four basic methods of sprint-assisted training are downhill sprinting; high-speed cycling; towing with surgical tubing, pulley devices, and the Sprint Master®; and high-speed treadmill sprint training. Not every method is equally effective. Some are also less costly and more practical than others. Read this section carefully and decide how you want to proceed. Table 9.1 describes the advantages and limitations of each sprint-assisted training technique.

Sprint-assisted training has been shown to efficiently and naturally increase both stride rate and length. Athletes have also improved 40-yard dash times by as much as .6 second during an 8- to 12-week period. Track athletes in the 100-meter dash have improved times by more than .8 second. Keep in mind that such improvement won't happen overnight. Neuromuscular training takes time, so stay with the program a minimum of 8 weeks. Eventually, you will move to an ongoing maintenance program of one or two workouts per week to avoid losing acquired gains.

Combining sprint-assisted training with sport loading (sprint-resisted) and finishing the workout with regular maximum effort sprints is a form of contrast training that targets neuromotor patterns and helps improve speed.

Table 9.1   **Comparison of Six Sprint-Assisted Training Programs**

Method	Cost	Advantages	Disadvantages	Effectiveness
Downhill sprinting	$0	Practical. Only slight chance of injury from falls or muscle pulls. Easy to reduce pace and stop if balance is lost.	Does not provide as much assistance. Less increase in stride rate and stride length than some other methods. Difficult to find proper slope.	Good. Will increase stride rate, stride length, and sprinting speed.

(continued)

Table 9.1

(continued)

Method	Cost	Advantages	Disadvantages	Effectiveness
High-speed stationary cycling	$500 to 1,200	Can be performed at home, at the gym, or outside on a road bike. Wind resistance and gravity eliminated to permit higher leg turnover than in sprinting.	Rather unproved. Increased rate of leg movement per second on the cycle should help increase stride rates in sprinting.	Fair. Focuses on leg turnover. More cycling research needed. Should be used with another method.
Towing (tubing)	$35 to 99	Inexpensive. Allows you to train alone safely indoors. Provides excellent controllable pull. Two tubings can be used to provide larger athletes with considerable pull.	Falls may occur. No bailout since tubing is fastened at the waist. Tubing occasionally breaks or comes loose at the belt.	Excellent. Increases stride rate, stride length, and speed in short distances.
Sprint Master	$2,500 or more	Operator controls the pull and can back off if form is broken or athlete stumbles. Athlete can bail out by merely releasing the grip.	Very expensive. Not practical for group sessions because of time requirement. Only one athlete can train at a time.	Excellent. Same as for towing.
High-speed treadmill sprinting	$8,000 to 15,000	Can be performed inside. Elicits very high stride rates. You can grab guard rails or allow safety belt to protect you if you lose your balance.	Very expensive. Requires use of spotting belt, an assistant, and time to learn how to step on and off at very high speeds (greyhound effect).	Excellent. Produces high stride rates and a long stride. Increases speed over short distances.
Ultra Speed Pacer	$100 to 150	Can be performed inside. Capable of producing high stride rates. Inexpensive.	More difficult to conduct group sessions indoors or outdoors. Expensive for the simple technology. Cannot perform sport-specific drills like surgical tubing.	Excellent. Produces high stride rates. Contains a bailout system if balance is lost or the pull is too great.

Downhill Sprinting

Downhill sprinting is one of the safest, most practical forms of sprint-assisted training and requires no special equipment. The trick is to find the proper slope and distance. Try to locate a 50-yard area with a slope no greater than 1 percent. Consult your coach for suggestions. A 1- to 2.5-degree slope will keep you within the 10-percent zone and avoid a braking effect, incorrect form, increased ground contact, and falling, which are much more likely to occur with higher slopes. The ideal area will allow you to sprint 20 yards on a perfectly flat surface (to accelerate to near-maximum speed), sprint down a 15-yard 1-degree slope (to force higher than normal stride length, stride rate, and speed), and then end by sprinting 15 yards on a flat area (to allow you to attempt to maintain the higher speed rates without the assistance of gravity). The crown on a football field is close to a 1 percent grade and can be used for both sprint-assisted training and sport loading by sprinting from one sideline of the field to the crown, up the slope, and down the other side at high speed to the opposite sideline. Combined downhill-uphill sprinting has been shown to force runners to take more steps per second than flat-surface sprinting.

Table 9.2 shows a sample eight-week program that incorporates downhill sprinting, surgical tubing, the Ultra Speed Pacer®, and the Sprint Master. Unless you have a solid conditioning foundation, avoid sprint-assisted training until after completing the first three weeks of a speed endurance training program (chapter 7), which will prepare you for the high-speed stride rates and stride length experienced in this part of a speed improvement program.

The first two weeks (four workouts) will help you adjust to the use of surgical tubing, to other towing devices, to downhill sprinting, and to the pulling action as you maintain proper sprinting form at all times. Do not exceed a three-quarter-speed striding action in any of the first four workouts. The sprint-assisted distance represents the distance towed or the actual downhill distance covered and does not include the 20- to 25-yard distance used to accelerate to maximum speed or the final 10-yard sprint without assistance at the end of each repetition.

Because of the assisted action of the pull, starting with week three you will be sprinting at submaximal speed in each workout. Although the preconditioning period has prepared you for this training, you can expect to experience muscle soreness the first five to seven days of sprint-assisted training. The distance covered should reflect the average distance sprinted in your sport (see table 7.3, page 151). Keep in mind that sprint-assisted training is NOT a conditioning activity and that full recovery between each repetition is important.

Carefully examine the grounds of your school, university, park, or neighborhood, looking for soccer and football fields and other grassy areas, or ask your coach to consider building an area specifically for downhill sprint training. Once you find a suitable place to train, follow the program shown in table 9.2; pay attention to the recovery period between each repetition.

Table 9.2

Week	Workout	Overspeed distance[a]	Repetitions	Rest interval
1	1	1/2-speed runs toward the pull for 15 yd., emphasizing correct sprinting form	5	1 min.
		1/2-speed backward runs toward the pull for 20 yd.	3	1 min.
1	2	3/4-speed runs for 20 yd. with perfect sprinting form	5	2 min.
		3/4-speed backward runs toward the pull for 20 yd.	3	2 min.
2	3	3/4-speed runs for 25 yd.	5	2 min.
		3/4-speed backward runs toward the pull for 25 yd.	3	2 min.
		3/4-speed turn-and-runs at a 45-degree angle for 25 yd. (left and right)	3	2 min.
2	4	Same as workout 3		
3	5	3/4-speed runs toward the pull for 15 yd.	3	2 min.
		Maximum-speed sprints toward the pull for 15 yd.	5	2 min.
3	6	3/4-speed runs for 20 yd.	3	2 min.
		Maximum-speed sprints for 20 yd.	6	2.5 min.
4	7	3/4-speed runs for 25 yd.	3	2 min.
		Maximum-speed sprints for 25 yd.	6	3 min.
4	8	3/4-speed sprints for 30 yd.	3	2 min.
		Maximum-speed sprints for 30 yd.	6	3 min.
5	9	3/4-speed runs toward the pull for 15 yd.	3	1 min.
		Quick feet, short step, low knee lift sprint for 15 yd. with rapid arm-pumping action	3	2 min.
		Quick feet, short step, high knee lift sprint for 15 yd. with rapid arm-pumping action	3	2 min.
		Maximum-speed pulls for 30 yd.	4	3 min.
5	10	Same as workout 9		
6	11	High-speed stationary cycling. With the resistance on low to average, warm up for 5 to 7 min. until you perspire freely. Pedal at 3/4 speed for 30 sec.	3	1 min.
		Pedal at maximum speed for 2 sec. as you say "one thousand and one, one thousand and two"	7	2 min.
		Pedal at maximum speed for 3 sec. as you say "one thousand and one, one thousand and two, one thousand and three"	3	2 min.
		Pedal at maximumspeed for 5 sec.	6	2.5 min.

Week	Workout	Overspeed distance[a]	Repetitions	Rest interval
6	12	Same as workout 11		
7	13	Repeat workout 11		
		Two-man pull-and-resist drill for 100 yd.	2	4 min.
		Maximum-speed sprints for 25 yd.	6	3 min.
7	14	Same as workout 11		
8	15	3/4-speed runs toward the pull for 15 yd.	3	1 min.
		Quick feet, short step, low knee lift sprint for 15 yd. with rapid arm-pumping action	5	2 min.
		Quick feet, short step, high knee lift sprint for 15 yd. with rapid arm-pumping action	5	2 min.
		Maximum-speed pulls for 30 yd.	5	3 min.
8	16	Maintenance program		
		3/4-speed runs toward the pull for 15 yd.	2	2 min.
		Quick feet, short step, high knee lift sprint for 15 yd. with rapid arm-pumping action	2	2 min.
		Maximum-speed pull forward for 20 yd., plant right foot and sprint diagonally left for 20 yd. Repeat, planting the left foot and sprinting diagonally right for 20 yd.	3	2 min.
		Maximum-speed pulls forward for 30 yd.	3	2 min.

[a]Overspeed distance is the actual yards you are being towed or sprinting downhill after reaching maximum speed.

High-Speed Stationary Cycling

During high-speed cycling, wind resistance, gravity, and body weight are eliminated to allow you to complete more revolutions per second (similar to steps in sprinting) than you are capable of completing during the sprinting action. This sprint-assisted training technique should be used with one other method, such as towing or downhill sprinting, to guarantee success of increasing stride rate and length. Preliminary evidence indicates that high-speed cycling programs may increase stride rate in sprinting. A sample program is described in table 9.3.

A tapering off period of about 5 to 10 seconds occurs after each sprint-assisted pedaling repetition. This tapering off period returns you to a slow cadence in preparation for the next repetition. Do not stop pedaling. Continue in the slow cadence of about 25 to 30 revolutions per minute while in the two-minute recovery period.

Cycling can be performed indoors using a stationary cycle or outdoors using a 10- to 30-speed racing bicycle that allows you to use the lower gears and low-resistance pedaling. As speed increases, a higher gear will be needed to complete the sprint-assisted phase.

Table 9.3   **Eight-Week High-Speed Cycling Program**

Week	Workout	Repetitions	Acceleration time (sec.)	Pedaling speed	Overspeed time[a] (sec.)	Rest (min.)
1	1	2	1.5 to 2.0	1/2	1.0 to 1.5	2
	2	3	Same	Same	Same	2
2	3	3	1.5 to 2.0	3/4	1.0 to 1.5	2
	4	3	Same	Same	Same	2
3	5	4	2.0 to 2.5	9/10	1.5 to 2.0	2
	6	4	Same	Same	Same	2
4	7	5	2.5 to 3.0	Maximum	1.5 to 2.0	2
	8	5	Same	Same	Same	2
5	9	6	2.5 to 3.0	Maximum	1.5 to 2.0	2
	10	6	Same	Same	Same	2
6	11	7	2.5 to 3.0	Maximum	2.0	2
	12	7	Same	Same	Same	2
7	13	8	2.5 to 3.0	Maximum	2.0	2
	14	8	Same	Same	Same	2
8	15	9	2.5 to 3.0	Maximum	2.0 to 2.5	2
	16	9	Same	Same	Same	2

[a]Overspeed time is the actual time you are pedaling at high speeds.

Towing

Towing, or pulling, athletes to sprint faster is not new. Before the use of surgical tubing and two-person pulleys, outdated methods such as motor scooters, motorcycles, and even cars were used. In 1956, Olympic medal winner Al Lawrence trained by holding a rigid bar attached to a car four times per week for 100 to 600 yards. In the 1960s, towing was successfully used in Australia to reduce the 100-meter time of one subject who held to the side of a tram car. Young sprinters increased stride length considerably (an average of six inches) and improved 100-yard dash time from an average of 10.5 to 9.9 seconds. In 1976, a four-station tow bar attached to an automobile was used to improve 40-yard dash times with a flying start. Towing has also been a regular part of our annual speed camps since 1970, and sprint-assisted training has been an important part of our training programs to improve 40-yard dash times for team sports.

Towing produces higher stride rates and increases stride length more effectively than downhill sprinting and high-speed cycling. Towing to force runners to take more steps than would otherwise be possible has improved stride rate and 40-yard dash times by more than .6 second. It also will improve your 20-, 30-, 40-, or 60-yard dash time more than most other sprint-assisted training techniques. You can choose from three methods: towing with surgical tubing, towing with the Ultra Speed Pacer, or towing with the Sprint Master, if available.

Surgical Tubing

Surgical tubing can force you to take faster and longer steps and complete a 40-yard dash at world-record speed simply by providing you with a slight pull throughout the high-speed portion of your sprint. A 20- to 25-foot piece of elastic tubing is attached to your waist by a belt. The opposite end can be attached to another athlete or to a stationary object such as a tree or a goal post to allow you to work out alone. Back up to stretch the tubing 15 yards (about 25 yards total from your partner or the stationary object); run at three-quarter speed with the pull until you learn to adjust by keeping your balance and using proper sprinting form. After four or five practice runs, you should be ready for the full ride.

Once you are accustomed to the tubing, back up until you are approximately 30 to 35 yards from your partner or the stationary object before sprinting at high speed with the pull. Most good surgical tubing will safely stretch to six times its unstretched length (20 feet × 6 = 120 feet, or 40 yards). Avoid stretching the tubing beyond this recommended limit. You also can make stationary runs from a three-point or track start. Athletes in our speed clinics and camps have completed 40-yard dashes in less than 3.9 seconds when being pulled with surgical tubing. Remember to apply the 10 percent rule to each athlete.

Surgical tubing allows you to train any time with or without a partner. You can use a number of different drills:

✦ Attach one end of the tubing to a goal post and the other to your waist with the tubing tied in front. Stretch the tubing by walking backward about 20 yards. Jog forward toward the goal post with the pull. Repeat four times, two with a three-quarter-speed run and two with a full-speed sprint. Within the next three sprints, back up an extra 5 to 8 yards each time to increase the pull and the speed of your sprint.

✦ Repeat the previous drill, emphasizing a high knee lift.

✦ At the close of the session, complete four or five all-out sprints using the exact rest interval recommended for your sport in table 7.3 (page 151). Allow the tubing to pull you at no more than .5 second faster than your best 40-yard dash time. It takes only a slight pull to produce this effect, and pulls that produce more than a 10 percent improvement in your 40-yard time are dangerous and counterproductive. Place two markers 40 yards apart and have someone time you as you are being towed.

✦ For athletes who are required to do so in their sport (defensive backs in football; basketball, baseball, field hockey, lacrosse, rugby, soccer, and tennis players), repeat the preceding drills by sprinting backward or sideways. Turn your belt around to the center of your back or to your hip.

✦ Choose a faster athlete and race him while you are being towed. You will be amazed at how fast you are sprinting. You also will win the race.

✦ Do the quick feet drill by measuring one of your strides before placing 20 sticks at a distance two to three feet shorter than your normal stride. Repeat the first drill described in this section, emphasizing rapid stride frequency.

✦ Complete the two-person drill by attaching one end of the tubing to your waist and the other to your partner's back. Have your partner sprint 25 to 30 yards ahead against the resistance and then stop. You now sprint toward your partner in a sprint-assisted training run. Continue for two or three more repetitions before reversing the position of the belt. You are now sprinting against resistance (sport loading), and your partner is sprinting with assistance (sprint-assisted training). This drill should be the last drill in your sprint-assisted training workout because it does not allow adequate time between each sprint to fully recover.

Follow the sprint-assisted training program in table 9.2 (page 190) two or three times per week (every other day) during the preseason and one or two times per week during the season.

Surgical tubing can be dangerous and requires adequate supervision at all times. Tubing can break if stretched too far. Belts can come loose if they are carelessly fastened. Too much pull can produce falls, soft tissue injuries, braking, increased ground-contact time, and inappropriate loading of the nervous system. Runners can get tangled at the end of the run as the tubing returns to its unstretched length. You can greatly reduce the risk of injury and other undesirable effects by carefully following these tips:

✦ Make certain the tubing is tied securely to the belt. After tubing is used a few times, the knots will tighten. Newly tied belts must be inspected before each run. After putting on the belt, there will be an extra length of leftover belt (the tail). It is important to wrap the tail around your waist, then thread it again through the loop formed before pulling securely to form a knot. This process should be repeated until most of the leftover belt is used.

✦ Inspect the tubing on the first run, by letting it slide through your hand as you back up, to locate any nicks or rough marks. If a nick is detected, discard and replace with new tubing.

✦ Avoid stretching the tubing more than six times its unstretched length.

✦ Inspect the knots on both belts and retie them if they are not tight or appear to be coming loose.

✦ Avoid standing with the tubing fully stretched for more than a few seconds. During this stretched phase, knots come loose and tubing breaks.

✦ If you must assume a three-point stance with the tubing fully stretched (e.g., at the start of a test), protect your face and avoid staying in the set position for more than .5 second. If the opposite end comes lose, it could recoil into your face.

✦ Use tubing that attaches to a belt around your waist rather than a harness. With only slight differences in height between you and your partner, a broken tubing or a loose belt could snap upward and strike you in the eye. Tubing attached to the waist that comes loose when stretched is unlikely to produce any serious injury.

✦ Use shoes without spikes for the first several workouts until you have fully adjusted to the high speed and can complete each repetition with correct form.

✦ Use surgical tubing on soft grassy areas only.

✦ Adhere to the 10 percent rule at all times. Deny requests to use more than one tubing on athletes under 200 pounds, and never allow the use of three pieces of surgical tubing.

Ultra Speed Pacer

The Ultra Speed Pacer uses thin elastic cord and a simple pulley device that relies on leverage to produce assisted-sprinting. The pulley (fulcrum) is fastened to a fixed object in the gym or on the athletic field. Each side of the rope going through the pulley is attached to an athlete using a belt. As one athlete sprints at a 45-degree angle away from the pulley, the other athlete is forced to sprint toward the pulley while receiving considerable pull.

After a few trials, you and your partner will easily determine how fast the angle sprinter should run to increase or decrease the pull. The device has the potential to tow the athlete at a speed twice that of the outgoing runner. Since the outgoing runner controls the speed of the pull, the 10 percent stimulus window can be monitored by timing the towed runner.

The Ultra Speed Pacer provides a strong pull and produces very high stride rates, stride lengths, and sprinting speed. It has a bailout system that allows the towed athlete to slap the pulley from his waist harness and release the tension and pull. A Velcro® safety strip can also be adjusted to release if the load on the towed runner is too great.

Sprint Master

After a summer speed camp in 1981 at Virginia Commonwealth University, there was frustration over problems with the use of a motor scooter to tow athletes at high speeds. It was then that Dr. Dintiman indicated the need for a motorized device that could be attached to a wall and used indoors or outdoors to tow athletes at high, regulated speeds. John Dolan, who assisted in the speed camp, was immediately enthusiastic. He and a highly mechanical friend, Michael Watkins, constructed more than 20 prototypes before the Sprint Master was perfected.

The machine is precisely engineered to pull athletes at speeds faster than any human can sprint. It attaches to the goal posts of a football or soccer field or to a gym wall and provides controlled, variable speed for each athlete. It is a safe device that eliminates the cumbersome, dangerous use of a vehicle and allows the athlete to merely release her grip if balance is lost. The Sprint Master also allows full use of the arms while being towed at speeds of up to one second faster than the athlete's best flying 40-yard dash time. The athlete grasps the two handles and is literally reeled in by the Sprint Master.

To start a sprint-assisted program with the Sprint Master, use the workout schedule shown in table 9.2 (page 190) two or three times per week (every other day). Have your coach or friend pull you at approximately .5 second faster than your best flying 40-yard dash time. The operator quickly learns to judge pace and can group athletes of similar speed together. It is also quite simple to place two markers 40 yards apart and time athletes as they are being pulled. The set screw on the machine can then be fixed at the proper speed.

When you are being pulled, grasp the tow-rope handles and accelerate slowly for 10 to 15 yards. The Sprint Master will then exert its proper pull as you reach full speed and will continue to pull you for the recommended 20 to 25 yards; longer distances tend to produce fatigue and cause a loss of balance. Pump your arms as you would in normal sprinting instead of placing your hands and arms in front of your body and letting yourself be pulled in water-ski fashion.

Practice the art of letting go of the rope handles if you lose your balance. On an athletic field, especially in full uniform, a high-speed fall and roll is generally safe. Few runners fall at any towing speed once the operator learns the technique.

Operating the Sprint Master is easily learned and is described precisely in a brochure. Speeds can be individually determined for each athlete, and the operator can make the pull safely. Most of the towing drills described for surgical tubing cannot be used with the Sprint Master because it allows only straight-ahead sprinting at various speeds.

Treadmill Sprinting

In the Virginia Commonwealth University Laboratory, the A.R. Young high-speed treadmill (capable of speeds of 0 to 26-plus miles per hour and a 100-meter dash under 10 seconds) has been used to improve stride length, stride rate, form, speed endurance, and sprinting speed. Cinematography identified differences in stride length and rate at various speeds in both treadmill and unaided flat-surface sprinting. Form was corrected by an expert standing on a stool facing and looking downward at the subject during high-speed sprinting. The treadmill is also an excellent piece of equipment for sprint-assisted training. High-speed treadmill sprinting (up to a 9.8-second 100-meter dash) improves stride rate and speed over short distances.

Before getting on the treadmill, use a standard warm-up procedure and stretch. Use a harness that attaches to the support rails and allows free arm movement, balance, and safety. One spotter is placed on each side of the tread belt. Use a one-week acclimation period to adjust to getting on the tread belt when it's moving at high speeds and to treadmill sprinting. Because the tread belt accelerates slowly and would introduce a fatigue factor if sprinters were required to jog, stride, and sprint until higher belt speeds were reached, tread belt speeds are preset before entry. After six to eight practice attempts, sprinters can easily enter at high speeds. The so-called greyhound effect allows athletes to reach maximum speed in approximately two seconds.

The sample program shown in table 9.4 has been used in a number of experiments at Virginia Commonwealth University. The high-speed cycling program described in table 9.3 (page 192) can also be used in treadmill sprint training. Overspeed distances are converted to seconds on the treadmill (10 yards = 1.0 second; a 25-yard sprint requires 2.5 seconds on the treadmill). The number of repetitions, length of the rest interval, and progression are similar for both techniques.

Treadmill sprinting is not without its special problems; the sprinting action produces a slight slowing effect each time the foot strikes the tread belt. However, aiding factors predominate and allow a faster rate for most individuals even without training. The braking effect when each foot strikes the tread belt is greater for heavier athletes (over 200 pounds) and for athletes of all sizes in the initial stages of training. It tends to be eliminated after acclimation and form instruction. At high speeds beyond maximum (in early training sessions), the braking effect almost reduces tread belt speed to a sprinter's maximum speed. This problem is soon overcome.

Additional problems exist, however. It is difficult to determine true tread belt speed with and without a sprinter on the treadmill. In one study (Dintiman 1984), a highly accurate surface speed indicator was used to determine belt speed variations with a sprinter (a 159-pound runner and a 197-pound runner) and without a sprinter. Several findings deserve attention:

+ A heavier sprinter has a greater braking effect.
+ The percent of braking increases as tread belt speed increases for both light and heavy subjects.
+ As training progresses over several weeks, the amount of braking is reduced in both light and heavy sprinters at the higher speed rates.
+ At speeds in which the sprinter is being supported by the belt and is unable to maintain belt speed, only a normal expected braking occurs.

Table 9.4   High-Speed Treadmill Sprint Program

Purpose	Speed	Repetitions
Acclimation	90% of maximum	6 to 20 at 2-min. intervals for 10 sec.
Entry practice	75% of maximum 90% of maximum Maximum	10 to 30 for 2 sec.
Improve stride and length	1 to 2 mph and 3 to 4 mph above maximum	2 to 6 for 3 to 5 sec., allowing full recovery after each

Most of the problems of treadmill sprint training can be overcome for athletes of all sizes by using an ample number of practice sessions at various speeds (acclimation), seeing that athletes master proper sprinting form, and avoiding a tread belt speed too far beyond the subject's present maximum speed (the point at which proper sprinting form cannot be maintained). Ongoing research with high-speed treadmill sprinting continues to show improvements in stride rate and length, with this effect carried over to unassisted sprinting.

Advanced Sprint-Assisted Training Techniques

A number of effective sprint-assisted variations have been tested with athletes at the middle school, high school, university, and professional levels. These advanced methods are designed only for older, mature athletes who meet the leg strength standard (2.5 times body weight) described in chapter 2 and have completed at least four weeks of a preconditioning program that included speed endurance training. Two different types of advanced sprint-assisted training are recommended: contrast training and exaggerated stride rate and length.

Contrast training combines sprint-assisted and sprint-resisted training (sport loading) in the same workout and finishes with regular maximum-velocity, unaided sprinting repetitions. Sport-loaded towing involves the completion of two to five repetitions at high speeds with weight added to the body (one to five pounds using the weighted vest described in chapter 6). This method should be used no more than twice weekly and never in consecutive workouts. The use of contrast training on Monday and Thursday or Tuesday and Friday for six to eight weeks meets the recommended length of time for a training effect and 72 hours of rest for this type of training. Experts indicate that the nervous system is slower to recover than the cardiovascular system and suggest a longer rest period for this demanding routine.

To train using an exaggerated stride rate and length, add two to six repetitions at the end of your sprint-assisted workout and focus on fast and long strides. Use towing with a shortened stride that allows you to consciously increase stride rate as much as possible. Complete two or three more repetitions while you consciously lengthen your stride by no more than three to six inches. For each drill, place sticks or markers close together for the stride rate repetitions and three to six inches farther apart than your normal stride for the stride length pulls.

Sprint-assisted training is one of your most important training programs. All athletes can benefit from this training, regardless of their 20-, 40-, or 60-yard dash times. It is nearly impossible to reach maximum speed potential without this type of training. A six- to eight-week program can produce dramatic results.

Chapter 10

STARTING AND STOPPING

Proper starting and stopping form is a major part of quickness in team sports and must be taught through the use of sport-specific drills that closely resemble the actual movements during competition. These techniques do not occur naturally. In performing the actions of sprinting, starting, and stopping, most athletes have some faulty traits that need to be corrected or relearned. No two athletes sprint exactly the same, nor do two athletes start and stop exactly the same. There also is no perfect style that fits all body types. The key is to improve basic technique without trying to mimic the exact form of others. Learn the ideals of starting, stopping, and sprinting in theory and adapt them to your personal traits. Unless start and stop and cut form is flawless, take the time to master the techniques and drills described in this chapter, and eliminate your major errors in each area.

Correct starting, stopping, and sprinting form is important for team sport athletes and can result in significant improvement in acceleration, maximum speed, quickness, agility, and overall times in short distances.

Starting and Stopping Strength

Combining speed and strength into a training program involves three components. First is explosive strength, developing the greatest force in the shortest time frame. Second is starting strength. Third is absolute strength, the maximum amount of weight you can lift, excluding time.

Starting strength is one of the keys to speed strength and refers specifically to the power required to begin a movement, such as the initial push to initiate a sprint or the stopping or cutting action commonly used in team sports. Speed-strength training in the weight room, plyometrics, and the drills in this chapter develop starting and stopping strength. Exercises in each of these three training areas must be sport-specific in terms of the mechanics of the movement and velocity. Each drill and exercise must closely relate to the demands of the sport.

Starting From a Stationary Position

Although not all team sport athletes use three-point or four-point stationary starts during competition, timed 20- to 60-yard dashes are a key part of the evaluation process when selecting players for university scholarships or the pro draft and for making the team in the high school, university, and professional ranks. Unfortunately, team sport athletes rarely take the time to work on an

effective start and the proper way to run a short dash even though this is critical for achieving their best times in these tests. During competition, only football uses a three-point or four-point stationary start to begin play. Athletes in baseball, basketball, field hockey, lacrosse, rugby, and soccer accelerate to maximum speed from a standing stationary position, slow walk, or jog and need to develop the best preparatory posture to perform as effective a start as possible.

Because speed tests of 20 to 60 yards cover very short distances, the stationary start is critical to peak performance. The first phase to examine in the start is the stance. Choose either the three-point or four-point stance.

For the three-point stance (figure 10.1), have your stronger leg, usually the leg you jump with, in front. For most athletes, if you are right-handed, your left leg will be your stronger leg.

From a kneeling position, place the stronger foot forward so that the edges of your toes are approximately 16 to 20 inches behind the starting line. With the knee of your back leg on the ground, position it even with the ball of your front foot. Extend your right arm just behind the line, and raise your body to a position where the angle of the front leg is about 90 degrees and the angle of

Figure 10.1   Starting from a three-point stance: *(a)* ready position with stronger leg in front; *(b)* push off both legs to begin the sprint.

the rear leg is close to 135 degrees. Extend the right hand on the fingertips with the fingers far apart to provide more stability. The left arm should rest on the thigh of your left leg or in a position behind your body as if in running position. Assume a relaxed position with most of your body weight on the legs and a small amount of your weight on the extended front arm.

The power of the start comes from your legs, not your arm, so don't lean so far forward that too much weight is on your arm. If most of your body weight is on your arm, there will not be enough pressure on your legs to drive and push out properly. If there is too much pressure on your arm, you will stumble out and catch yourself before regaining balance. Drive and push out with both legs when starting; don't try to throw your arms out and forward. Your arms are just working to create proper stride length and frequency; they do not replace the power of the legs.

After the initial thrust off both feet, the rear leg leaves the ground first, followed by the drive off the front leg in a straight line from your foot through the top of your head. A good start will combine a balanced and stable position followed by correct driving and pushing with the legs. Emphasize pushing backward and downward to set the body in motion.

The four-point stance (figure 10.2) is the same as the three-point stance except both arms are extended to the ground. From a kneeling position, place your stronger leg forward with toes approximately 16 to 20 inches behind the starting line. With the knee of your back leg

Figure 10.2 Starting from a four-point stance: *(a)* ready position with both arms extended to the ground; *(b)* push off both legs to begin the sprint.

on the ground, position it even with the ball of your front foot. Extend and spread out both arms behind the starting line about shoulder-width apart. Keep your fingers spread and arms straight. Rise to a set position where the front leg is at a 90-degree angle and the back leg is at a 135-degree angle.

Keep most of the weight on your legs so that you are comfortable and balanced. The driving action will come from the legs. Keep your arms straight in the set position and do not bend at the elbows. The two key factors when starting the 40-yard dash or other short sprint are balance and the driving and pushing action. As in the three-point stance, forward momentum is created by an initial thrust off both legs before the drive off the front leg in a line through the top of your head. Emphasize pushing backward and downward with both feet to set your body in motion.

When racing the 20-, 40-, or 60-yard dash, it is important to accelerate from start to finish. Although this sounds simple or even obvious, athletes who fail to understand acceleration are cheating themselves of their best times. The scientific analysis of sprinting has proven that you cannot run at your very top speed for much more than one second. In the 20-, 40-, or 60-yard dash, most athletes believe they have to run at maximum speed over the entire distance. They also believe that if they focus on increasing stride frequency, they will run a fast time. The more efficient approach to running a 20- to 60-yard dash is to accelerate over the entire distance and through the finish in order to reach your top speed toward the end of the race. Your fastest times will be recorded when you feel yourself accelerating through the finish line.

Checklist for the Stationary Three- and Four-Point Start

Each practice repetition of the start should cover a minimum of 10 to 15 yards or 8 to 10 strides. The checklist includes important aspects a coach or training partner can look for when analyzing your three- or four-point crouched start and the acceleration phase of sprinting.

Preparatory Position

+ Relaxed position with proper foot and arm spacing
+ Body weight evenly distributed between hands, knees, and feet
+ Straight arms are shoulder-width apart
+ Head aligned with the back, relaxed neck

Set Position

+ Movement of the center of gravity above the front foot
+ Front leg bent at 90-degree angle, rear leg near 135 degrees
+ Hips slightly higher than shoulders
+ Both feet apply pressure to the ground
+ Straight arms shoulder-width apart and in front of hands

Takeoff (Starting Action)

+ Explosive thrust exerted off both the lead and rear foot
+ Rear foot leaves the ground first
+ Fast, flat forward swing of the rear leg
+ Active alternate side-arm motion

Drive (Acceleration) Phase

+ Gradual straightening of the body and lengthening of the stride
+ Landing on the balls of the feet and limited lowering of the heels
+ Head down, looking at the ground
+ Straight line forward drive, no sideways placement of feet

In the first 20 yards of a short sprint, stride length increases are easily handled by most team sport athletes. At this stage, concentration is placed on leg turnover (stride rate). As the sprint continues beyond 60 yards, athletes shift their efforts from stride rate to stride length.

Drive out of the starting position and gradually come into full running position. Don't stay low or bent at the waist during the race because this will keep you from running with correct body position. In addition, you must stay relaxed. Speed over any distance requires the athlete to be disciplined enough to relax through the entire race.

Reaching maximum speed requires training. Many sport professionals believe that running is a natural act that needs no special focus. This belief has prevented many athletes from improving performance. As you consider your training, concentrate on the principles of sprinting mechanics and your speed will improve.

Starting From a Standing Position

The standing start may be more suitable for younger athletes who do not possess the necessary strength and power to produce the forceful push off of both feet and the powerful leg action required to accelerate from a crouched position. It also may be the best choice for athletes in sports such as baseball, basketball, soccer, lacrosse, and field hockey who are forced to use a type of standing start during competition. Others who are unaccustomed to a crouched start or who have not taken the time to master the technique will also benefit from the standing start.

The errors of an improper crouched start result in poor times. The standing start is easier to learn, places the lead foot closer to the starting line, is more forgiving if executed improperly, and is likely to result in a better time than that recorded after incorrectly performing a crouched start. However, high school and college athletes should not use the standing start for the 40-yard dash or other speed tests. The fastest time will occur through the use of a perfected crouch start.

Assume a standing position with the foot of your strongest leg as close as possible to the starting line. Kneel down and place the knee of your rear leg even with the toe of your lead leg. Stand up, keeping the rear foot in that same spot, feet about shoulder-width apart; this is proper foot spacing. Bend your knees, lower your head, and lean forward with approximately two-thirds of your weight on the front foot. Experiment with straight arms or with bending both elbows to 90 degrees to see which way works best for you. The arm opposite the lead leg is in front and the arm opposite the rear leg is in back (figure 10.3a).

Push-off begins with both feet to get the body moving forward before the rear foot is lifted and the remaining push-off is performed by the lead leg. As described in the three-point and four-point start, drive out of the start and gradually come into full running position. Don't stay low or bent at the waist during the race because this will keep you from running with correct body position. The rear arm is thrust forward and the lead arm backward as you push off both feet and begin the sprinting cycle.

Checklist for the Standing Stationary Start

Preparatory Position

+ Relaxed position with proper foot spacing
+ Body weight evenly distributed on both feet
+ Arms bent at right angles and shoulder-width apart

Figure 10.3 The standing start: *(a)* ready position with knees and elbows bent; *(b)* push off with both feet.

Set Position

+ Movement of the center of gravity above the front foot
+ Front leg bent at slightly less than a 90-degree angle
+ Opposite arm of lead leg back, other arm forward
+ Arms bent at 90 degrees or straight
+ About two-thirds of weight on the lead foot
+ Both feet apply pressure to the ground

Takeoff (Starting Action)

+ Explosive thrust exerted off both the lead and rear foot
+ Rear foot leaves the ground first
+ Fast, flat forward swing of the rear leg
+ Forward thrust of the rear arm

Drive (Acceleration) Phase

+ Gradual straightening of the body and lengthening of stride
+ Landing on the balls of the feet and limited lowering of the heels
+ Head down, looking at the ground
+ Limited bending at the waist

Regardless of the type of start you choose, read and practice the tips provided in the 40-Yard Dash Clinic sidebar to improve 20-, 40-, and 60-yard dash times. You will be surprised at how much you can improve by practicing these tips.

40-Yard Dash Clinic

The timed 20-, 40-, or 60-yard dash is a very important test in team sports, yet the test is taken by athletes who know very little about proper starting techniques. The following tips can immediately improve times.

For both the crouched and standing start, place your stronger leg in front; the lead leg is responsible for about two-thirds of the velocity at the start. To identify your stronger leg, compare your scores in the single-leg press, single-leg extension, and single-leg kickback tests described in chapter 2.

A common error is to step forward with the back foot as the front foot pushes off. No track athlete would ever make this mistake. Near equal thrust off the front and back foot must be exerted to initiate the drive phase of sprinting and get out of the starting stance. The force exerted by the rear foot is about 65 to 75 percent of the force applied by the lead foot. This thrust off both feet occurs before the rear foot steps forward. To form the habit of pushing off both the lead and rear foot requires hours of concentrated practice and the use of the special drills described in this chapter. Begin by having your workout partner block both feet with his feet and tell you about the thrust you are applying on each start.

If possible, stay with the four-point track start since it makes it easier to support your forward weight. Place considerable weight on both hands in the set position without being so forward that your feet cannot exert a forceful thrust against the ground. Lean forward until your shoulders are over the line, keeping your right knee on the ground. It is easier to hold your weight over the line with one knee on the ground until you move to the set position.

Rise up slowly. Maintain the set position (keeping your shoulders over the starting line) only a very short time to reduce the strain on your hands. Unlike the start of the 100-meter dash in track, the start of the clock in team sports occurs on your first noticeable movement forward, and the set position with extra weight forward needs to be held for only one- to two-tenths of a second rather than one to two seconds. Eyes should be fixed on the running surface as you keep your head down and lean forward for the start and drive (acceleration) phase of your sprint. Wear spiked shoes to improve push-off power if permitted to do so.

If you are being tested on natural turf, dig two small holes in the ground to increase your traction during the push-off, or have a friend block your feet with her feet while standing behind you.

Use vigorous, smooth arm movements for the first 10 yards. Continue to work the arms hard throughout the sprint. To sprint fast, you must concentrate on sprinting fast; it does not occur automatically. Stay low for the first 8 to 12 yards with your head slightly down in a natural position. Sprint 5 to 8 yards past the finish line.

If you get a bad start, are having a bad run, or slip, stop and ask for another trial. If you complete the test, you may not get a second chance.

Starting From an Upright Moving Position

In team sports such as basketball, soccer, rugby, field hockey, and lacrosse, athletes continuously move and need to develop efficient techniques for making the transition from a slow walk or jog to an all-out sprint. The sprinting form techniques during acceleration, or the drive phase of a sprint (after clearing the ground and completing the initial two or three steps), apply to the walk- or jog-to-sprint transition (see chapter 12). The transition requires a quick shift in the center of gravity, slight forward lean with little bend at the trunk, vigorous arm action, and forceful push-back at ground contact with both legs (figure 10.4). The pushing action of the legs comes from the balls of the feet, not the toes. Pushing from the toes causes loss of power, stability, and speed. Read the section on the stride cycle in chapter 12 (page 233), and study the technique carefully before practicing the transition drills in this chapter.

Figure 10.4 The moving start: *(a)* from a slow jog or walk, *(b)* push off the balls of the feet to generate speed.

Checklist for the Moving Start

Preparatory Position

- ✦ Relaxed walking or jogging form
- ✦ Proper arm use during walking or jogging
- ✦ Only a slight, natural forward lean is evident

Drive (Acceleration) Phase

- ✦ Explosive thrust exerted off both the lead and rear foot
- ✦ Gradual straightening of the body and lengthening of stride
- ✦ Landing on the balls of the feet and limited lowering of the heels
- ✦ Head slightly down, looking at the ground
- ✦ Strong use of the arms in synch with the legs

Starting Drills

These drills develop the explosive leg power required in starting. They are stressful enough to be a workout,or can be part of a workout. They are not designed as warm-up or cool-down drills. Starting strength can be improved by using exercises with weights and resistance of 60 to 80 percent of maximum strength at high speed.

STRAIGHT BOUNDING

Beginning from a slow jog, try to bound as high into the air as possible, using a running form that emphasizes a high knee lift (figure 10.5). Land on the opposite leg and continue bounding down the field.

The intensity of this drill is controlled by altering the height and number of repetitions. For beginners and heavier players, the height of the bound should be limited and the number of bounds kept at no more than four per leg. As experience and training progress, increase the height and number of repetitions.

Figure 10.5

OUTSIDE BOUNDING

Outside bounding is similar to straight bounding except that the foot is placed laterally outside the normal landing position and the body is projected laterally as well as up and forward (figure 10.6). You should have experience with straight bounding before trying this drill.

Figure 10.6

INSIDE BOUNDING

Inside bounding (figure 10.7) is similar to outside bounding except that the foot is placed laterally inside the normal landing position and the body is projected laterally as well as up and forward. You should have experience with straight bounding before trying this drill.

Figure 10.7

TWO-FOOT PUSH-OFF AND DIVE

Assume a crouched start and move to the set position. Exert as much initial thrust as possible off both feet and dive forward onto a grassy or matted area (figure 10.8). Complete 15 to 20 repetitions each session. Pushing off both feet to get the body moving from your starting posture is the most difficult habit to form; it is also the most important.

Figure 10.8

TWO-FOOT PUSH-OFF AND DRIVE

From the crouched set position, exert maximum thrust off both feet momentarily to get your body in motion. Now make the transition by continuing the thrust with the lead foot and stepping forward with the back foot to begin the sprint cycle. Sprint 8 to 10 yards in each of 15 to 20 repetitions. Your task is to develop the feel for thrusting off both feet to establish the initial forward movement then driving the back leg forward to begin the sprint cycle.

FALLING STARTS

From a stationary start, move your body weight forward on the command *Set* by falling to about 90 degrees without moving your feet (figure 10.9a). On the command *Go,* swing your forward arm back and your back arm forward as you drive off your back leg and front leg simultaneously and then your front leg independently to initiate the first stride (figure 10.9b).

Figure 10.9a

Figure 10.9b

PARTNER-ASSISTED STARTS

Have a partner hold you at the waist from behind after you assume the standing start position (figure 10.10). Lean forward 45 degrees and complete four or five strides as your partner provides enough resistance to allow you to move slowly forward before releasing the hold and permitting an all-out sprint for 8 to 10 yards.

Figure 10.10

HARNESS STARTS

Using a shoulder harness held by a partner, assume the crouched or standing start position. Move into the set position, holding it for only a short time. On the *Go* command, execute a powerful push-off and start as your partner provides enough resistance to allow you to cover approximately 10 to 15 yards in two to three seconds.

HARNESS AND RELEASE STARTS

Repeat the drill for harness starts with your partner using a quick release harness or bullet belt after the count of "one-thousand-and one, one-thousand-and two" to permit one to two seconds of heavy resistance, followed by an 8- to 10-yard sprint.

SPRINT-ASSISTED START USING TUBING

Attach surgical tubing to your waist and your partner's waist in the front. Walk back to stretch the tubing about 25 yards. Assume the proper standing start, then execute a high-speed 10- to 15-yard start and sprint with the pull. Repeat using a crouched start, taking special care to ensure that knots and belts are securely fastened and the tubing is free of nicks and cuts. A spotter should stand just in front of you to protect your head and face if the tubing snaps from your partner's side. The crouched position is immediately assumed after the tubing is stretched, and the start is quickly executed to shorten the time you are in this vulnerable position.

SPRINT-ASSISTED START USING A DOWNHILL AREA

Assume a crouched or standing start position in the center mound (50-yard line) of a football field. Complete three to five starts for 10 to 15 yards, using the force of gravity to aid your movement.

START AND SPRINT

From the stationary crouched or standing position, start quickly and feel the power being applied behind your body. After 10 yards, quickly shift from running in back of the body to sprinting in front of the body. This drill should emphasize the difference between starting technique (behind the body) and sprinting technique (in front of the body).

Transition Starting Drills

GEARS

Place five cones 20 yards apart. Each cone represents a higher gear. Run in first gear (starting speed) between cones one and two, third gear between cones two and three, and fourth gear (maximum speed) between cones four and five. Now use an easy standing start to a jog to cone one, one-half speed to cone two, and maximum speed to cone three before reducing intensity and trying to maintain stride frequency through cones four and five.

Figure 10.11

INS AND OUTS

Place five cones 20 yards apart. Progress from a slow walk to a jog by cone one, accelerate to near-maximum speed by cone two, then to maximum speed (figure 10.11) by cone three. At cone three, attempt to sprint faster than ever before. At cone four, reduce intensity and try to maintain stride frequency to cone five.

PICKUP SPRINTS

Walk 10 yards, jog 10 yards, and sprint 10 yards around a track or field, concentrating on the rapid transition from a jog to a sprint. Complete 15 to 20 repetitions. Later, use longer distances of 15 to 25 yards and a walk-jog-stride-sprint cycle (use three-quarter speed for the stride), emphasizing proper transition form on each repetition.

DOWNHILL SPRINTING

Locate a downhill area. Complete four or five repetitions of a jog-stride-downhill sprint-hold cycle. (On the hold element, reduce intensity as you attempt to maintain the sprint-assisted downhill speed on a flat area for 15 to 20 yards.)

Stopping in Team Sports

High-speed stopping in team sports produces extremely high forces on the body that must be countered by the muscular system to prevent injury and bring a moving body to a complete stop or pause before executing a change in direction. A football, basketball, or soccer player who is sprinting at high speed often must come to a rapid stop to execute a tackle, change direction, or secure the ball. The reactive forces of the ground or floor hit the athlete's body with the same force that hits the ground and must be rapidly absorbed to counter the shock and stress.

Even with proper technique, it may be difficult to extend the time to soften the impact. Special equipment and padding in football, soccer, field hockey, and lacrosse provide additional assistance; however, proper technique produces most of the needed delay for extending the time force is absorbed and spreading the force to allow explosive stopping and starting action in team sports.

Stopping Technique

The technique to produce an injury-free, high-speed stop after a rebound or after reaching maximum sprinting speed involves proper flexing of the ankles, hips, and knees at landing or during the first one or two steps of the stopping action; this extends the time the force is absorbed and spread throughout the body. Most athletes bend their knees as they land after a jump and during the stopping action while sprinting. The stopping action loads the legs with elastic energy as muscles stretch (lengthen) to absorb and control the high-speed stop. The countermovement must now take place as quickly as possible to avoid losing this elastic energy as heat. The faster the countermovement is made after stopping, the more explosive the concentric contraction and the quicker the countermovement in another direction is made.

During a rapid stop in team sports, the quadriceps are stretched and loaded eccentrically to produce stored elastic energy. If the stretch (stop) is too slow, no energy is stored and the countermovement will be slow. To improve quickness, an athlete must possess sufficient strength in the muscles involved to decelerate and stop rapidly.

Explosive stopping is the key to quickness in team sports and paves the way to executing rapid changes in direction under all types of competitive conditions. The objective is to train the neuromuscular system and teach the muscles to fire more quickly. The nervous system will eventually increase the firing rate of motor neurons, causing maximum recruitment of fast-twitch fibers, quicker reaction, and improved explosive force of the stop and start.

Figure 10.12 shows the proper technique for coming to a stop (pause), shifting body weight and center of gravity, and rapidly moving laterally or in the opposite direction. This technique is used over and over in team sports. Coming to a complete stop is not as common. More often, high-speed forward movement is shifted by executing a "plant" with the right or left foot and a high-speed cut in the opposite direction. This action and the various types of "cuts" and "fakes" used in team sports are described in chapter 11.

Figure 10.12   *(a)* Coming to a stop; *(b)* moving in another direction.

Stopping Drills

Each stopping drill must involve a rapid countermovement and minimum pause between the stopping and starting actions to produce quickness. According to Twist (2001), a simple test can be used to determine whether an athlete is ready for this type of training.

> When the player performs a simple lateral stop-and-start drill, does he land evenly with both feet at the same time? Is the footprint consistent, or does the athlete land at different places throughout the drill?

Athletes who do not meet these criteria may need to improve their quickness foundation through the use of additional speed endurance training, weight training, balanced flexibility training, and plyometrics.

Keep in mind that quickness is improved by teaching and practicing correct form and technique in sport-specific stopping and starting quickness drills that emphasize quality, not quantity. As in sprint-assisted training, the emphasis is on training the neuromuscular system; it requires all-out maximum effort in each drill and repetition, followed by near-complete recovery. Inadequate recovery time between repetitions and drills will produce fatigue and slow movement time, leading to incorrect form and technique. Athletes without excess body fat who possess adequate strength and power in the legs and abdominal muscles, lower back, adductors, abductors, hip rotators, hip flexors, hip extensors, and glutes will benefit the most from this type of training.

START, STOP, AND CUT DRILL

The start, stop, and cut test in figure 2.2 (page 15) is an excellent drill to develop the ability to accelerate quickly and execute high-speed stops, backward and forward sprints, and 90-degree cuts. Each repetition is timed to compare performance as improvement in technique and skill occurs. Proper form is emphasized on each of the four separate maneuvers in the test (stationary start; high-speed stop and backward sprint; side shuffle; and plant, cut, and sprint). A three- to four-minute rest is taken between each repetition.

BACKWARD TO LATERAL AND FORWARD MOVEMENT

Sprint backward using proper arm action. At the command *Left,* plant your right foot to initiate the stopping action, rotate your left foot outward, execute a right-foot crossover step, and laterally sprint five to eight yards. Complete five to eight repetitions to the left and right.

Once again sprint backward. At the command *Forward,* plant either your right or left foot behind your body to create the stopping action, followed by a vigorous push-off. Sprint forward for five to eight yards.

BOX JUMP DROP AND CUT

Begin with a box 12 to 15 inches high. Step off the box, absorbing the landing on both feet, then cut and sprint to the left or right for four or five strides, depending on the signal given by your partner (figure 10.13). Repeat the drill after stepping off the box backward, rotating one leg outward, and sprinting four or five strides.

HIGH-SPEED STOPS WITH SURGICAL TUBING

Attach surgical tubing around your waist and your partner's waist. Stretch it 20 to 25 yards. Sprint toward the pull to a cone 20 yards from the starting line. Execute a high-speed stopping action by shifting your center of gravity before planting either your right or left foot, then use the opposite foot to push off and execute a five- to eight-yard backward sprint, lateral sprint, and 90-degree-angle sprint in three separate repetitions.

SIDE, FRONT, AND BACK SHUFFLE

Begin the side shuffle (figure 10.14) by standing with your left foot on an angle board and your right foot on the flat run. Take a short lateral step with your right foot, then step with the left foot before hitting the opposite angle board with the right foot. Take a short lateral step with your left foot, then step with the right foot before hitting the opposite angle board with the left foot. Continue for 8 to 10 repetitions. This drill requires a hard foot-plant on the angle board to initiate the stopping action and a strong push-off to change the direction of momentum.

Figure 10.13

Figure 10.14

Begin the front shuffle (figure 10.15) by standing with both feet on the flat run facing one of the angle boards. Take a short forward step onto the angle board with your left foot, then execute a shuffle step with your right foot onto the angle board. Step back to the flat run with your left foot before repeating the action on the same angle board, beginning with the other foot.

Begin the backward shuffle (figure 10.16) by standing with both feet on the flat run facing away from one of the angle boards. Take a short step back to the angle board with your left foot, then execute a shuffle step with your right foot onto the angle board. Step on the flat run with your left foot before repeating the action on the same angle board, beginning with the other foot.

Figure 10.15 **Figure 10.16**

FOUR-CORNER DRILL

Mark a 10-yard square on a field or gymnasium floor using four cones. Begin in the top left corner of the square in a standing start. Sprint for 10 yards to the right. At cone one, make an inward pivot to begin a crossing-leg movement (carioca) for 10 yards to the bottom right corner (cone two). Pivot again and sprint backward to cone three. Pivot and sprint to the top left corner of the square past cone four to complete the test.

Chapter 11

CUTTING AND ACCELERATING

*I*f there were any secrets to high-level sports performance, any keys that unlock doors to higher achievement, they would be found in this chapter. However, finding one of these secrets is just the beginning of a long journey of practice and integration to turn the secret into action. Gaining the control over these skills that maximizes their use takes many hours of practice. You can't practice for this kind of magic in the traditional way. Rather, it is a matter of learning the language of movement and then writing sentences, paragraphs, chapters, and books on the playing field. Only then will you have a chance to play the game as an echo to every situation that arises on the field. Players who do this seem to live in another dimension and appear to have a sixth sense beyond sight, sound, smell, touch, and taste. They are in the zone. These spectacular players take your breath away with dazzling plays.

This magic is part of the big plays that everyone enjoys. Fans know that big plays are rare and that consistent, small plays keep you in the game, but we still admire the kings of the big play, players such as Shaquille O'Neal, Michael Jordan, Barry Bonds, Walter Payton, Barry Sanders, and Emmitt Smith.

Great players can keep fans on the edge of their seats, expecting that at any moment an explosive cut here, a cut there, and a burst into daylight can turn an impossible situation into a big game-winning play. A big run, a fast break, a dazzling dribble, or a stolen base is a fan's delight and can win big games and bring in big dollars to a professional athlete. It's the skills, the language, that enable the athlete to break away to pay dirt with blinding speed. It is the athlete's ability to evade the opponent by being aware of the situation and alert to the possibilities, anticipating the reactions of opponents, feinting, faking, cutting, and accelerating, all wrapped into the language of maneuvering or playing the game.

Consider the 2002 LSU–Kentucky game at Kentucky. Only two seconds remained on the clock. LSU had the ball, but they were behind and 75 yards from pay dirt. What else was there to do but the old Hail Mary, made famous by Roger Staubach? With Kentucky fans on the field ready to bring down the goal posts and fireworks already going off, LSU's quarterback launched the ball 75 yards from the end zone. Numerous players converged on the ball. After several tips, the ball finally fell into the out-stretched hands of an LSU player, who hauled it in and raced into the end zone. Can you plan for a situation like this? Quite simply, yes you can.

Boundaries of Human Performance

Every one of the senses provides important information for rapid decision making on the playing field. In addition, the sixth sense offers a powerful dimension that can add immensely to the quality of performance or make up for deficiencies in other qualities. No dimensions of sport benefit more from this than feinting, faking, cutting, and accelerating.

Table 11.1 clarifies how fast and at what level of force common sporting events happen. Study the table to gain a better understanding of why attention, focus, decision making, and movements are so crucial during the game. A careful study of the events listed and their times of occurrence helps us understand how critical a blink of the eye or a millisecond can be.

It is interesting to speculate as to what is happening to time when outstanding athletes say that time slows down during their best games. Rest assured that events are still happening in the physical realm at the same high speeds.

Power and a Game of Steps

It is unusual to win one championship at any level of competition. It is especially rare to put together a streak of championships. Even when teams have the same players, situations are different and so are the results. Consider the Los Angeles Lakers for a moment. What more can you ask a professional basketball team to do? Win a fourth consecutive NBA championship? When asked what makes the Lakers tick—other than talent, a good coach, a good front office, and rabid fans—trainer Gary Vitti got right to the source.

Gary Vitti explained that the Lakers believe power output and quickness are extremely important in identifying and training players. The qualities and measures they generally look for are related to power output and quickness (acceleration). Remember, quickness is determined by an athlete's awareness and explosiveness. Great athletes are able to generate blinding quickness and use a higher percentage of their explosiveness at various speeds of movement than average athletes. Walter Payton, for example, would use a feint to get the defender off balance and then run right over him to make extra yards or break away for a touchdown. Other running backs, guards in basketball, soccer players, hitters, or baserunners also draw on this quality when they explode from a stationary position or cut at very high speed.

Vitti went on to say that the first and second steps, the first and second jumps, and the sustained power and quickness of repeated steps or jumps are what the Lakers measure, assess, and try to develop through their conditioning program. Special equipment is fitted with devices (transducers) to measure

Table 11.1   Speed and Force of Sporting Events

Contact event	Time of foot contact (sec.)	Force (lb.)
Awareness threshold	>.0000	
Reaction	.09 to .016	
Reaction time	.090	
Sprinting	.090	1,050
Sprinter ground contact	.090	1,034
Sprint Master	.128	700
Sled (full load)	.175	488
Sprint load sled pulling	.175 to .195	590
Bounding	.175	1,200
Bound	.175	1,182
High jumper	.130	1,000 to 1,300
Long jumper, takeoff	.110	1,371
Hop	.180	585
Hopping	.180	585
Cut 20 degrees	.250	682
Cut 60 degrees	.250	700
Cut 90 degrees	>.250	350
Depth jump, 16 to 100 cm	.200 to .285	945 to 1,327
Depth jump, 16 cm	.210	945
Depth jump, 40 cm	.200	990
Depth jump, 100 cm	.300	585
Kicker, plant foot	.285	503
Race walker	.400	
Marathon[a]	<.400	
Quarterback, back foot throw	.500	364
Quarterback, front foot throw	.500	268
Impact	Time	
Golf ball hit by driver	.001	
Baseball hit off tee	.013	
Handball serve	.013	
Baseball hit from pitcher	.020	
Soccer ball header	.023	
Softball hit off tee	.035	
Tennis forehand	.050	
Football kick	.080	
Striking force (boxer, martial artist)	.088	800 to 2,000

[a]Marathon: +10,000 steps × 2 × .400 sec = 8,000 sec. (133.3 min., or 2 hr. 13.3 min.)

power output as players do their various lifts. The Lakers are on the cutting edge, and we are impressed by how they train players and emphasize the truly important areas of performance.

Still, the big question remains: What information can be used to accurately identify a player's power and quickness? One approach involves using the research completed by Paul Ward at Indiana University in 1973 on the ability of a sprinter to accelerate in the first three steps. Results of his study allow us to make some useful comparisons. Another excellent source of information is the data collected by Ralph Mann and Bob Ward in 1993 on how football players maneuver on the field. A computer graphic method (OFAS, 1985 to 1993) developed by Mann was used to evaluate many NFL and college players' movement patterns during actual games.

There is little doubt that today's coaches have an advantage in technology that makes the future look very bright for measuring a player's movements during competition. In addition, there are companies that estimate the amount of energy expended and measure heart rate, stride length, stride rate, and split times for important distances. In the near future, players may be connected to satellite technology (global positioning satellite, or GPS) to track their movements on the field. New methods are rapidly evolving for those who want the facts to help explain performance in a more objective way.

The times in table 11.2 serve as a reference point for how fast male and female athletes move in the first three steps. Females complete the first three steps more slowly mainly because muscle mass and hormone levels (testosterone) are lower in women, reducing strength, speed, power, and sustained power output required in explosive sports. On average, a woman's ability to compete in highly explosive and contact sports is diminished primarily because of this.

Table 11.2   Speed, Length, and Force of the First Three Steps in Track and Football

	First step		Second step		Third step	
	Male	**Female**	**Male**	**Female**	**Male**	**Female**
Track[a]	10.50 to 13.89 fps	7.40 to 13.50 fps	12.54 to 16.33 fps	12.00 to 18.40 fps	16.57 to 20.00 fps	14.40 to 18.40 fps
Football[b]	8 to 15 fps (8.7 40 yd.)	(9.5 40 yd.)	13 to 16 fps (9.7 40 yd.)	(10.5 40 yd.)	16 to 20 fps (6.7 40 yd.)	(7.3 40 yd.)
Step length (in.)	2.98 to 4.02		3.00 to 4.26		3.74 to 5.10	
Force (lb.)	222 to 523	186 to 450				

Note: Gender estimations based on percent differences found in Adrian and Cooper 1989.

[a]Ward, P. 1973. An analysis of kinetic and kinematic factors of the standup and the preferred crouch starting techniques with respect to sprint performance. Unpublished dissertation.

[b]On-field analysis, 1993.

Table 11.3 shows a time analysis of a play. On-field analysis can easily produce this kind of breakdown for every play of the game. However, it is rather difficult and tedious to make visual observations and notations on the subtleties of each play. Video analysis done by most coaches today is "notice and note."

Few experts have tried to identify the nuclear glue that makes things work on the playing field. Most people who try come up with subjective ideas that leave a lot of room for error. Some scientists and sports team administrators call these unknowns "intangibles." We believe the key element is akin to psychological warfare, which establishes uncertainty in your opposition. What makes a bully successful? Fear based on alleged strengths. But when you put the bully to the test, these strengths usually melt away because they are based on smoke and mirrors with no flames.

Table 11.3   **Time Analysis of a Play**

Total time (sec:ms)	Preplay and playing speed events	Split time (sec:ms)
00:000	Awareness threshold anticipation lag time ± big performance advantage	00:000
00:000	Play starts (clock starts)	00:000
00:150	Time reacting to a key	00:150
00:350	Starting (first step)	00:200
00:000	Second step	00:000
00:000	Third step	00:000
00:000	Breakdown (cha-cha-cha)	00:000
00:000	Red zone (6 inches)—engaging the opponent	00:000
00:000	Contact, focus, distance	00:000
00:000	Holding, controlling, blocking, tackling, catching	00:000
00:000	Driving, touching, muscle sensing	00:000
00:000	Disengaging, playing quickness	00:000
00:000	Avoiding, maneuvering, running, pursuing, playing speed	00:000
00:000	Breakdown (cha-cha-cha)	00:000
00:000	Red zone (6 inches)—engaging the opponent	00:000
00:000	Contact, focus, distance	00:000
00:000	Driving, touching, muscle sensing	00:000
05:000	Play ends	05:000
00:000	Rest period between plays begins	45:000
50:000	Play starts (clock starts)	00:000

Psychological warfare starts with your previous performance (your myth, or image), which is always game-dependent. Every new game is a new display of talent. During the game, you can and must establish or reestablish this uncertainty in the opposing team and players. This level of uncertainty deals with the application of your tactical skills in running a particular play to implement a strategy. The nuclear glue that holds everything together is developed in two dimensions. Intrinsic qualities are the psychological aspects within the athlete—what the athlete brings to the game. Extrinsic qualities are the external elements presented to the athlete from the outside, such as opponents, tactics, strategies, and game conditions.

All you have to do is play a game to recognize the disparity between game plans and the actual play-by-play. There can be some resemblance to what you thought the opponent and you would do, but rarely does it go as planned. It is impossible to prepare for such a game when the opponent's philosophy is "Here I come, ready or not." Learn to use the skills you possess and express your speed and quickness—that is expected. The other side of the coin is the unexpected actions that you or your opponent add to obtain an advantage. For example, an expected element of a team might be that the players will try to run to daylight and outrun or overpower the opponent. What may be unexpected are the false cues the team shows the opponent and the rapid changes of speed and direction the players are capable of.

Any biomechanist will confirm that coordinated timing of the accelerations and decelerations of each body part remains more important than absolute strength or speed of movement of each independent basic element of performance. Likewise, the coordinated timing of total body resources and segments is more important than your ability to independently generate maximum power, speed strength, speed, or strength in those segments.

Maneuvering on the field or court is similar to how a boxer uses combinations to defeat his opponent. The boxer uses a jab to set up other combinations. If he never lands a punch or if his punch isn't very effective, the opponent is going to react offensively. On the other hand, if the boxer lands a staggering left jab or two at the very beginning, the opponent will respond defensively to the slightest hint of a jab because the boxer laid the groundwork for future uncertainty. In fact, this approach uses the same science of conditioning that Pavlov used when he trained his dogs to salivate to the ringing of a bell.

Stances of Readiness: Geometry of Movement

Shapes in nature tell us a lot about structure, function, and object stability. I'm sure you've seen a huge rock with a small base perched on a rock formation and wondered how it was able to stay standing. Laws of physics explain how a very unstable-looking formation can still stand. Similarly, the shapes our bodies assume during sports activities reveal a lot about how we are able to move on the field from a stationary position, from moving slowly, and from moving at high speed.

In fact, we suggest that you study how animals move and make notes of the shapes and positions their bodies assume as they move through various activities. Go to a zoo or just tune in to TV shows to find animal subjects. You'll be pleasantly surprised at what you learn about movement and how to apply the things you see to your game.

Maneuvering on the Field

Learn to apply the following six principles to improve your level of play considerably. These principles are based on fact (actual deeds during competition) or fiction (propaganda about alleged, rumored, or potential deeds).

Invariably, dominance brings negative thinking, fear, and hesitation into the minds of the opponent. Consequently, you could say it facilitates the implementation of the other principles. The principles are listed in their order of importance.

First, establish dominance by adding uncertainty and discouragement to the concerns of your opposition. Use your playing skills, speed, power, and strength to get the job done. In overmatched situations, this may be all that is necessary to win the game. However, few games present a complete mismatch. Therefore, other skills have to be employed.

Second, be the first to display sufficient force. This is one of the golden rules of sport. In other words, if it takes 250 pounds of force to move a player in a desired direction, then get in there before he has a chance to do the same to you.

Third, neutralize the defender by slowing his movement, breaking his concentration, altering his center of gravity, delaying his total commitment, and placing doubt in his mind. Fourth, change direction. Make the defender move away from where you want to go. Fifth, practice skillful misdirection. Trick your opponent into moving in the wrong direction.

Finally, draw the defender into the danger zone, which allows you to manipulate the situation. For instance, an effective cut must occur two to three yards from the defender. A fake straight-ahead break will draw him into an effective range. Keep in mind that faking or feinting is used first to neutralize the opponent and then to allow you to go by untouched. Any fake will help neutralize, and any fake is better than no fake at all.

Just as every language has its alphabet and grammar, so too does the language of maneuvering. In this chapter, we offer you some of these elements that we have developed and those we have taken from individual and team sports that will help you develop your own form of movement on the field.

There can be no better time to lay the foundation of movement than in early childhood (elementary school). Coaches at all higher levels will reap the benefits from such programs. You must practice all types of total body, head, shoulder, arm, and leg fakes daily to develop the proper skill. These basic moves and cuts should be mastered to increase your vocabulary of movement. Dancing of all kinds and gymnastics are highly recommended for developing the fine, subtle shifts of body weight needed to refine movement patterns.

Sufficient force has been previously defined. All principles are directed to delivering sufficient resources to a task before your opponent can. Stillness, or absence of movement, is key. A time will come in the progress of play when you realize that stillness is the best choice. You'll learn that your opponent can take himself out of the play.

Try dancing in your shoes. Shift your weight back and forth without lifting your feet. This can be classified as a simpler version of the slow phasic bent-knee position. The slow phasic bent-knee position was first promoted by Bruce Lee, who recognized that it is best if an athlete is in a ready position. This was nothing new. However, if the body is moving slightly it is easier to overcome inertia and improve performance. Experiment with shuffling. Move in any direction for a short distance without lifting your feet off the ground. In other words, slide your shoes on the ground.

The cha-cha-cha movement and related actions are important. Bruce Lee was an accomplished cha-cha dancer in Hong Kong and reputedly won many dance competitions. Experiment, too, with broken rhythm. Insert a half beat or a slight variation into the rhythm.

Think back to the basic movement patterns you learned in elementary school, such as starting from stationary positions; stopping the body while moving; sliding left or right, including a step to the side with a hop; leaping (jumping from one foot to the other), which is the first step in learning to long jump; skipping (a step and hop sequence that can be used with many variations in rhythm and movement); galloping (a step and a jump before landing with the same foot forward); hopping (jumping and landing on the same foot); turning or spinning (pivoting on one foot), which enables you to change directions and avoid opponents; and using combinations, which involves sequencing any number of basic moves. In fact, the cha-cha-cha is one of the most practical combinations in sport. Any number of movements can be added to this critical combination.

Add a creative warm-up to your usual routine. Jog, skip, hop, or gallop. Practice established patterns with pacing, matching the movements of your opponent. Watch your cadence. Make your movement coincide with your opponent's. Try forcing your opponent to slow down and follow your cadence.

Basic footwork is developed through all forms of movement. Various elementary school games such as hopscotch were designed with this end in mind. All forms of dance are excellent for footwork development.

Classic training drills are useful, too. Run forward with a zigzag, run backward with a zigzag, and move side to side, from left to right. Watch your tempo. Choose the exact psychological and physical moment of weakness in your opponent. Stop and hit. Attack an opponent's attack in order to arrest his attack. Use the straight arm (long range), establishing it as a jab for keeping your opponent at a distance and as a movement for feinting and faking. Use your forearm to keep your opponent at a distance in close range.

Overpower your opponent. This may seem out of place in a faking chapter, but it is an excellent example of how to establish uncertainty. Once established, it can become a visual cue that can be used as a part of your maneuvering vocabulary. It is referred to as "conditioning the opponent."

Develop effective tactics for contact, such as the hit and side step, the hit and spin, the full spin, and the fake spin. The hit and side step is based on making good solid contact then using the energy the opponent gives you to initiate the side step. Walter Payton was a brilliant runner and a good example of a player who was so advanced that he dictated all aspects of play, even the use of contact. In all aspects of play, make sure you develop the ability to go left or right. The hit and spin is based on making good solid contact first and then using the energy the opponent gives you to initiate the spin. The full spin is a precontact spin that is especially good for moving around a clutter of players or changing directions. The fake spin is just that: a fake spin.

Use a ball change. Practice switching arms with the ball to become highly skilled. Then you can use the ball change to make your opponent think you will be going a certain direction.

© Steve Woltmann/SportsChrome

A well-executed cut in the proper zone will stall the defender and open the way to the goal.

For the single cut, angle away from the defender to force his commitment before planting the outside foot and cutting in the opposite direction. For the double cut, run at the opponent before planting the left foot and breaking right, only to plant that foot also and return left to go by the defender. The first cut will neutralize, the second cut will draw, and the third will be one he'll only be able to watch.

Once you master these basic skills in various situations at maximum speed, you can advance to more complicated faking by building various combination much as a boxer does.

Every sport has critical elements of performance. Learning to estimate distance to the opponent or target is one of them. Being able to estimate this distance is crucial if you are to maneuver effectively on the field. Players must match their resources with those of their opponents if they are to be effective.

Fencers, boxers, and martial artists know the importance of distance better than any other athletes. Their survival depends on staying in or out of their opponents' range as the situation demands. Certainly, athletes in most sports draw on the principles of distance in order to win. If the principles of distance are important to successful play in all sports, it would be wise for all team sport athletes to study one or all of these arts to learn their secrets.

Maneuvers must be used in the proper zone. Attempts in an inappropriate zone, where the opponent is too close or too far away, negate the effects of the feint, fake, or movement. Therefore, athletes must practice in varying situations that duplicate actual game conditions to input important information into their biological computers. This information will form the database for making split-second decisions in future games. Each zone or distance requires specific skills to manage the situation.

In the contact zone, you are in contact with your opponent. Close-range skills are needed. In the touch zone, you are close enough to touch your opponent (arm's length). In the evasion zone, you are one or two steps away from your opponent. The one-step zone is any distance beyond the touch zone with a closing distance of one step. The two-step zone is any distance beyond the touch zone with a closing distance of two steps. The three-step zone is any distance beyond the touch zone with a closing distance of three steps.

Feinting

Athletes in team sports can benefit from the experience and tips of Bruce Lee on the principles of control, breakdown, feinting, and faking.

The objective of the feint is to open the line in which you intend to move, make the opponent hesitate, and defeat the movement the feint produced. The feint can be defined as a movement designed to mislead an opponent as to your intention, conceal your intended movement, distract your opponent's attention, lead your opponent to believe an action is coming, and induce a reaction. Body movements that aren't an immediate threat but bring a reaction must be long enough to suggest intent, including speed and rhythm changes.

Bruce Lee (1975) suggested several principles for feinting. Leads should be preceded by a feint. A slight wave of the hand, a stomp of the foot, or a sudden shout can produce sensory distractions sufficient to reduce coordination. A feint is composed of a false move and a real or evasive move. The false move must appear so real that it will threaten the opponent to make a move. No feint can be considered effective unless it forces the opponent to move. The feint must appear as an attack. Good feints are decisive, expressive, and threatening. Good feints establish proper distance to accomplish the intended action. Feinting is an essential part of an attack.

Practice one-two feints (inside/outside, outside/inside, forward/backward, and diagonal). Change your cadence (short, long, short). If your opponent doesn't respond to feints, attack by hitting your opponent in contact sports or by making positive directional moves.

According to Lee (1975) and Lukovich (1971), there is a great risk of counteraction if too many feints or inappropriate feints are made. The fewest number of feints is best. In addition, keep your real intention secret and be fast and explosive with an appropriate sense of tempo. Act without hesitation. Perform a straight action, keeping aware of your opponent's action. Remember, your intention is to score. Use a longer (slower) feint against an opponent who doesn't react aggressively. Use a shorter (quicker) feint against an opponent who can respond more quickly. A single feint ends on the same side.

If you train all the tools your body possesses (the total body joint system), your success rate will be phenomenal. Let's illustrate this point using basketball. What if you weren't able to dribble effectively with your left hand? The answer is simple: You would be a one-dimensional basketball player. In fact, the level of dexterity that is demonstrated on the courts of America is a wonderful sight to behold. Not only do many players display ambidexterity, they use a variety of creative ways to move the ball to the left and right sides.

On the other hand, move a football player to the other side, even at the pro level, and you'll see dramatic differences in performance. Coaches should provide activities that train hitting actions, pushing actions, guiding actions, circling actions, figure-eight actions, and pulling actions.

Response Time

In your search for automatic actions, trained reflexes, and successful decisions, you will have to commit to many hours of technical work. Without exception, everyone treads on the common ground of hard work. Reputedly, noted concert pianist Van Cliburn practiced eight to nine hours a day. Two of those hours were spent on finger exercises. To gain freedom in performance, your mind must be free of the response you just made, right or wrong. Otherwise, you won't be able to attend immediately to the next signal, which is the most important.

Nerve impulses don't travel fast enough to sort out all the possible alternatives required in playing Beethoven, Rachmaninoff, or any other musical masterpiece. The master pianist isn't thinking about his fingers; he is contemplating the masterpiece. An athlete must contemplate the surroundings and be ready to apply the acquired skill that has been conditioned into her nervous system. Skills are based on a language that can be applied at any time, whether the situation is expected or unexpected. Just a simple eye blink at the wrong time can bring disastrous results. Therefore, the action must be conditioned, or brought under the voluntary control of the athlete. Mastery of total body control takes many years of training. Application of a vast library of learning experiences will become a part of immediate results when they are forgotten and called on automatically as needed. Wisdom comes from realizing that you can add more elements to your dictionary of movement tasks to get the job done more effectively.

The player's response to a single stimulus or a complex group of stimuli can be broken down into a reaction time of less than .37 second, a process time of about .20 second, and a movement time of .17 second, for a total time of .74 second. It will take more than world-record speed to become all-league or all-pro or to even make first team.

Training for Total Control

Acceleration produces great feats on the field but can also generate the forces that cause injuries. Quickness is the most critical factor in sports, not only for level of performance but also for protection. It is expressed in the repeated starts, stops, and changes of direction that the player is called on to make. Therefore, an athlete must strengthen his whole body. The trunk (57 to 59 percent) and legs (about 16 percent) make up about 85 percent of the body's total weight.

Many games can be used to develop faking and cutting skills. These games require little organization, are free form and free flowing, and require a multitude of body movements and postures for escape and evasion. The simple elementary school game of tag is one example. Both sides of the body are forced into action, thereby producing a well-rounded library of multidirectional movements.

Games are important for a variety of reasons. They condition the body in sportlike movements and at the same time teach the art of competition. Coaches can use games to develop a winning attitude in their athletes and to teach the importance of giving all you have at all times. It is better for athletes to learn these things in games that have only intrinsic value rather than those that have extrinsic value, such as league games. Badminton, handball, basketball, and various forms of soccer are a few games that have a lot to offer for training athletes of all ages and skill levels, from young, growing athletes to pros.

The beauty of badminton is that it combines a feinting, soft touch with accuracy, includes quick starts and stops with good footwork and body position, and involves explosive hits that send a speeding birdie toward the opposition at over 200 mph.

The most obvious benefit of handball is that both sides of the body have to be used. It is rugged enough in singles matches, but in cutthroat and doubles matches players must manage other players and space. Quick thinking and action are essential traits of a good handball player and a good athlete as well.

There isn't a better way to train the anaerobic and neuromuscular systems of the body than basketball. The player has to control the ball and relate to teammates, opponents, and the basket. However, a few assumptions must be made: balanced use of both sides of the body, varied patterns of foot- and handwork, and high-speed effort.

Soccer (handball rules) is a fantastic game for building sound footwork, leg control, and overall quickness. Bob Ward devised this game while with the Dallas Cowboys. It is a great way to efficiently train players because it is possible to get more kicks in a given training session. The court precludes having to chase the ball, and at the same time the players have to deal with a variety of shots from both sides of the body.

Soccer tennis is another game Bob Ward used when he was with the Cowboys. The game requires higher skill than the handball version and better conditioning because longer distances must be covered. Therefore, it would be prudent to develop some level of efficiency in the handball court before venturing out on the tennis court.

Plan for Everything, Expect Nothing

In 1986 at the NASE Symposium, Dr. Les Fehmi introduced the concept of open focus. This is the perfect way to summarize this chapter. Think of the times when you were integrating the total control principles and excelling in performance. You'll know you're on the right road toward total control when you experience some of the following situations:

+ Witnessed your own performance
+ Functioned effortlessly while remaining effective
+ Felt that time sped up or slowed down
+ Experienced a sense of team unity during the game
+ Effortlessly responded to game situations in a creative manner
+ Rose to high performance levels on high-demand occasions
+ When struggling, remained patient until a flow state was achieved
+ Increased power to prolong endurance
+ Performed at full speed effortlessly
+ Chose the point of impact and effortlessly exploded through it
+ Dissolved physical and emotional pain
+ Experienced high levels of motivation and confidence and performed effortlessly
+ Executed specific acts and actions and remained in the center while observations, motives, and sensations remained in the background
+ Experienced the presence and direction of movement of all players on the field simultaneously
+ Simultaneously focused on a narrow key and the total play action while witnessing your play

If you have experienced most of these situations, you are well on your way to taking control of the game and becoming a master performer.

Chapter 12

SPRINTING FORM AND TECHNIQUE

*A*n analysis of correct sprinting form has allowed researchers to identify key factors contributing to efficient movement. It has also revealed a diversity of styles and techniques among champion athletes. This diversity suggests the need for athletes to improve their basic styles without trying to mimic the exact techniques of others.

Although no two people sprint precisely the same way, basic sprinting mechanics should remain the same for all team sport athletes. Form and technique are important in a holistic speed improvement program. Athletes need to take the time to develop proper sprinting mechanics and eliminate faulty actions that do not contribute to forward movement.

This chapter explains the mechanics of sprinting, including stride length, stride frequency, and arm action during the acceleration and maximum effort phase for team sport athletes. Proper starting techniques for football, soccer, baseball, basketball, field hockey, rugby, and lacrosse were presented in chapter 10.

Running is instinctive, but misinterpretation of the fundamental phases of running sometimes interferes with natural and correct form. Athletes must be aware of what is natural and what is unnatural. If you are unaware of this difference, your efforts can make you run slower.

Often athletes feel that they have to bear down and stay low and pull in order to run fast. Scientific analysis of running suggests just the opposite. Reaching maximum speed depends greatly on staying relaxed in a naturally upright position. The human machine is much better at pushing than pulling, partly because the formation of the leg is unsuitable as a pulling force. Therefore, the suggestion to stay low and pull prevents maximum speed. If you want to run faster, remember that sprinting is primarily a pushing action against the ground.

Sprinting Speed: Stride Length × Stride Frequency

Sprinting involves a series of jumps from one foot to the other. Stride is lengthened by increasing the power of the push-off and jumping farther

Figure 12.1 Lengthen the stride naturally by driving the center of mass forward.

Figure 12.2 The foot is directly under the center of gravity when it contacts the ground.

without touching the lead foot down ahead of the center of gravity. Stride length also is increased by exerting more force during high-speed movement. This force requires additional strength, power, and flexibility.

Sprinting speed is the product of stride length and stride frequency. Maximum speed is achieved only when these components are in correct proportion. Stride length is best improved by increasing force against the ground. The resulting reaction drives the body's center of mass farther forward, lengthening the stride naturally (figure 12.1). When the foot makes contact with the ground, it must be directly under the body's center of gravity (figure 12.2). If the foot lands too far out in front and ahead of the center of gravity when sprinting (a condition known as overstriding), it will cause a braking effect, resulting in a loss of speed.

Stride frequency is the time required to complete a stride and is limited by the length of the stride. Whereas stride length is determined when force is applied by pushing against the ground, stride frequency is merely the time required to complete that stride. Forcing a stride frequency of more than 10 percent above the natural rate will produce only a shorter stride length and reduce speed. Emphasis should be on improving stride length (through form, strength, and power training to improve technique and increase the push-off force against the ground without overstriding) and on practicing the techniques to increase stride frequency presented in chapter 9.

Stride Cycle

During any running stride, the leg cycles through three different phases: the drive phase, when the foot is in contact with the ground; the recovery phase, when the leg swings from the hip while the foot clears the ground; and the support phase, when the runner's weight is on the entire foot.

During the drive phase, power comes from a pushing action off the ball of the foot (figure 12.1). Recall that stride length, and therefore sprinting speed, results from a pushing action. The goal of the drive phase is to create maximum push off the ground. The ball is the only part of the foot capable of creating an efficient and powerful push. Some misinformed sport professionals believe that the drive phase's pushing action comes from the toes. However, pushing from the toes reduces both power and stability and slows the runner. The drive phase contributes to overall speed only when the runner pushes off the ground using the ball of the foot.

During the recovery phase, the knee joint closes and the foot cycles through as it comes close to the body (figure 12.2). As the knee joint opens and the leg begins to straighten, the foot comes closer to the ground in preparation for the support phase. The runner does not reach for the ground or force a stamping action. The leg should remain relaxed; the runner should allow the foot to naturally strike the ground.

During the support phase, the foot makes initial contact with the ground on the outside edge of the ball of the foot. The weight of the body is then supported at a point that varies according to the speed of the athlete (figure 12.3). The faster the speed, the higher the contact point on the ball of the foot. Striking the ground first with this part of the foot maximizes speed but takes great energy. At slower speeds (jogging, for example), the contact point moves toward the rear of the foot between the arch and heel. During longer and slower runs, energy is saved by using a flat foot. At all running speeds, the support phase begins with a slight load on the support foot that then rides onto the full sole. Even during sprinting, the heel makes a brief but definite contact with the ground. This analysis of the support phase shows how it is impossible to reach your maximum speed by running on your toes.

Figure 12.3 The foot makes contact with the ground in the support phase.

The drive of the supporting leg during the sprinting action takes approximately .09 to .11 second, even though it takes .7 to .9 second to reach maximum strength in contracted muscles. Obviously, maximum strength is not reached during the sprinting action. Fast training that improves speed strength, therefore, has the best chance of decreasing supporting leg time and improving sprinting speed. After an adequate strength foundation has been acquired, direct your attention toward the improvement of speed strength. Poor form and lack of leg extensor strength can result in a poor stride length pattern.

Arm Action

Arm action in sprinting is critical when developing the most efficient stride length. The arms work in opposition to the legs, with the right arm and left leg coming forward as the left arm and right leg go backward and vice versa. The shoulders should be as relaxed as possible, with the swing coming from the shoulder joint. The shoulders should stay square (perpendicular) to the direction of the run. The swing should be strong but relaxed. The hands should also be relaxed. On the upswing, the hand should rise naturally to a point just in front of the chin and just inside the shoulder (figure 12.1, page 232). During the upswing, the arm angle is about 90 degrees or less, coordinating with the quick recovery of the forward swing of the leg (figure 12.2, page 232).

During the downswing, a natural straightening at the elbow corresponds with the longer leverage of the driving leg on the opposite side of the body to allow horizontal drive. As the arm swings down, the elbow extends slightly (figure 12.1, page 232). At the bottom of the swing, the hand is next to the thigh. However, toward the end of its backward movement, the arm bends and speeds up again to match the final, fast stage of the leg drive. The elbows should stay close to the body. Attempts to keep the elbows away from the body will prevent relaxation of the shoulders and limit efficient running mechanics. The arm action in sprinting is never forced or tense.

The mechanics of sprinting dictate that athletes who want to run faster must concentrate on pushing off the ground, landing with the proper foot placement, using the correct arm action, and staying relaxed.

Troubleshooting Sprinting Mechanics

If you run with tense arms, try practicing loose swinging movements from a standing position. Remember to swing from the shoulder and keep your arms relaxed at all times. Although your arms work in opposition to your legs, they must be coordinated with your leg action for maximum sprinting efficiency.

Many athletes and some sport professionals suggest too much body lean. Your body should have a slight lean in the direction you are running. It is important to note that the lean comes from the ground and not from the waist. The lean is only a result of displacing the center of gravity in the direction you are running. Leaning by bending at the waist interferes with the correct mechanics of sprinting.

Don't run up on your toes. The toes have no power or stability. If you run on your toes, you will not be able to run fast. Stay on the balls of your feet and push against the ground. Don't reach for and pull toward the ground; this will cause injuries and result in poor sprinting mechanics and slow times. Allow your heel to make contact with the ground when running at any distance.

Overstriding is the worst and most misunderstood element of sprinting. Don't reach and overstride to increase stride length. Push against the ground and let your foot land underneath your center of gravity. Any placement of the foot in front of the center of gravity will cause the body to slow down.

Avoid understriding as well. Try not to be too quick. Too much turnover will cause you to run fast in one place, and you will not cover any ground. Quality sprint speed is a combination of both stride frequency and stride length. One does not replace the other.

Don't try to power your way through a race or sprint effort. You will not run fast if you are tight. To run fast, you must stay relaxed.

Key Sprinting Form Drills

Sprinting form drills help establish correct neuromuscular movement patterns. Establishing as near error-free movement as possible may improve stride rate and stride length and eliminate wasted energy that does not contribute to forward movement.

Four muscle groups highly associated with fast sprinting are the quadriceps, plantar flexors, hamstrings, and dorsiflexors. The flexor muscles overcome limb weight and inertia; the extensors overcome their own weight and gravity. Form training and speed-strength training concentrate on these four groups. Since speed improvement occurs through well-developed, efficient reflex patterns of action, correct repetitions using proper form are essential in every drill.

Other factors that are a part of the total speed improvement program described in this book also improve form and technique. Increasing the strength of the knee extensors and plantar flexor muscles of the feet, for example, helps the legs handle the workload during the drive phase, or push-off at ground contact. When these muscles are stronger, the less distance the center of mass drops and the faster the muscles contract with each stride. A strong upper body and trunk also help maintain good sprinting posture. All key muscle groups involved in sprinting, such as the hip flexors, are strengthened through plyometrics, strength and power training, speed-strength training, sport loading, and other training programs. While some training programs focus on specific areas, others have a positive effect on many different aspects of speed improvement.

Ralph Mann, former Olympic silver medalist in the 400-meter hurdles and current speed improvement specialist, evaluated more than 1,000 drills for downtime, proper technique, and duplication of skills. The following bounding, sprinting, and workout drills have been successfully used by Mann and coach Tom Tellez to improve speed over short distances.

Sprinting Drills

These drills are designed to develop the mechanics, strength, and power needed to produce maximum performance in sprinting. Use these drills while warming up before a workout. The length and difficulty of each drill can be altered to any desired distance and intensity.

BUTT KICKERS

From a jog, allow your lower leg to swing back and bounce off your buttocks (figure 12.4). Your upper leg should stay vertical and not move much. Place emphasis on allowing (not forcing) your heel to come up to your butt.

Figure 12.4

WALL SLIDE

From a jog, complete the same action as you did for the butt kickers drill, but do not let the heel of your recovery leg travel behind your body (figure 12.5). Imagine a wall of glass running down your back, and do not allow your heel to break the glass. This will produce knee lift without forcing the action. As in butt kickers, when this drill is done properly, your heel will bounce off your butt.

QUICK FEET DRILL

From a jog, increase your stride rate so that you take as many steps as possible in a 10-yard interval. Jog for 10 yards and repeat. Emphasize quick turnover with your legs moving in front of, not behind or under, your body.

Workout Drills

These drills were designed as a workout or as part of a workout. Typically, three sets of each drill are performed. Start each of these drills on your toes, and make an effort to remain in this position during the drill.

Figure 12.5

CYCLING

While leaning against a wall, bar, or any support, cycle one leg through a sprinting action. Emphasize keeping your leg from extending behind your body, allowing your foot to kick your butt during recovery, and pawing the ground to complete the action. Complete 10 cycles with each leg to make up one set.

BUTT KICKERS

This drill is the same as butt kickers in the sprinting drills except that the emphasis is more on quickness. Complete 10 kicks with each leg to make up one set.

DOWN AND OFFS

Jog in place using high knees (figure 12.6). Emphasize decreasing foot contact by hitting the ground with the ball of your foot and getting off as quickly as possible. The effort on the ground should bounce your leg up into the high knee position. Complete 10 down and offs for one set.

Figure 12.6

PULL-THROUGHS

Extend your leg in front of your body as a hurdler does. Bring your leg down and paw at the ground in a power motion (figure 12.7). Complete 10 pull-throughs with each leg to make up one set.

Figure 12.7

STICK DRILL

Place 20 sticks (18 to 24 inches long) 18 inches apart on a grass surface. Sprint through the sticks as fast as possible, touching one foot down between each stick. Emphasize high knee lift and quick ground contact. Coaches can time athletes by starting a stopwatch when the foot contacts the ground between the first and second stick and by stopping the watch when the foot contacts the ground after passing the final stick. One completion of the drill makes up one set.

AFRICAN DANCE

While running forward, raise each leg to the side of your body as in hurdling and tap each heel with your hand (figure 12.8). A 10-yard run equals one set. Start this drill easily and gradually build up the intensity. For variety, you can run using the same leg motion but keep your arms at your sides in a sprinting action.

DRUM MAJOR

While running forward, rotate your leg in to the midline of your body and tap your heel at the midline (figure 12.9). A 10-yard run equals one set. For variety, you can run using the same leg motion but keep your arms at your sides in a sprinting action.

Figure 12.8

Figure 12.9

Chapter 13

SPORT-SPECIFIC TRAINING PROGRAMS

You now have enough information in four main areas to begin your personal program: you understand the key areas to emphasize for improving speed in your sport, you know how important each of these areas is to your specific sport, you are aware of your weaknesses based on test results, and you know how to properly utilize each training program to eliminate weaknesses and improve speed through a holistic approach to speed improvement.

The speed improvement attack areas for your sport and the specific training programs designed to strengthen these areas were presented in chapter 1, tables 1.1 and 1.2 (pages 4-5). Take a moment now to write the areas for your sport in a column on the left side of a piece of paper. Now list the specific training programs designed to improve the attack areas. In general, you don't need to concentrate on any of the training programs specified in table 1.2 unless test results revealed a weakness. You do, however, need to maintain what you already have. Sometimes it is beneficial to focus on speed improvement in an area such as stride rate even when a weakness has not been revealed because further improvement is likely to occur with training. However, such areas should not be the major focus of your program.

Preseason Speed Improvement

Although there are some differences of opinion among conditioning coaches, there is a logical research-supported sequence for the placement of different training programs in a workout session (see table 13.1).

After a formal warm-up, complete stretching exercises. Form training is next, followed by sprint-assisted training, which must be done when the body is still free of fatigue and capable of very high speed. Conditioning activities such as calisthenics, speed endurance training, sport loading, plyometrics, and weight training are completed near the end of the workout. A final 5- to 10-minute cool-down period is followed by static stretching to end the workout.

Research supports a system introduced by Italian coach Carlo Vittori for the proper order of conditioning activities in the latter part of a workout: weight training followed by plyometrics, ending with a series of short all-out sprints.

Table 13.1   **Order of Training Programs for Team Sport Athletes**

Training program[a]	Length (min.)	Order	Frequency	Explanation
General warm-up	8 to 12	1	Before each workout	Warm-up continues until you are perspiring freely. You are now ready to begin the stretching or flexibility session.
Stretching	10 to 15	2	Each workout	Avoid stretching cold muscles by warming up first. Use some dynamic stretching and some static stretching exercises.
Form training	15 to 20	3	Each workout	Practice starting, accelerating, and sprinting form using the Olympic form drills.
Sprint-assisted training	10 to 15	4	2 or 3 times a week	Complete before you are fatigued from other conditioning. Rest between each repetition should result in near-full recovery. The objective is not to condition but to exert submaximal stride rates and train the neuromuscular system.
Speed endurance training	15 to 20	5	2 or 3 times a week	The main objective is to improve your ability to make repeated short or long sprints in your sport without slowing because of fatigue.
Sport loading	10 to 15	6	2 times a week	Include uphill sprinting, sleds, or lightly weighted vests.
Strength, power, and speed-strength training	30 to 60	7	3 times a week	Conditioning items 7, 8, and 9 are grouped in sequence at the end of the workout. Although other systems are in use, research indicates that this order has both a practical and scientific basis. Upper-body strength training coupled with lower-body plyometrics and vice versa is recommended when both weight training and plyometrics are used in the same workout.

(continued)

Table 13.1   **(continued)**

Training program[a]	Length (min.)	Order	Frequency	Explanation
Plyometrics	15 to 20	8	1 or 2 times a week	Plyometric exercises closely mimic the starting, accelerating, and sprinting action and attempt to use a ground contact time shorter than that during the sprinting action.
Short all-out sprints	10 to 12	9	Each workout	Perform a series of 4 to 10 30- to 40-yd. sprints.
Cool-down and stretching	10	10	Each workout	Light jogging and a second stretching session (static) follows weight training, plyometrics, and short sprints.

[a]Not all training programs will be used in the same workout.

Your workout schedule uses a variation of this method in some sessions. Keep in mind that other approaches have also been shown to yield good results. Study the logic behind this suggested order, and follow it as carefully as possible during the eight-week preseason period.

The preseason period presented in this book begins two months before the first scheduled practice day. For best results, count back eight weeks from the start of your in-season period (first day of regularly scheduled practice). It is assumed that you have maintained a solid aerobic, strength, and power foundation before beginning this eight-week period.

Tables 13.2 through 13.5 describe the general speed improvement training programs to follow in a typical workout week (in the order they are presented). Specific programs for foundation training (chapter 3); strength, power, and speed-strength training (chapter 4); ballistics and plyometrics (chapter 5); sport loading (chapter 6); speed endurance training (chapter 7); and sprint-assisted training (chapter 9) were presented throughout this book.

These programs are designed so you will approach peak performance by the first official practice day in your sport. You then are in the hands of the coaching staff, who will bring you to peak performance by mid-season without losing any of the gains acquired through your preseason speed improvement program.

This eight-week time period allows you to concentrate specifically on the foundation areas that may be preventing you from sprinting faster and moving quicker and the strength and power, speed-strength, sport loading, speed endurance, sprint-assisted training, starting and stopping, cutting and accelerating, and sprinting form programs that will take you to the next speed level. You will not have time during the season to improve these areas; your only hope is

Table 13.2   Weekly Preseason Schedule for Football Players

Day	Training programs	Guidelines
Daily	General warm-up Dynamic stretching Olympic form drills Static stretching	Slow jogging 1/2 to 3/4 mile, increasing the pace the final 100 yd. of each 1/4 mile. Use dynamic stretching before completing the form drills. End each workout with a static stretching session.
Monday	Sprint-assisted training Starting and stopping drills Football speed endurance Strength, power, and speed-strength training	Follow the program in table 9.2. Follow the program in chapter 10. Use the stance required by your position for the start. Use repeated high-speed sprints following the program described in table 7.3. Use some backward high-speed sprints on both a level surface and a slight incline to develop the hamstring muscle group. Follow the programs in tables 4.3 to 4.7.
Tuesday	Aerobics Football skill session Football cutting and acceleration drills Sport loading Plyometrics Short all-out sprints	Continuous work at target heart rate for 20 to 30 min. Integrate speed into your football drills. High-speed sprinting is the major objective; think speed and quickness as you work out. Include drills using the three-point and four-point stances, emphasizing a two-foot push-off for offensive backs and linemen and the standing start for defensive backs and linebackers. Practice the feints, cuts, and drills in chapter 11 for 20 min. Master at least eight different cuts and fakes if you are a running back, defensive back, or receiver. Follow the program in table 6.6. Use weighted vests, harnesses, or parachutes to execute power starts from the three-point, four-point, or standing start depending on your position. Follow the program in table 5.2. Complete 4 to 10 repetitions of 10- to 20-yd. sprints with a 30-sec. rest interval.

(continued)

Day	Training programs	Guidelines
Wednesday	Starting and stopping drills	Follow the program in chapter 10. Use the stance required by your position for the start.
	Football speed endurance	Use repeated high-speed sprints following the program described in table 7.3. Use some backward high-speed sprints on both a level surface and a slight incline to develop the hamstring muscle group.
	Strength, power, and speed-strength training (upper body)	Follow the programs in tables 4.3 to 4.7.
Thursday	Aerobics	Continuous work at target heart rate for 20 to 30 min.
	Football skill session	Integrate speed into your football drills. High-speed sprinting is the major objective; think speed and quickness as you work out. Include drills using the three-point and four-point stances, emphasizing a two-foot push-off for offensive backs and linemen and the standing start for defensive backs and linebackers.
	Sport loading	Follow the program in table 6.6. Perform hillbursts using 2.5- to 7-degree stadium steps or a hill for 10 to 60 yd. Use weighted vests, harnesses, or parachutes to execute power starts from the three-point, four-point, or standing start depending on position.
	Strength, power, and speed-strength training (lower body)	Follow the programs in tables 4.3 to 4.7.
Friday	Sprint-assisted training Football speed endurance	Follow the program in table 9.2. Use repeated high-speed sprints following the program described in table 7.3. Use some backward high-speed sprints on both a level surface and a slight incline to develop the hamstring muscle group.
	Strength, power, and speed-strength training Short all-out sprints	Follow the programs in tables 4.3 to 4.8. Complete 4 to 10 repetitions of 10- to 20-yd. sprints with a 30-sec. rest interval.

Day	Training programs	Guidelines
Saturday	Aerobics	Continuous work at target heart rate for 20 to 30 min.
	Starting and stopping drills	Follow the program in chapter 10. Use the stance required by your position for the start.
	Football cutting and acceleration drills	Practice the feints, cuts, and drills in chapter 11 for 20 min. Master at least eight different cuts and fakes if you are a running back, defensive back, or receiver.
	Football skill session	Integrate speed into your football drills. High-speed sprinting is the major objective; think speed and quickness as you work out. Include drills using the three-point and four-point stances, emphasizing a two-foot push-off for offensive backs and linemen and the standing start for defensive backs and linebackers.
	Plyometrics	Follow the program in table 5.2.
	Muscle endurance	Circuit weight training. Do 3 sets at 50 to 85 percent 1RM, 8 to 12 reps, resting 15 to 40 sec. between exercises.

Note: Each workout begins with a general warm-up consisting of light jogging and striding until the athlete is perspiring freely and body temperature has risen one or two degrees, a relaxed session of dynamic stretching, and a series of walk-jog-stride-sprint cycles. Workouts end with a cool-down that includes static stretching.

Table 13.3   **Weekly Preseason Schedule for Baseball Players**

Day	Training programs	Guidelines
Daily	General warm-up Dynamic stretching Olympic form drills Static stretching	Slow jogging 1/2 to 3/4 mile, increasing the pace the final 100 yd. of each 1/4 mile. Use dynamic stretching before completing the form drills. End each workout with a static stretching session.
Monday	Sprint-assisted training Starting and stopping drills Baseball speed endurance Strength, power, and speed-strength training	Follow the program in table 9.2. Follow the program in chapter 10. Use the standing start and crouched position of a baserunner or fielder. Use repeated high-speed sprints following the program described in table 7.3. Use some backward high-speed sprints on both a level surface and a slight incline to develop the hamstring muscle group. Follow the programs in tables 4.3 to 4.8.
Tuesday	Aerobics Baseball skill session Baseball cutting and acceleration drills Sport loading Plyometrics Short all-out sprints	Continuous work at target heart rate for 20 to 30 min. Integrate speed into your baseball drills. High-speed sprinting is the major objective; think speed and quickness as you work out. Include drills using the standing start, emphasizing a two-foot push-off for baserunners and explosive lateral starting movement for all players. Practice the feints, cuts and drills in chapter 11 for 20 min. Master proper baserunning technique and high-speed changes of direction. Follow the program in table 6.6. Use weighted vests, harnesses, or parachutes to execute power starts from a standing start and from the batter's box, first and second bases, and infield and outfield positions. Follow the program in table 5.2. Complete 4 to 10 repetitions of 30- to 40-yd. sprints with a 30-sec. rest interval.

Day	Training programs	Guidelines
Wednesday	Starting and stopping drills	Follow the program in chapter 10. Use the standing start and crouched position of a baserunner or fielder.
	Baseball speed endurance	Use repeated high-speed sprints following the program described in table 7.3. Use some backward high-speed sprints on both a level surface and a slight incline to develop the hamstring muscle group.
	Strength, power, and speed-strength training (upper body)	Follow the programs in tables 4.3 to 4.7.
Thursday	Aerobics	Continuous work at target heart rate for 15 to 30 min.
	Baseball skill session	Integrate speed into your baseball drills. High-speed sprinting is the major objective; think speed and quickness as you work out. Include drills using the standing start, emphasizing a two-foot push-off for baserunners and explosive lateral starting movement for all players.
	Sport loading	Follow the program in table 6.6. Perform hillbursts using 2.5- to 7-degree stadium steps or a hill for 10 to 60 yd. Use weighted vests, harnesses, or parachutes to execute power starts from a standing position.
	Strength, power, and speed-strength training (lower body)	Follow the programs in tables 4.3 to 4.7.
Friday	Sprint-assisted training	Follow the program in table 9.2.
	Baseball speed endurance	Use repeated high-speed sprints following the program described in table 7.3. Use some backward high-speed sprints on both a level surface and a slight incline to develop the hamstring muscle group.
	Strength, power, and speed-strength training	Follow the programs in tables 4.3 to 4.7.
	Short all-out sprints	Complete 4 to 10 repetitions of 30- to 40-yd. sprints with a 30-sec. rest interval.

(continued)

Table 13.3 (continued)

Day	Training programs	Guidelines
Saturday	Aerobics	Continuous work at target heart rate for 20 to 30 min.
	Starting and stopping drills	Follow the program in chapter 10. Use the standing start and crouched position of a baserunner or fielder.
	Baseball cutting and acceleration drills	Practice the feints, cuts, and drills in chapter 11 for 20 min. Master proper baserunning technique and high-speed changes of direction.
	Baseball skill session	Integrate speed into your baseball drills. High-speed sprinting is the major objective; think speed and quickness as you work out. Include drills using the standing start, emphasizing a two-foot push-off for baserunners and explosive lateral starting movement for all players.
	Plyometrics	Follow the program in table 5.2.
	Muscle endurance	Circuit weight training. Do 3 sets at 50 to 85 percent 1RM, 8 to 12 reps, resting 15 to 40 sec. between exercises.

Note: Each workout begins with a general warm-up consisting of light jogging and striding until the athlete is perspiring freely and body temperature has risen one or two degrees, a relaxed session of dynamic stretching, and a series of walk-jog-stride-sprint cycles. Workouts end with a cool-down that includes static stretching.

Table 13.4 **Weekly Preseason Schedule for Basketball Players**

Day	Training programs	Guidelines
Daily	General warm-up Dynamic stretching Olympic form drills Static stretching	Slow jogging 1/2 to 3/4 mile, increasing the pace the final 100 yd. of each 1/4 mile. Use dynamic stretching before completing the form drills. End each workout with a static stretching session.
Monday	Sprint-assisted training	Follow the program in table 9.2.
	Starting and stopping drills	Follow the program in chapter 10. Execute stops and starts from a defensive stance and an offensive posture.
	Basketball speed endurance	Use repeated high-speed sprints following the program described in table 7.3. Use some backward high-speed sprints to develop the hamstring muscle group.
	Strength, power, and speed-strength training	Follow the programs in tables 4.3. to 4.7.

Day	Training programs	Guidelines
Tuesday	Aerobics	Continuous work at target heart rate for 20 to 30 min.
	Basketball skill session	Integrate speed into your basketball drills. High-speed sprinting is the major objective; think speed and quickness as you work out. Include drills using the defensive stance.
	Basketball cutting and acceleration drills	Practice the feints, cuts, and drills in chapter 11 for 20 min. Master the basic fakes and cuts with and without the ball and accelerate for 8 to 10 yd.
	Sport loading	Follow the program in table 6.6. Use weighted vests, harnesses, or parachutes to execute power starts from a defensive stance and from an offensive posture with and without the ball.
	Plyometrics	Follow the program in table 5.2.
	Short all-out sprints	Complete 4 to 10 repetitions of 10- to 20-yd. sprints with a 30-sec. rest interval.
Wednesday	Starting and stopping drills	Follow the program in chapter 10. Execute stops and starts from a defensive stance and an offensive posture.
	Basketball speed endurance	Use repeated high-speed sprints following the program described in table 7.3. Use some backward high-speed sprints to develop the hamstring muscle group.
	Strength, power, and speed-strength training (upper body)	Follow the programs in tables 4.3 to 4.7.
Thursday	Aerobics	Continuous work at target heart rate for 20 to 30 min.
	Basketball skill session	Integrate speed into your basketball drills. High-speed sprinting is the major objective; think speed and quickness as you work out. Include drills using the defensive stance.
	Sport loading	Follow the program in table 6.6. Perform hillbursts using 2.5- to 7-degree stadium steps or a hill for 10 to 60 yd. Use weighted vests, harnesses, or parachutes to execute power starts from a defensive stance and from an offensive posture with and without the ball.
	Strength, power, and speed-strength training (lower body)	Follow the programs in tables 4.3 to 4.7.

(continued)

Table 13.4 (**continued**)

Day	Training programs	Guidelines
Friday	Sprint-assisted training	Follow the program in table 9.2.
	Basketball speed endurance	Use repeated high-speed sprints following the program described in table 7.3. Use some backward high-speed sprints to develop the hamstring muscle group.
	Strength, power, and speed-strength training	Follow the programs in tables 4.3 to 4.7.
	Short all-out sprints	Complete 4 to 10 repetitions of 10- to 20-yd. sprints with a 30-sec. rest interval.
Saturday	Aerobics	Continuous work at target heart rate for 20 to 30 min.
	Starting and stopping drills	Follow the program in chapter 10. Execute stops and starts from a defensive stance and an offensive posture.
	Basketball cutting and acceleration drills	Practice the feints, cuts, and drills in chapter 11 for 20 min. Master the basic fakes and cuts with and without the ball and accelerate for 8 to 10 yd.
	Basketball skill session	Integrate speed into your basketball drills. High-speed sprinting is the major objective; think speed and quickness as you work out. Include drills using the defensive stance.
	Plyometrics	Follow the program in table 5.2.
	Muscle endurance	Circuit weight training. Do 3 sets at 50 to 85 percent 1RM, 8 to 12 reps, resting 15 to 40 sec. between exercises.

Note: Each workout begins with a general warm-up consisting of light jogging and striding until the athlete is perspiring freely and body temperature has risen one or two degrees, a relaxed session of dynamic stretching, and a series of walk-jog-stride-sprint cycles. Workouts end with a cool-down that includes static stretching.

Table 13.5 **Weekly Preseason Schedule for Soccer Players**

Day	Training programs	Guidelines
Daily	General warm-up Dynamic stretching Olympic form drills Static stretching	Slow jogging 1/2 to 3/4 mile, increasing the pace the final 100 yd. of each 1/4 mile. Use dynamic stretching before completing the form drills. End each workout with a static stretching session.
Monday	Sprint-assisted training Starting and stopping drills Soccer speed endurance Strength, power, and speed-strength training	Follow the program in table 9.2. Follow the program in chapter 10. Use a standing and walking start. Use repeated high-speed sprints following the program described in table 7.3. Use some backward high-speed sprints on both a level surface and a slight incline to develop the hamstring muscle group. Follow the programs in tables 4.3 to 4.7.
Tuesday	Aerobics Soccer skill session Soccer cutting and acceleration drills Sport loading Plyometrics Short all-out sprints	Continuous work at target heart rate for 20 to 30 min. Integrate speed into your soccer drills. High-speed sprinting is the major objective; think speed and quickness as you work out. Include drills using a walk and jog to a sprint for 10 to 30 yd., emphasizing proper acceleration form and technique. Repeat with the ball. Practice the feints, cuts, and drills in chapter 11 for 20 min. Master the basic cuts and fakes used in soccer with and without the ball. Follow the program in table 6.6. Use weighted vests, harnesses, or parachutes to execute power starts from a walking, jogging, and 3/4 striding action. Follow the program in table 5.2. Complete 4 to 10 repetitions of 10- to 20-yd. sprints with a 30-sec. rest interval.
Wednesday	Starting and stopping drills Soccer speed endurance Strength, power, and speed-strength training (upper body)	Follow the program in chapter 10. Use a standing and walking start. Use repeated high-speed sprints following the program described in table 7.3. Use some backward high-speed sprints on both a level surface and a slight incline to develop the hamstring muscle group. Follow the programs in tables 4.3 to 4.7.

(continued)

Table 13.5 (continued)

Day	Training programs	Guidelines
Thursday	Aerobics	Continuous work at target heart rate for 20 to 30 min.
	Soccer skill session	Integrate speed into your soccer drills. High-speed sprinting is the major objective; think speed and quickness as you work out. Include drills using a walk and jog to a sprint for 10 to 30 yd., emphasizing proper acceleration form and technique. Repeat with the ball.
	Sport loading	Follow the program in table 6.6. Perform hillbursts using 2.5- to 7-degree stadium steps or a hill for 10 to 60 yd. Use weighted vests, harnesses, or parachutes to execute power starts from a walking, jogging, and 3/4 striding action.
	Strength, power, and speed-strength training (lower body)	Follow the programs in tables 4.3 to 4.7.
Friday	Sprint-assisted training	Follow the program in table 9.2.
	Soccer speed endurance	Use repeated high-speed sprints following the program described in table 7.3. Use some backward high-speed sprints on both a level surface and a slight incline to develop the hamstring muscle group.
	Strength, power, and speed-strength training	Follow the programs in tables 4.3 to 4.7.
	Short all-out sprints	Complete 4 to 10 repetitions of 10- to 20-yd. sprints with a 30-sec. rest interval.
Saturday	Aerobics	Continuous work at target heart rate for 15 to 30 min.
	Starting and stopping drills	Follow the program in chapter 10. Use a standing and walking start.
	Soccer cutting and acceleration drills	Practice the feints, cuts, and drills in chapter 11 for 20 min. Master the basic cuts and fakes used in soccer with and without the ball.
	Soccer skill session	Integrate speed into your soccer drills. High-speed sprinting is the major objective; think speed and quickness as you work out. Include drills using a walk and jog to a sprint for 10 to 30 yd., emphasizing proper acceleration form and technique. Repeat with the ball.
	Plyometrics	Follow the program in table 5.2.
	Muscle endurance	Circuit weight training. Do 3 sets at 50 to 85 percent 1RM, 8 to 12 reps, resting 15 to 40 sec. between exercises.

Note: Each workout begins with a general warm-up consisting of light jogging and striding until the athlete is perspiring freely and body temperature has risen one or two degrees, a relaxed session of dynamic stretching, and a series of walk-jog-stride-sprint cycles. Workouts end with a cool-down that includes static stretching.

to maintain them. Take each training program seriously, and practice proper recovery nutrition (chapter 8) during this critical period. This is the key time to focus only on improving speed over short distances. No other period of time allows you to totally devote your efforts to one objective. Make it pay off. Use the time wisely, and it will pay big dividends next season.

Plan to retest yourself at the end of the first four-week period and again after completing the eight-week period. Use the speed profile form discussed later in this chapter to chart your progress. Your coach may also test you at the start of the in-season period.

In-Season Speed Improvement

Normal practice sessions during the in-season period in most sports are not long enough to bring about great improvement in most basic training areas. Coaches may also have difficulty finding enough time and deciding where to place the key maintenance programs that will prevent athletes from losing much of their off-season gains. This section provides some guidelines for the proper placement of various training programs and a reasonable time frame that does not significantly detract from the practice schedule and still maintains off-season gains in speed, quickness, strength, power, flexibility, and speed endurance.

A good in-season maintenance program will help athletes keep speed gains made during the off-season, allowing them to excel on the field.

Without a well-designed in-season program, it is common in most sports for athletes to lose a percentage of the gains acquired in the off-season. Although additional improvement can occur in an attempt to peak for a specific game or tournament at the latter part of the season, the primary objective of an in-season program is to prevent loss of strength, power, flexibility, speed endurance, speed, and quickness.

Fortunately, there is also a logical order for coaches and athletes to consider. Let's review this order along with the conditioning and training objectives of each program.

1. General warm-up (jogging, striding, and light sprinting) and dynamic stretching exercises have little conditioning value. Their main contribution is to increase range of motion, help prevent injuries, and warm the body in preparation for the more vigorous aspects of the program. These exercises are completed at the beginning of each workout.

2. Sprint-assisted training is specifically designed to improve stride rate (number of steps per second) and stride length. Because sprint-assisted training requires the complete absence of fatigue, it should be scheduled second in the workout, immediately after the general warm-up and stretching exercises.

3. Scrimmage should follow sprint-assisted training. Keep in mind that the body is still unfatigued, less apt to be injured, and more likely to execute skills at high speed under game conditions.

4. Sport-specific drills for the purpose of skill development are fourth. At this point in the practice session, you are still relatively free from fatigue and can execute at high speed under game conditions. These drills could also precede scrimmage if the emphasis is on mastery of skills rather than conditioning.

5. Calisthenics improve general conditioning, develop strength and muscular endurance, and improve aerobic fitness. They are conditioning-oriented and should not be at the beginning of the workout. After 30 minutes of hard calisthenics, a fresh athlete will turn into a fatigued athlete. Such fatigue will interfere with skill and timing and make you more susceptible to injury.

6. Speed endurance training such as interval sprint training commonly used in football, baseball, basketball, soccer, and other team sports is also a conditioning activity. Because such training brings about a high level of fatigue and makes it difficult to continue a workout much longer, speed endurance training should be near the end of the workout, rather than at the beginning.

7. Ballistics can be incorporated here if practice time allows. Because this is also a conditioning activity, it should occur near the end of the workout.

8. Strength and power training (weight training, plyometrics, and sport loading) is the most fatiguing of any program. It leaves you weak and vulnerable to injury. It is therefore placed close to the end of the workout.

9. A cool-down period is desirable as the last item in a workout and may involve a slow jog or walk and a relaxed static stretching period, particularly after strength and power training.

Under conditioning coach Bob Ward, the Dallas Cowboys used a unique method referred to as speedweek that remains an effective approach during the in-season period for team sports. The program is easy for players to understand and apply and is very effective. Speedweek divides each seven-day period into three phases:

1. Early nonfatigued phase (Monday, Tuesday, Wednesday morning): No leg work (strength and power training or endurance training) is permitted during this period. High-intensity work with sprint-assisted training (tubing, downhill sprinting) dominates this three-day period while athletes are relatively fatigue-free. The proper order described previously is still followed. Upper-body strength and power training takes place.

2. Late fatigued phase (Wednesday afternoon, Thursday, Friday): Training now moves to strength and power training activities (sprint loading, weight training, plyometrics) and speed endurance. During the final four to eight weeks of the preseason period, plyometrics involve only short jumps and hops for 30 to 50 meters at very high speed as opposed to longer jumps at a moderate pace. Sprint-assisted training is not used during this period. Again, the proper order described previously in this chapter is carefully followed.

3. Rest period (Saturday): A light workout is combined with team strategy sessions and one-on-one meetings with specialty coaches.

Maintenance Programs

A maintenance program for strength and power training, plyometrics, speed strength, speed endurance, and sprint-assisted training is presented in each of those chapters in your eight-week program. The Olympic form and stopping, starting, and cutting drills should be performed twice weekly during the in-season period. (See table 13.6 for a sample in-season maintenance program.) Although time becomes precious during the competitive season in most sports, it is not difficult to work with these maintenance loads to prevent loss of speed. Only a slight adjustment and departure from the normal practice routine will be necessary to work the maintenance program into your regular practice schedule. If practice time is a problem, check with your coach about completing your maintenance schedule at the close of a workout one or two times weekly. To make this adjustment, coaches may also consider the following suggestions:

+ Commit a part of each practice day to speed improvement.

+ Include testing at least twice per season in the major areas described in chapter 2 to locate weaknesses that are restricting fast and quick movement and preventing athletes from reaching their genetic speed potential.

+ Assign a sprint coach specifically to the task of maintenance and testing. A track coach is generally an excellent choice.

Table 13.6   **Maintenance Loads During the Season**

Quality	In-season maintenance loads
Flexibility	Daily sessions of dynamic stretching as part of the warm-up and static stretching as part of the cool-down at the end of the workout
Speed	Two 15- to 20-min. sprint-assisted workouts per week (five to eight towing pulls each session)
Strength, power, and speed strength	One vigorous weight training workout weekly plus one plyometric session
Speed endurance	Two pickup sprint training workouts weekly to replace wind sprints
Starting, stopping, cutting, and accelerating	Two 15-min. sessions using the drills specific to your sport that were presented in chapters 10 and 11

+ Eliminate traditional wind sprints from the program. Substitute one of the speed endurance programs described in chapter 7 that maintains adequate records and guarantees progress and improvement.

+ Use explosive power and strength training and sprint-assisted training one or two times weekly to maintain the strength, power, quickness, and speed acquired during the preseason.

+ Use plyometric training no more than one or two times weekly.

+ Use the speed improvement maintenance programs in the proper order.

Tracking Your Progress

To properly track your progress, isolate the factors responsible for your improvement or lack of improvement and find out where you need to work harder through additional emphasis. Proper tracking involves careful record keeping in two areas: test score results and the actual workout schedule you complete.

Follow these simple steps in each of the two areas to make certain you are fully aware of what you are doing, how it is affecting your speed test scores, and what you need to change to stay on course to improve speed for your sport.

Record your initial scores on the speed profile form (figure 13.1). Make a copy and place it on a clipboard. Retest yourself in each area after the fourth workout week. Compare scores in each area for improvement. If no improvement has occurred, alter your workout by increasing the number of times a specific program is used and the intensity of that phase of the workout. If you now meet the standard where you were previously deficient and feel you no longer need as much effort, reduce the use and intensity and resort to the maintenance load specified in each training program to merely keep the gains you have acquired. At the close of the eight-week preseason training period, retest yourself once again in each area and make comparisons and changes.

Make two copies of the workout record form (figure 13.2). Place one on a clipboard and take it with you to each training session. The first copy covers weeks one to four and the second copy covers weeks five to eight. Record the information requested for each speed improvement training program immediately after completing each separate program in a workout. This information is now available for review and analysis to help you understand why test score improvement in some areas may not have occurred or was lower than anticipated. This record keeping also ensures that you are applying the principle of progressive resistance exercise to each speed improvement training program by increasing the number of repetitions, distance covered, and intensity and altering the rest interval between each repetition to complete more work (volume) and more work per unit of time (intensity) each session. Study the workout record form carefully until you understand how to record what you actually did each workout.

You are now ready to begin a personalized program designed specifically for you. Don't put it off. This is your chance to move to a higher level for your sport and significantly improve speed and quickness. Take a serious approach and master each training program. You will be amazed at the results.

Fig 13.1 Speed Profile Form

Name _____

Sport _____ Position _____ Age _____ Height _____ Weight _____

Second test date (end of fourth training week) _____ Initial test date _____

Third test date (end of eighth training week) _____

Test item	Initial score	Second test	Difference	Third test	Difference
Sprinting speed					
Stationary 120-yd dash					
20-yd time					
Flying 40-yd time					
60-yd time					
80-yd time					
120-yd time					
Speed endurance					
Speed endurance (flying 40-yd time minus 80- to 120-yd time)					
NASE repeated 20s, 30s, or 40s					
High-speed directional changes					
Start, stop, and cut test					

(continued)

Fig 13.1 *(continued)*

Test item	Initial score	Second test	Difference	Third test	Difference
Strength					
Leg strength: double-leg press (strength/weight ratio)					
Two-leg curl (quads)					
Leg extension (quads)					
Single-leg kickback					
Stride					
Stride length	R _____ L _____	R _____ L _____	R _____ L _____	R _____ L _____	R _____ L _____
Flexibility					
Sit-and-reach					
Practical ROM tests					
Explosive power and quickness					
Standing triple jump					
Quick hands test					
Quick feet test					
Right and left leg hops	R _____ L _____	R _____ L _____	R _____ L _____	R _____ L _____	R _____ L _____
Body composition					
Biceps					
Triceps					
Subscapula					
Suprailiac					
Total					
Percent body fat					
Other tests					
Stride rate					
Start and acceleration (flying 40-yd time minus stationary 40-yd time)					

Starting and sprinting technique

Starting form errors
1.	1.	1.	1.
2.	2.	2.	2.
3.	3.	3.	3.

Sprinting form
1.	1.	1.	1.
2.	2.	2.	2.
3.	3.	3.	3.

Aerobic fitness

1.5-mile run _____ _____ _____ _____

Advanced testing

NASE future 40 _____ _____ _____ _____

Muscle balance (1RM scores)	R_____ L_____	R_____ L_____	R_____ L_____	R_____ L_____
Right and left leg extension (quads)	R_____ L_____	R_____ L_____	R_____ L_____	R_____ L_____
Right and left leg curl (hamstrings)	R_____ L_____	R_____ L_____	R_____ L_____	R_____ L_____
Right and left leg kickback	R_____ L_____	R_____ L_____	R_____ L_____	R_____ L_____
Single-arm curl	R_____ L_____	R_____ L_____	R_____ L_____	R_____ L_____
One-arm military	R_____ L_____	R_____ L_____	R_____ L_____	R_____ L_____
Leg press	R_____ L_____	R_____ L_____	R_____ L_____	R_____ L_____

Improvement observations (after second testing session) _____

Improvement observations (after third testing session) _____

Figure 13.2 Workout Record Form

Name _____ Age _____ Height _____ Weight _____

Sport _____ Position _____ Starting date _____

Second test date _____ Third test date _____

Training area	Weeks 1 and 5	Weeks 2 and 6	Weeks 3 and 7	Weeks 4 and 8	Total
Number of workouts	_____ _____	_____ _____	_____ _____	_____ _____	_____ _____
Starting form Two-foot pushoff (reps) and starting repetitions	_____ _____ _____ _____ _____	_____ _____ _____ _____ _____	_____ _____ _____ _____ _____	_____ _____ _____ _____ _____	_____ _____ _____ _____ _____
Sprinting form Olympic drill sessions Completed	_____ _____ _____ _____ _____	_____ _____ _____ _____ _____	_____ _____ _____ _____ _____	_____ _____ _____ _____ _____	_____ _____ _____ _____ _____
Sprint-assisted training Completed	_____ _____ _____ _____ _____	_____ _____ _____ _____ _____	_____ _____ _____ _____ _____	_____ _____ _____ _____ _____	_____ _____ _____ _____ _____
Stop and start drills (reps) Completed	_____ _____ _____ _____ _____	_____ _____ _____ _____ _____	_____ _____ _____ _____ _____	_____ _____ _____ _____ _____	_____ _____ _____ _____ _____

Figure 13.2 *(continued)*

Training area	Weeks 1 and 5	Weeks 2 and 6	Weeks 3 and 7	Weeks 4 and 8	Total
Cutting and acceleration (reps) Completed	_____ _____ _____ _____ _____	_____ _____ _____ _____ _____	_____ _____ _____ _____ _____	_____ _____ _____ _____ _____	_____ _____ _____ _____ _____
Speed endurance training Distance, reps, rest	_____ _____ _____ _____ _____	_____ _____ _____ _____ _____	_____ _____ _____ _____ _____	_____ _____ _____ _____ _____	_____ _____ _____ _____ _____
Speed-strength training Completed	_____ _____ _____ _____ _____	_____ _____ _____ _____ _____	_____ _____ _____ _____ _____	_____ _____ _____ _____ _____	_____ _____ _____ _____ _____
Sport loading Completed	_____ _____ _____ _____ _____	_____ _____ _____ _____ _____	_____ _____ _____ _____ _____	_____ _____ _____ _____ _____	_____ _____ _____ _____ _____
Plyometric training Completed	_____ _____ _____ _____ _____	_____ _____ _____ _____ _____	_____ _____ _____ _____ _____	_____ _____ _____ _____ _____	_____ _____ _____ _____ _____
Sprinting form training Completed	_____ _____ _____ _____ _____	_____ _____ _____ _____ _____	_____ _____ _____ _____ _____	_____ _____ _____ _____ _____	_____ _____ _____ _____ _____

BIBLIOGRAPHY

Abe, T., S. Fukashiro, Y. Harada, and K. Kawamoto. 2001. Relationship between sprint performance and muscle fascicle length in female sprinters. *Journal of Physiological Anthropology and Applied Human Science* 20:141-7.

Adrian, M., and J. Cooper. 1989. *Biomechanics of human movement.* Indianapolis: Benchmark.

Albert, M. 1995. *Eccentric muscle training in sports and orthopaedics.* 2nd ed. New York: Churchill Livingstone.

Allerheligen, W.B. 1994. Speed development and plyometric training. In *Essentials of strength training and conditioning,* ed. T.R. Baechle, 314-44. Champaign, IL: Human Kinetics.

Alter, Michael J. 1998. *Sport stretch.* Champaign, IL: Human Kinetics.

Anderson, J. 2000. Muscle, genes, and athletic performance. *Scientific American.* Sept.

Baechle, T., ed. 1994. *Essentials of strength training and conditioning.* Champaign, IL: Human Kinetics.

Baechle, T., and R.W. Earle. 1989. *Weight training: A text written for the college student.* Omaha: Creighton University Press.

Baker, D. 1995. Selecting the appropriate exercises and loads for speed-strength development. *Strength and Conditioning Coach* 3(2):8-16.

Bell, S. 2000. Drills which lead to better sprint performance. In *Sprints and relays: Contemporary theory, technique and training.* 5th ed., ed. J. Jarver, 91. Mountain View, CA: Tafnews Press.

Berg, K., R.W. Latin, and T. Baechle. 1990. Physical and performance characteristics of NCAA Division I football players. *Research Quarterly for Exercise and Sport* 61(4):395-401.

Blattner, S., and L. Noble. 1979. Relative effects of isokinetic and plyometric training on vertical jumping performance. *Research Quarterly for Exercise and Sport* 50(4):583-8.

Bompa, T., and L. Cornacchia. 1999. *Serious strength training: Periodization for building muscle power and mass.* Champaign, IL: Human Kinetics.

Bosco, C., H. Rosko, and J. Hirvonen. 1986. The effect of extra-load conditioning on muscle performance in athletes. *Medicine and Science in Sports and Exercise* 18(4):415-9.

Chelly, S.M., and C. Denis. 2001. Leg power and hopping stiffness: Relationship with sprint running performance. *Medicine and Science in Sports and Exercise* 33:326-33.

Chu, D. 1983. Plyometrics: The link between strength and speed. *NSCA Journal* 5(2):20-1.

———. 1998. *Jumping into plyometrics.* 2nd ed. Champaign, IL: Human Kinetics.

———. 1999. *Explosive power and strength.* Champaign, IL: Human Kinetics.

Clarke, D., and F. Henry. 1961. Neuromotor specificity and increased speed from strength development. *Research Quarterly for Exercise and Sport* 32:315-25.

Costa, L. 1994. *Explosive fire power.* Optimum Training Systems.

Costello, F. 1985. Training for speed using resisted and assisted methods. *NSCA Journal* 7(1): 74-5.

Counsilman, J.E., and B.E. Counsilman. 1994. *The new science of swimming.* 2nd ed. Englewood Cliffs, NJ: Prentice Hall.

Davis, G., D. Kirkendall, D. Leigh, M. Lui, T. Reinbold, and R. Wilson. 1981. Isokinetic characteristics of professional football players: Normative relationships between quadriceps and hamstring muscle groups relative to body weight. *Medicine and Science in Sports and Exercise* 13:76.

Delecluse, C. 1997. Influence of strength training on sprint running performance: Current findings and implications for training. *Sports Medicine* 24(3):147-56.

Dintiman, G.B. 1964. The effects of various training programs on running speed. *Research Quarterly for Exercise and Sport* 35:456-63.

————. 1966. The relationship between the leg strength/body weight ratio and running speed. *Bulletin of the Connecticut Association for Health, Physical Education, and Recreation* 11: 5.

————. 1970. *Sprinting speed: Its improvement for major sports competition.* Springfield, IL: Charles C Thomas.

————. 1974. *What research tells the coach about sprinting.* Reston, VA: AAHPERD.

————. 1980. The effects of high-speed treadmill training upon stride length, stride rate, and sprinting speed. Unpublished work. Virginia Commonwealth University.

————. 1984. *How to run faster: Step-by-step instructions on how to increase foot speed.* Champaign, IL: Leisure Press.

————. 1985. Sports speed. *Sports Fitness* August 70-3, 92.

————. 1985. A survey of the prevalence, type, and characteristics of supplementary training programs used in major sports to improve running speed. Unpublished work. Virginia Commonwealth University.

————. 1987. A faster athlete is a better athlete. *Sportspeed* Vol. 1. April. pp. 3-5.

Dintiman, G.B., and J. Unitas. 1982. *The athlete's handbook: How to be a champion in any sport.* Englewood Cliffs, NJ: Prentice Hall.

Dintiman, G.B., and R. Ward. 1988. *Train America! Achieving championship performance and fitness.* Dubuque, IA: Kendall/Hunt.

————. 1999. *The Mannatech Exercise Program (MEP).* Coppel, TX: Mannatech.

Dintiman, G.B., R. Ward, and T. Tellez. 1997. *Sports speed.* 2nd ed. Champaign, IL: Human Kinetics.

Douillard, J. 1995. *Body, mind, and sport: The mind-body guide to lifelong fitness and your personal best.* New York: Crown.

Dowson, M.N., M.E. Nevill, H.K. Lakomy, A.M. Nevill, and R.J. Hazeldine. 1998. Modelling the relationship between isokinetic muscle strength and sprint running performance. *Journal of Sports Science* 16:257-65.

Field, R.W. 1991. Explosive power test scores among male and female college athletes. *NSCA Journal* 13(3):50.

Figoni, S., C.B. Christ, and B.H. Mossey. 1988. Effects of speed, hip, knee angle, and gravity on hamstring to quadriceps torque ratios. *Journal of Orthopedics, Sports, and Physical Therapy* 9(8):287-91.

Foran, B., ed. 2001. *High-performance sports conditioning.* Champaign, IL: Human Kinetics.

Francis, C., and P. Patterson. 1992. *The Charlie Francis training system.* Ottawa: TBCI Publications.

Gambetta, V. 1991. *The complete guide to medicine ball training.* Sarasota, FL: Optimum Sports Training.

————. 1997. Quick to the ball. *Training and Conditioning* 7(6):31-5.

————. 1998. *Soccer speed.* Sarasota, FL: Gambetta Sports Training.

Garhammer, J. 1991. A comparison of maximal power outputs between elite male and female weight lifters in competition. *International Journal of Sports Biomechanics* 7:3-11.

Goldfarb, A.H., et al. 1985. The effects of endurance training on myocardial glycogenolysis. *ACSM Annual Medical Abstracts* 17(2):204.

Grace, T., E.R. Sweetser, M.A. Nelson, L.R. Ydens, and B.J. Skipper. 1984. Isokinetic muscle imbalance and knee joint injuries. *Journal of Bone and Joint Surgery* 66A:734.

Häkkinen, K., and P.V. Komi. 1982. Specificity of training-induced changes in strength performance considering the integrative functions of the neuromuscular system. *World Weightlifting* 3:44-6.

Henry, F. 1960. Factorial structure of speed and static strength in a lateral arm movement. *Research Quarterly for Exercise and Sport* 31:440-7.

Herman, D. 1976. The effects of depth jumping on vertical jumping and sprinting speed. Master's thesis. Ithaca, NY: Ithaca College.

Hilsendager, D., M.H. Strow, and K.J. Acklerman. 1969. Comparison of speed, strength, and agility exercises in the development of agility. *Research Quarterly for Exercise and Sport* 40:71-5.

Hitchcock. Recovery of short-term power after dynamic exercise. *Journal of Applied Physiology* 67:677-87.

Inglis, R. 2000. Training for acceleration in the 100m sprint. In *Sprints and relays: Contemporary theory, technique and training*. 5th ed., ed. J. Jarver, 35-9. Mountain View, CA: Tafnews Press.

Jakalski, K. 2000. Parachutes, tubing and towing. In *Sprints and relays: Contemporary theory, technique and training*. 5th ed., ed. J. Jarver, 95-100. Mountain View, CA: Tafnews Press.

Jarver, J., ed. 1995. *Sprints and relays: Contemporary theory, technique and training*. 5th ed. Mountain View, CA: Tafnews Press.

Keller, T.S., A.M. Weisberger, J.L. Ray, S.S. Hasan, R.G. Shiavi, and D.M. Spengler. 1996. Relationship between vertical ground reaction force and speed during walking, slow jogging, and running. *Clinical Biomechanics* (Bristol, Avon) 11:253-9.

Klinzing, J. 1984. Improving sprint speed for all athletes. *NSCA Journal* 6(4):32-3.

Komi, P.V. 1991. Stretch-shortening cycle. In *Strength and power in sport*, ed. P.V. Komi, 181-93. Oxford: Blackwell Scientific.

Kondraske, G., and B. Ward. 1999. Comprehensive sports training model. *Technical Report*. Human Performance Institute, University of Texas, Arlington.

Korchemny, R. 1985. Evaluation of sprinters. *NSCA Journal* 7(4):38-42.

Kraemer, W.J. 2000. Physiological adaptations to anaerobic and aerobic endurance training programs. In *Essentials of strength training and conditioning*. 2nd ed., ed. T.R. Baechle and R.W. Earle, 137-68. Champaign, IL: Human Kinetics.

Kraemer, W., and S. Fleck. 1993. *Strength training for young athletes*. Champaign, IL: Human Kinetics.

Kukolj, M., R. Ropret, D. Ugarkovic, and S. Jaric. 1999. Anthropometric, strength, and power predictors of sprinting performance. *Journal of Sports Medicine and Physical Fitness* 39: 120-2.

Kumagai, K., T. Abe, W.F. Brechue, R. Ryushi, S. Takano, and M. Mizuno. 2000. Sprint performance is related to muscle fascicle length in male 100-m sprinters. *Journal of Applied Physiology* 88:811-6.

Laird, D.E. 1981. Comparison of quadriceps to hamstring strength ratios of an intercollegiate soccer team. *Athletic Training* 16:666-7.

Lawson, G. 1997. *World record breakers in track & field athletics*. Champaign, IL: Human Kinetics.

Lee, B. 1975. *Tao of Jeet Kune Do*. Burbank, CA: Ohara.

Leutholtz, B., and R.B. Kreider. 2001. Exercise and sport nutrition. In *Nutritional health*, ed. by T. Wilson and N. Temple, Totowa, NJ: Humana Press. 207-39.

Lopez, V. 2000. An approach to strength training for sprinters. In *Sprints and relays: contemporary theory, technique and training*. 5th ed., ed. J. Jarver, 58-63. Mountain View, CA: Tafnews Press.

Luhtanen, P., and P.V. Komi. 1978. Mechanical factors influencing running speed. In *Biomechanics VI*. Vol. B, ed. E. Asmussen and E. Jorgensen, 23-9. Baltimore: University Park Press.

Lukovich, I. 1971. *Electric foil fencing*. Budapest: Corvina Press.

Mann, R. 1984. Speed development. *NSCA Journal* 5(6):12-20, 72-3.

McAnalley, B. 1998. A solid scientific foundation. *Breakthroughs* 2(1):5-7.

McFarland, B. 1984. Speed: Developing maximum running speed. *NSCA Journal* 6(5):24-8.

————. 1985. Special strength: Horizontal or vertical. *NSCA Journal* 7(1):64-6.

Meduski, J. Promoters of the anabolic state. *American Fitness.* 17-19.

Mero, A. 1988. Acceleration in the sprint start. *Track Technique* 105:3359-60.

Mero, A., P.V. Komi, and R.J. Gregor. 1992. Biomechanics of sprint running: A review. *Sports Medicine* 13:376-92.

Moore, J., and G. Wade. 1989. Prevention of anterior cruciate ligament injuries. *NSCA Journal* 11(3):35-40.

Novacheck, T.F. 1998. The biomechanics of running. *Gait Posture* 7:77-95.

Ostemig, L.R., J.A. Sawhill, B.T. Bates, and J. Hamill. 1981. Function of limb speed on torque ratios of antagonist muscles and peak torque joint position. *Medicine and Science in Sports and Exercise* 13:107.

Parker, M.G., D. Holt, E. Bauman, M. Drayna, and R.O. Ruhling. 1982. Descriptive analysis of bilateral quadriceps and hamstring muscle torque in high school football players. *Medicine and Science in Sports and Exercise* 14:152.

Pauletto, B. 1986. Let's talk training: Periodization peaking. *NSCA Journal* 8(4):30-1.

Plagenhoef, S. 1971. *Patterns of human motion.* Englewood Cliffs, NJ: Prentice Hall.

Plagenhoef, S., and L. McBryde. 1994. Application of anatomical strength curves to function and rehabilitation. *Southwest Ergonomic Systems.*

Plisk, S. 1991. Anaerobic metabolic conditioning: A brief review of theory, strategy, and practical application. *Journal of Applied Sports Science Research* 5(1):22-34.

Rogers, J. 1967. A study to determine the effect of the weight of football uniforms on speed and agility. Master's thesis. Springfield, IL: Springfield College.

Sale, D.G., J.D. MacDougall, S.E. Alway, and J.R. Sutton. 1983. Muscle cross-sectional area, fiber type distribution, and voluntary strength in humans (abstract). *Canadian Journal of Applied Sport Sciences* 2:21.

Schlinkman, B. 1984. Norms for high school football players derived from Cybex data reduction computer. *Journal of Orthopedics, Sports, and Physical Therapy* 5:410-2.

Schmolinsky, G., ed. 1993. *Track and field: The East German textbook of athletics.* Toronto: Sport Books.

Schroder, G. 2000. Basics of the sprint start. In *Sprints and relays: Contemporary theory, technique and training.* 5th ed., ed. J. Jarver, 11-4. Mountain View, CA: Tafnews Press.

Seiver, D. 1996. *The rediscovery of light and sound stimulation.* Edmonton, Alberta: Comptronic Devices.

Shirreffs, S.M., and R.J. Maughan. 1997. Whole body sweat collection in man: An improved method with some preliminary data on electrolyte composition. *Journal of Applied Physiology* 82:336-341.

Smith, L. 1961. Individual differences in strength, reaction latency, mass, and length of limbs and their relation to maximal speed of movement. *Research Quarterly for Exercise and Sport* 32:208-20.

Snell, P., and B. Ward. 1999. The importance of creatine monohydrate. *Proceedings of the Fisher Institute for Medical Research* 1(2):19-23.

Spassov, A. 1989. Bulgarian training methods. Paper presented at the symposium of the National Strength and Conditioning Association in Denver, CO, June.

Subduhi, A.W., S.L. Davis, R.W. Kipp, and E.W. Askew. 2001. Antioxidant status and oxidative stress in elite alpine ski racers. *International Journal of Sports Nutrition and Exercise Metabolism* 11(1):32-41.

Tarnopolsky, M. 1999. *Gender differences in metabolism: Practical and nutritional implications.* Boca Raton, FL: CRC Press.

Thomas, L. 1984. Isokinetic torque levels for adult females: Effects of age and body size. *Journal of Orthopedics, Sports, and Physical therapy* 6:21-4.

Twist, P. 2001. Lightning quickness. In *High-performance sports conditioning*, ed. B. Foran, 99-118. Champaign, IL: Human Kinetics.

Uusitalo, A. 2001. Overtraining: Making a difficult diagnosis and implementing targeted treatment. *The Physician and Sports Medicine* 29(5):50.

Verkhoshansky, Y.V. 1973. Depth jumping in the training of jumpers. *Track Technique* 51: 1618-9.

———. 1996. Quickness and velocity in sports movements. *New Studies in Athletics* 11(2-3): 29-37.

———. 1996b. Speed training for high level athletes. *New Studies in Athletics* 11(2-3):39-49.

———. 2000. Recommended methods of speed development for elite athletes. *Sprints and relays: Contemporary theory, technique and training.* 5th ed., ed. J. Jarver, 79-82. Mountain View, CA: Tafnews Press.

Volkov, N. 1975. The logic of sports training: Track and field. *Fitness and Sports Review International* 10(2):29-34.

Ward, B. 1987. Training models for sport. *NASE* 1(1):6-9.

Ward, B., and G.B. Dintiman. 1986. *Speed and explosion consultant manual.* Kill Devil Hills, NC: National Association of Speed and Explosion.

Ward, P.E., and R.D. Ward. 1997. *Encyclopedia of weight training.* Laguna Hills, CA: QPT.

Ward-Smith, A.J. 2001. Energy conversion strategies during 100 m sprinting. *Journal of Sports Science* 19:701-10.

Wathen, D. 1993. NSCA position stand: Explosive/plyometric exercises. *NSCA Journal* 15(3): 16.

Weinberg, R., and D. Gould. 1999. *Foundations of sport and exercise psychology.* Champaign, IL: Human Kinetics.

Wells, C.L. 1991. *Women in sport and performance.* 2nd ed. Champaign, IL: Human Kinetics.

Weyand, P.G., D.B. Sternlight, M.J. Bellizzi, and S. Wright. 2000. Faster top running speeds are achieved with greater ground forces not more rapid leg movements. *Journal of Applied Physiology* 89:1991-9.

Williams, M. 1995. *Nutrition for fitness and sport.* Dubuque, IA: Brown & Benchmark.

Wilmore, J., and D. Costill. 1994. *Physiology of sport and exercise.* Champaign, IL: Human Kinetics.

Wolinsky, I., and J. Driskell, eds. 2001. *Nutritional applications in exercise and sport.* Boca Raton: CRC Press.

Young, W., B. McLean, and J. Ardagna. 1995. Relationship between strength qualities and sprinting performance. *Journal of Sports Medicine and Physical Fitness* 35:13-9.

Young, W.B., R. James, and I. Montgomery. 2002. Is muscle power related to running speed with changes of direction? *Journal of Sports Medicine and Physical Fitness* 42:282-8.

Young, W.B., M.H. McDowell, and B.J. Scarlett. 2001. Specificity of sprint and agility training methods. *Journal of Strength and Conditioning Research* 15:315-9.

Videos

Coaching speed. 1998. Champaign, IL: Human Kinetics.

Dintiman, G.B., and L. Isaacs. 1995. *Speed improvement for soccer.* Kill Devil Hills, NC: National Association of Speed and Explosion.

Speed for sport and fitness. 1998. Champaign, IL: Human Kinetics.

Ward, B., and G.B. Dintiman. 1995. *Speed and explosion.* Kill Devil Hills, NC: National Association of Speed and Explosion (www.sportsscience.com).

White, R., V. Espiricueta, and B. Ward. 1994. *Creating big plays.* (www.sportsscience.com).

INDEX

Note: The italicized *f* and *t* following page numbers refer to figures and tables, respectively.

ABOUT THE AUTHORS

George B. Dintiman, a professor emeritus of health and physical education at Virginia Commonwealth University, has more than 30 years' experience working on speed improvement with athletes at all levels. The author of 40 books and four videos on speed improvement and health and wellness, Dintiman also is cofounder and president of the National Association of Speed and Explosion and an internationally recognized authority on speed improvement for team sports. Dintiman received an EdD from the Teachers College of Columbia University in 1964. In 1993 he was an inductee in the Capital Area chapter of the Pennsylvania Sports Hall of Fame.

Bob Ward was conditioning coach for the Dallas Cowboys from 1976 to 1989. He is director of sports science for Advocare in Dallas. An author, columnist, and lecturer, Ward has coached several Olympic champions and numerous championship football and track teams. Ward has authored other books on sport speed and has lectured extensively on conditioning, track and field, and nutritional support for athletes. He developed a software program based on many forms of the martial arts that is currently used in the NFL and at many colleges. Ward also developed a sport martial arts video, *Creating Big Plays*, with NFL Hall-of-Famer Randy White and world-class martial artist Valentine Espiriceuta. Ward received a PED from Indiana University in 1973. He is a member of the National Strength and Conditioning Association.